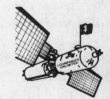

GAUNTLET Exploring The Limits Of Free Expression

ARTISTS UNDER FIRE

ANYTHING GOES

FICTION

BOOK REVIEWS

Published by *Gauntlet*, Inc.
Barry Hoffman, President

Founder/Editor-in-Chief
Barry Hoffman

Editorial Consultant
R. M. Hoffman

Assistants to the Editor
David Reed, Cheryl Meyer

Research Assistant
Dara Lise, D. Kingsley Hahn

Columnists
John Sutherland, Tom McDonald,
Matthew Costello

Correspondents
Mike Baker, S.C. Ringgenberg,
Duane Swierczynski, Debbie Wilker

Investigative Reporters
Ed Cafasso, Mark Di Ionno

Layout and Design
Kara Tipton

Cover Editor
Leslie Sternbergh

Front Cover Photo
Adam Alexander © 1992

Front Cover Layout
Mark Michaelson

Back Cover
Arlen Schumer

Editorial Cartoons
Michael Taylor Charles Dougherty,
John Longhi, Skip Newton

Address all letters/queries/orders to:
Gauntlet, Dept. B92, 309 Powell Rd.,
Springfield, Pa. 19064

EDITORIAL MEANDERINGS

If you've picked up *Gauntlet* at your local comic or book store in the past, you're probably wondering why there is a *second* volume of this *yearly* anthology in 1992.

For a number of reasons, we've decided to put out two volumes a year. We've had to face the harsh economic reality that an annual 300+ page publication is just beyond our means. I discussed this at length in issue #3; suffice it to say, printing costs make this slimmer version easier to swallow.

We have, however, turned a potential negative into a positive. You're the final judge, but we believe this leaner issue is tighter - less quantity, more quality.

Distributors are pleased with our more frequent publishing schedule. The lower price and greater frequency should also please our regular readers and subscribers. [Please note, that our next issue will be out late-April or early-May.]

The major free expression issue of 1992, to date, has been the media - both manipulation of and manipulation by the media. While an easy target (especially for politicians) at no time has the media, itself, come under such scrutiny, attack and abuse. At no time have there been more instances where the media *made* news by its actions, as opposed to reporting or commenting on the news.

The medias digging into the personal lives of presidential candidates has become a hot potato(e) with both political parties. Presidential candidates sidestepping traditional TV news venues for the "softer" talk show circuit has drawn both praise and fire.

The 90s seems to have ushered in a new journalistic morality -tabloid journalism picked up and further sensationalized by the mainstream press and electronic media. Dailies and magazines are in competition with an increasing number of reality-based TV programs (i.e. *Current Affair* or *Inside Edition*), and talk shows (*Oprah, Arsenio, Donahue* to name just a few); all vying for ratings dominance and survival. Anything and anyone is fair game as sound-bite journalism replaces investigative reporting and a blurring occurs as to what is news and what is entertainment.

Hence, Arthur Ashe is *forced* to disclose he has contracted AIDS, and Oliva Newton-John that she has breast cancer to head off media leakage of what was once considered matters of utmost privacy. Lawyers orchestrate media events, using the media to extort out of court settlements. The press leaks details of alleged criminal behavior, even when no charges have been brought against the accused. Reputations are tarnished, which can never be reclaimed.

The medias personal agendas has also come into question. Bosnia is front page news; starvation in Somalia is ignored, at first, then relegated to the inside pages of newspapers.

This and more is covered in a variety of journalistic reports, commentary, debate and comics in this issue.

As always, wherever possible, we present both sides of the coin. As always we offer no easy solutions, but challenge the reader to make an informed decision. And as always, we confound liberals and conservatives alike, for *Gauntlet* does not goose-step to the agenda or pander to First Amendment purists.

It is also ironic that with our low budget we have broken stories now being investigated by media with deep pockets. In our last issue, we ran a first-person account of sexual harassment and rape in the armed forces during the Persian Gulf War. Months later, in the summer of 1992, such stories are all the rage. We may not get the credit, but it's there in black and white.

Before I close, I want to officially welcome cartoonist Leslie Sternbergh to our staff. She is in charge of covers (both back and front). She penned the back cover for issue #3 and chose both the back and front cover for this issue. [Note to retailers: you *may* display the back cover if its more suitable to your clientele. We believe in *choice*, so we gave you two covers with two drastically different looks].

We have one glaring need, and if you want to make our day and earn a bit of money, contact the editor if you are interested in handling advertising for forthcoming issues. With an eclectic audience, generating advertising is a challenge . . . but it can be rewarding.

Enough. Read on, and please give us your feedback to help us shape future issues.

Barry Hoffman
September 1, 1992

DC comics is killing off Superman! Give us a break. The *Philadelphia Inquirer*, for one, trumpets the headline "Superman will die, says DC Comics, and not even Jimmy Olson can save him." A crock, a ploy, a hoax and the media is eating it up.

The media has been manipulated by DC Comics (owned by Time Warner, Inc.) who admit readership is down. How to spur interest? Kill off the sucker, generate an avalanche of publicity (and sales), wait for an outpouring of indignation (which has already begun) and resurrect the old codger.

DC's ploy couldn't be more transparent. Does it deserve coverage in the *New York Times*, top-of-the-show reporting on *Entertainment Tonight* and play on every local news broadcast. Yes, *if*, and only if, Superman was truly dead and buried . . . *forever.*

The media has been suckered into providing DC with free publicity money could never buy . . . *for a non-story.* The media has been duped, because you can bet the house there are writers right now at DC resurrecting the fallen Superhero, contrary to any denials by DC spokesmen.

Superman dead. Right! . . . the day Madonna becomes a nun, or is invited to the White House as a spokeswoman for family values.

OPENERS

Right to Know

This came to us anonymously. Does the FBI have a file on you? Do you even want to know? Let us know what *they* know you weren't aware you knew. It might make for an interesting article in a future issue.

PRIVACY ACT & FREEDOM OF INFORMATION ACT REQUEST

_____   _____
_____   (date)
_____
(requester's name and address)

Federal Bureau of Investigation
Records Management Division - FOIA/PA Office
9th & Pennsylvania Avenue NW
Washington, DC 20535

Gentlemen:

This is a request for records under the provisions of both the Privacy Act (5 USC 552b) and the Freedom of Information Act (5 USC 522). This request is being made under both Acts.

I hereby request one copy of any and all records about me or referencing me maintained at the FBI. This includes (but should not be limited to) documents, reports, memoranda, letters, electronic files, database references, "do not file" files, photographs, audiotapes, videotapes, electronic or photographic surveillance, "june mail", mail covers, and other miscellaneous files, and index citations relating to me or referencing me in other files.

My full name is: _____. My date of birth was _____.

My place of birth was: _____. My social security #: _____.

I have lived in these places: _____

Other names, places, events, organizations or other references under which you may find applicable records:
_____.

As you know, FOIA/PA regulations provide that even if some requested material is properly exempt from mandatory disclosure, all segregable portions must be released. If the requested material is released with deletions, I ask that each deletion be marked to indicate the exemption(s) being claimed to authorize each particlar withholding. In addition, I ask that your agency exercise its discretion to release any records which may be technically exempt, but where withholding serves no important public interest.

I hereby agree to pay reasonable costs associated with this request up to a maximum of $25 without my additional approval,. However, I strongly request a fee waiver because this is, in part, a Privacy Act request.

This letter and my signature have been certified by a notary public as marked below.

Sincerely,

_____
requester's signature

_____   _____
requester's printed name   notary stamp and signature

Can You Say Hypocrisy?

For the past several years those who've supported "outing"—publicly naming celebrities and politicians suspected of being gay — have justified the practice as providing positive role models for the gay community, and those who have not yet come out of the closet. However *The Advocate*, in June, "outed" Dr. Anne-Imelda Radice, conservative chairwoman of the NEA, solely as a form of *humiliation*. Displeased with her rejection of a grant application for the Names Project Aids memorial quilt, *The Advocate* detailed a "long-time" living arrangement she supposedly had with a woman lover. It's obvious *The Advocate* sought simply to embarrass an opponent, as they certainly don't consider her a *positive* role model for other gays.

Would David Duke Have Done The Same?

Kudos to Louisiana Governor Edwin Edwards, who the *USA Today* reported, in June, promised to veto a law to outlaw the sale of certain music to minors. His reason? He didn't like the idea of government dictating "what books people can read, what poetry they can read, what songs they can sing." Edwards, you might recall, beat David Duke last year in a highly-publicized gubernatorial campaign.

Opening Pandora's Box

Citing that life begins at conception, a Kansas judge overturned the conviction of a woman arrested for trespassing at last summer's abortion protests in Wichita. Judge Paul Clark said the woman's "wrongful act is forgiven in the eyes of the law under the doctrine of justification by necessity." Aside from abandoning judicial precedent, his argument taken to the extreme would provide a competent defense for the murder of doctors who perform abortions or bombing of abortion clinics, "under the doctrine of justification by necessity."

Killing the Messenger

Abortion foes are driving doctors who perform abortions out of business by any means necessary — legal or otherwise. In the case of Operation Rescue it's harassment. "We're going to shame them, humili-ate them, embarrass them, disgrace them and expose them until they quit," *USA Today* quotes the groups founder Randall Terry. Operation Goliath, a radical Florida offshoot of the parent organization, has been the most militant, passing out "wanted" posters with at least one doctors home phone number, the license plate for him, his girlfriend and mother, as well as offering $1000 for further information. This doctor has been repeatedly harassed and vandalized, while the police stand idly by.

One result of this and such other forms of intimidation is that the National Abortion Federation estimates 83% of the nation's counties have no doctors who perform abortions.

Ice-T Fallout

Prior to Ice-T's pulling his song "Cop Killer" from his *Body Count* album, the *Wall Street Journal* reported Time Warner, Inc. had considered drafting a policy against distributing "inappropriate" music. Talk about bending to pressure. When the Ice-T flap is but a memory the significance of such a corporate policy (which could easily extend to other labels) may still be felt by underground and radical entertainers.

In a related development, former Geto Boys rapper Willie D released a song in July, chastising Rodney King for his appeal for calm amidst the Los Angeles riots. The song concludes, according to the *New York Post*, with obscenities directed at King followed by the rappers shooting him.

This begs the question just how far can you go before you incite someone to murder and mayhem? On the other hand, it has been pointed out that if such a plot appeared in a book or movie, it would go unchallenged. Why then, the argument goes, should music have to follow a different set of rules? Food for thought as many First Amendment supporters grapple with this thorny issue.

Losing His Magic

Magic Johnson's well-received book *What You Can Do to Avoid AIDS* is not reaching its target audience, according to Peter Osnos of Time Books, because its been banned from three of the nation's largest chain stores. Walgreen and Kmart wouldn't touch the book from the beginning, and Wal-Mart pulled it after deciding it was "not in keeping with what our customers tell us they want to read." While the book is frank and explicit, the bottom line, says Osnos, is it advocates abstinence. The book is missing young people 10 and older, as they don't hang out at bookstores, Osnos notes. "They're far more likely to go to drugstores or a variety store like Kmart." Once again, it appears a vocal minority have determined corporate policy. Not until the child of an executive from one of these chains contracts AIDS due to his/her ignorance will such protectors of family values understand AIDS doesn't discriminate; it's an epidemic, and education (no matter how frank) is one tool in halting its spread.

---

*Thanks to those who have sent material for our **Openers** section. Additional blurbs appear throughout the issue. If you come across an item of interest, send it to the editor.*

In the midst of the Woody Allen affair, New York TV station WNYW showed remarkable restraint and taste when an anonymous videotape Mia Farrow shot arrived. The *USA Today* reported the tape was of Miss Farrow's 7-year old daughter answering questions about an alleged incident of abuse by Woody Allen. While reporter Rosanna Scota commented on the tape, the station *refused* to air it. [It should be noted that no charges had been filed against Allen.] Thus the station passed on a golden opportunity to one-up the tabloids. Kudos to WNYW . . . and a lesson to others.

FLOYD BROWN'S DIRTY TRICKS AND THE BUSH CAMPAIGN

Ed Cafasso

He looks like Dennis the Menace, enjoys cookies and ice cream, loves Clint Eastwood movies and adores his children.

He is also one of the most despised men in American politics, a man whose work is publicly condemned by the leaders of both major parties, whose name alone brings campaign managers and political consultants to the verge of stroke.

Floyd Brown. Scion of radical loggers from the American Northwest. Student activist. Leader of a new generation of Republican conservatives. One of the most powerful manipulators of public opinion in the business.

Since the 1988 presidential race, it has been impossible not to mention Brown's name in the same breath as the name "Willie Horton."

And since Horton's name has become the ultimate symbol of negative campaign advertising, so has Brown's.

A candidate who employs "the Willie Horton approach" today seeks to distort an issue or event that touches people's basic fears in an effort to frame an opponent in the worst possible light.

Thus, if Brown turned up with a knife in his back tomorrow, only a small circle of friends and true believers would shed a tear.

But history — and a little dispassionate research — might well render a different judgment on Brown. In fact, it might judge him a First Amendment martyr.

After all, few know that it was Brown who encouraged the growth of student newspapers on college campuses, who made it possible for people to peacefully protest outside foreign embassies in Washington, D.C., or who helped drive a stake through the heart of David Duke's political career in Louisiana.

Fewer know that George Bush's 1988 commercial dealing with convicts who escaped Massachusetts' prisons while on furlough was arguably far worse — in terms of pure political distortion and manipulation — than the Brown ad that focused on the Horton case alone.

And even fewer understand that what Brown does for a living everyday, regardless of his right-leaning politics, aids the most liberal causes of free expression by reaffirming the right of all citizens to play an active role in the democratic process.

Put aside his politics and you might find that the 31-year-old Brown, who's happiest spending a week in Disney World with his two young sons, is a lot like us.

The problem is that Brown bleeds politics.

"Floyd is someone who's going to be around into the next century," said political consultant and pollster Tony Fabrizio, one of Brown's closest friends. "He's demonstrated time and time again that he's willing to get his hands dirty to get the job done."

✦   ✦   ✦

His grandfather came to Washington state from Oklahoma, fleeing the barren wasteland of the dustbowl for the lush forested hills of the Pacific Northwest.

"He became a logger and a WOBBLY, a member of the International Workers of the World," Brown said in an interview with *Gauntlet*. "The WOBBLYs were the radicals of the labor movement. They used to have regular gun battles with the owners of the logging camps. Basically, my grandfather was a socialist.

"He lost his job in the Great Depression," he adds. "In the end, he worked for the WPA up there in the Puget Sound Naval Shipyard during World War II. My mother often jokes that, in her family, they worshipped FDR."

When Brown was in the fourth grade, his 22-year-old aunt, a newly married aspiring nurse, was robbed and murdered. Her assailant was apprehended, convicted and jailed, but eventually released — some two decades before Brown stumbled upon the saga of Willie Horton in *Reader's Digest*.

"It made me just viscerally anti-crime," he said of his aunt's death. "If a man murders somebody, in my mind, he has given up his own right to live in this society. I honestly believe society has a right to purge itself of people who commit murder. I'm a strong advocate of the death pen-

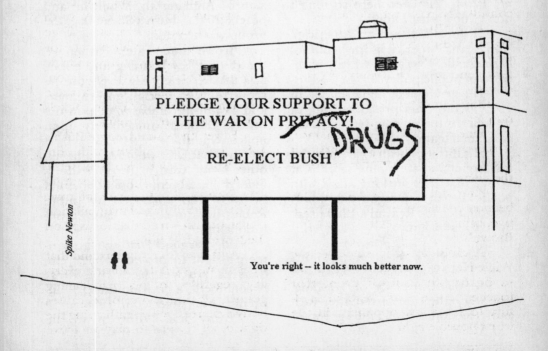

Spike Newton

PLEDGE YOUR SUPPORT TO
THE WAR ON ~~PRIVACY~~! DRUGS

RE-ELECT BUSH

You're right -- it looks much better now.

alty."

In high school in 1976, Brown found himself attracted to the Democratic presidential campaign of U.S. Sen. Henry "Scoop" Jackson.

"Even though my family was Democratic, we were socially conservative," he recalled. "Also, we were for a strong national defense. Scoop was nothing if not strong on defense."

But Jackson faded early in the Eastern primaries, so Brown and a few activist friends looked around for another candidate who "thinks most like we think."

They found Ronald Reagan and volunteered.

When it's suggested that most high school students in the mid-70s couldn't have cared less about politics, let alone the politics of an aging California governor and B-movie film star, Brown chuckled and agreed.

"I guess I have always just had a real interest in making my country better," he replied. "You know, there are Italian-Americans, African-Americans, Mexican-Americans, but my family has been here so long I don't know what I am.

"I guess I'm just an American-American. America is my cultural heritage, so I've always been interested in public policy."

He graduated high school in 1979 as the class president and, at six-foot-six, the starting center on the basketball team.

His flirtation with a career in the military ended after nine months at West Point. His life-long affair with politics began as Oregon state youth coordinator for Reagan's 1980 presidential campaign.

✦ ✦ ✦

At the University of Washington, where he transferred after Reagan's election, Brown and a group of fellow students started a monthly newspaper called *The Spectator* — one of more than two dozen conservative publications that sprung up on campuses nationwide in the early 1980s.

His fundraising talents already honed at jobs with "The Center for the Defense of Free Enterprise" and "Young Americans for Freedom," Brown described the new monthly tabloid as "an alternative to the local liberal rag" that "controls the discourse of ideas on campus."

He criticized the rival paper's publication of profanity and its explicit columns on sex, vowing that *Spectator*'s first investigative story would track student fees to campus groups that funded U.S. Out of El Salvador rallies and gay-lesbian dances.

"If they want to have these sexual perversions, it's fine with me. Just don't ask me to pay for it," Brown said on Thanksgiving 1982.

A year later, Brown led 70 delegates at a Young Americans conference in Washington, D.C., to the Soviet embassy to protest the invasion of Afghanistan. When he and others tried to burn a Soviet flag, the group was arrested.

Brown immediately challenged the district law banning any public acts that reflected negatively on the reputations of foreign governments and requiring embassy demonstrators to disperse immediately upon police request.

In what later would become another ironic twist in Brown's life, a federal appeals court opinion issued in 1987 and authored by Judge Robert Bork upheld the law's constitutionality.

Bork argued that the government's right to protect foreign embassies outweighed the First Amendment, a decision the U.S. Supreme Court reversed in 1988.

"Every time I drive by an embassy now and I see a demonstration outside, I feel a real sense of accomplishment. I am a strong advocate of freedom of expression," Brown said.

In 1985, as executive director of the U.S. International Youth Year Commission, Brown — upset at the "anti-American tone"—led a walk-out of several delegations at a Jamaica conference attended by 1,000 young people from 100 countries.

A cryptic flow chart found in Lt. Col. Oliver North's White House safe two years later raised questions about whether the U.S. Youth Year Commission was used to secretly funnel Reagan Administration money to the Contras, but no direct link was ever substantiated.

Brown would serve briefly as aide at the Agency for International Development — the only time, he says, he has ever set foot in the White House.

Then he entered the arena of presidential politics fulltime, becoming Midwest director for U.S. Sen. Robert Dole's bitter campaign for the White House against Vice President George Bush in 1988.

In addition to meeting the savvy youthful conservatives who would later form the Willie Horton ad team, Brown built a political network that brought Dole to victory in four Midwest states, including Iowa.

Brown still points to "winning Iowa for Dole" as "the highlight" of his career, perhaps because what followed has made him everyone's favorite political whipping boy.

✦   ✦   ✦

A Massachusetts convict named Willie Horton had been haunting the 1988 presidential campaign of Michael Dukakis for months before the emergence of the campaign commercial that would earn Brown an eternal place into the media spotlight.

Horton, sent to a Massachusetts prison for life for the brutal murder of a teen-age gas station attendant, had failed to return to jail after a weekend furlough. Instead, he fled to Maryland, where he broke into a couple's home, stabbing a man and forcing him to watch as he raped the man's fiancee.

Under intensive media scrutiny led by a suburban Massachusetts' newspaper, the *Lawrence Eagle-Tribune*, the Horton case quickly became a symbol for all the problems of the state corrections system under then-Gov. Dukakis.

Tennessee Sen. Al Gore, one of the most vicious primary campaigners in 1988 and this year's Democratic vice presidential nominee, was the first to raise the furlough issue against Dukakis during an April debate just before the New York primary.

Gore's assault intrigued Bush campaign research director James Pinkerton, who immediately began compiling news clippings on the Horton case and other potential pitfalls for Dukakis.

By June, Atwater was bluntly telling Republican activists in Washington: "If I can make Willie Horton a household name, we will win the election."

Afterwards, Bush mentioned Horton and the furlough issue on the stump a couple of times but, for the most part, held his fire.

It wasn't until three months before the 1988 presidential election that a conservative lobby known as the National Security Political Action Committee announced Horton would be used in a television commercial attacking Dukakis' record on crime.

NSPAC, created in 1986 by Elizabeth "Lilly" Fediay, had formed a political fund-raising arm called "Americans for Bush" to finance a

$10 million advertising push on behalf of the Republican nominee.

Americans for Bush was registered with the Federal Election Commission as an "independent expenditure group," meaning it could spend as much as it wanted on its pro-Bush agenda but could have absolutely no ties to the Bush campaign organization.

Its first ad, a low-budget commercial produced that June by Larry McCarthy, the ex-communication director of Dole's primary campaign, and marketed by Fabrizio, also a Dole refugee, had highlighted Bush's career as a Navy pilot, businessman, congressman, ambassador and vice president.

The toll-free number in the ad generated 80,000 calls from Bush supporters.

The spokesman of "Americans for Bush" was conservative whiz kid Floyd Brown, who, along with media specialist Craig Shirley, had signed on with Fediay as a political consultant after Dole's primary campaign fizzled.

The group — known to political insiders as an "IE," had already run afoul of the Bush campaign, whose general counsel, Jan Baran, claimed the name being used by Fediay was deceiving potential Bush contributors.

"The Vice President has asked me to tell you that he does not endorse nor approve of your activities," Baran wrote Fediay that June, threatening to file a complaint with the FEC, the Internal Revenue Service and, possibly, a lawsuit.

Brown glibly dismissed Baran's charge of deception as the Bush campaign's way of "keeping an arm's length distance" from the NSPAC's activities.

The dispute simmered until the campaign hit full stride in Septem-

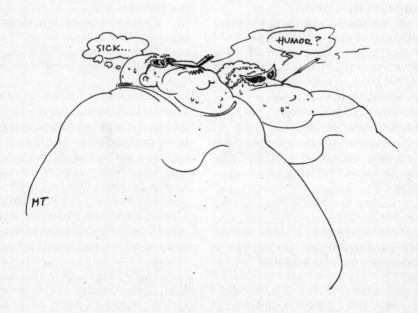

ber, when Fediay and Brown announced a month-long, $540,000 ad campaign featuring two McCarthy-produced, Fabrizio-marketed commercials attacking Dukakis for being soft on crime.

One ad contrasted Dukakis opposition to the death penalty with Bush's support for it. The second focused on the Horton case.

"When we're through," Brown said in a statement that still reverberates throughout American politics today, "people are going to think Willie Horton is Michael Dukakis' nephew."

Only $125,000 worth of air time had been secured for the Horton ad, but, as Brown and his colleagues had planned, the mere announcement that such commercials were on the way generated millions of dollars worth of free national publicity as the media scrambled to re-examine not only the Horton case but also Dukakis' law enforcement record as governor of Massachusetts.

It also eventually caused a re-examination of the role of independent expenditure groups in general and whether "Americans for Bush" was operating with the tacit — and illegal — approval of the Bush campaign.

By then, NSPAC had spent $1.5 million on Bush's behalf and had raised more than twice as much from Bush supporters, prompting Baran to file complaints with the FEC, IRS and U.S. Postal Service.

Fediay, pronounced "Feh-dye," went a step further, writing to Bush campaign Chairman James Baker: "While we have heard the grumbling . . . , senior level officials such as yourself have remained silent . . . We would be interested in your wishes with regard to our independent public advocacy of Mr. Bush for President."

She told reporters: "If he asks me to stop advocating the election of George Bush, I will."

But Baker's lukewarm reply merely reiterated what Baran had said publicly in June, leaving the air thick with the perception that Fediay, Brown and the others had been enrolled by Atwater and/or Baker as the Bush campaign's roaming political pit bulls.

Far beneath the surface of that debate, Brown, McCarthy, Shirley and Fabrizio were faced with another problem: How to get airtime for their Horton ad on CNN, the Nashville Network and other cable outlets?

They suspected the commercial was a political timebomb because it featured a grainy police mugshot of the glowering Horton — a photograph which, when combined with details of his brutal crimes against white victims, would play skillfully on the deep-seated racial fears of middle America.

Their solution to the problem was deceptively simple.

"We had two Horton spots," Fabrizio told *Gauntlet*. "They were almost identical except for eight or nine seconds in the middle where Horton's picture was supposed to be. So we sent the one with no picture out first.

"After that had aired for three or four days, we replaced it with the ad with Horton's picture in it and the networks sent it right through."

Not much could be done even after the switch became apparent.

"We had paid in advance and had written contracts," Fabrizio recalled. "It was the kind of thing you can only get away with once."

Added Brown: "I don't think the Horton ad would have cleared (TV advertising restrictions) unless we had done two versions of it."

Not long after the NSPAC ad began airing — generating even more free publicity for Brown and "Americans for Bush," as well as saturation coverage of the Dukakis record on crime — the Bush campaign began airing its own Horton commercial.

Bush's ad did not include Horton's picture, but it featured similarly devastating imagery — "prisoners" walking through a revolving door to freedom as a narrator claimed Dukakis's "revolving-door prison policy gave weekend furloughs to first-degree murderers not eligible for parole.

"While out, many committed other crimes like kidnap and rape, and many are still at large," the commercial claimed ambiguously.

The revolving door ad had been ready for weeks, long before Bush and his aides had begun publicly complaining about Brown's version.

In fact, the Bush campaign had begun working on it in May — four months before Brown even previewed the NSPAC commercial — when a discussion of the Horton case prompted Dukakis supporters to abandon their candidate during two focus group sessions assembled in suburban New Jersey by Bush strategist Lee Atwater.

Atwater, who watched the focus groups react with shock to the Horton saga from behind a two-way mirror, said afterward he realized then that "the sky was the limit on Dukakis's negatives."

By the eve of the 1988 election, any remaining distinctions between Americans for Bush as an independent political force and the Bush campaign had been badly blurred, creating a thin trail of circumstantial evidence pointing to illegal coordination between the two.

McCarthy, it was noted, once worked for Roger Ailes, the Bush campaign's superlative media hatchet man.

Americans for Bush was using the same direct-mail vendors as the Bush campaign.

Baker had passed on Fediay's offer to pre-empt the Horton ad.

And then there was that Oct. 22 letter to Fediay from vice presidential nominee Dan Quayle, in which Quayle offered thanks for a free copy of an attack ad aimed at Dukakis and praised Americans for Bush as "a source of real encouragement as well as a great boon to our efforts."

A Quayle spokesman said the letter was written by an intern and signed with an automatic pen, but that explanation didn't persuade many.

"Officially, the campaign has to disavow themselves from me," Fediay said at the time. "Unofficially, I hear that they're thrilled about what we're doing."

✦   ✦   ✦

Today, FEC records show that NSPAC, the mother of "Americans for Bush," was the single largest PAC spender of the 1988 campaign, shelling out $8.5 million to help fund conservative candidates, as well as to pay its own staff overhead, supply and equipment costs and expensive direct-mail solicitations.

Of that total, NSPAC reported spending $8 million on behalf of Bush's election.

The Horton ads still rankle the 1988 Dukakis braintrust, who continue to ponder whether Brown and Bush skipped hand-in-hand through the wide gray area of federal law that bars coordination between independent expenditure groups and presidential campaigns.

"The law in this area is such a mess that it may well be that they weren't in violation," Susan Estrich, Dukakis' campaign manager in 1988, told *Gauntlet*. "Anybody who was paying careful attention to the campaign could tell what the Bush strategy was and how to take it to the next step."

Citing how closely the Bush revolving door ad followed Brown's Horton ad and how Bush's rhetoric on the stump incorporated the same themes being plied by Brown and other IEs, Estrich said: "Whether they are illegally coordinated or not, one helps the other.

"What Brown is able to do is to take the assault to that level beyond good taste with a commercial that can drive the message home like a sledgehammer," she said. "Bush campaigns on family values and trust and questions Bill Clinton's character. Brown runs the Gennifer Flowers ad.

"It's symbiotic. Brown simply takes the extra step that any presidential campaign would get pilloried for doing."

The problem, Estrich said, is not Brown himself or the cut throat strategies typically employed by someone like Roger Ailes. It is the construction of the FEC law barring coordinated action between presidential campaigns and like-minded independent groups.

"The law here is a little ridiculous," said Estrich, now a law professor at the University of Southern California. "Its definition of coordinated action fails to take into account the realities of politics and how things work during a campaign.

"You don't need to violate the rules to understand how to help the other campaign," she added. "I don't blame Brown or Ailes for it, they're just pushing it to the limit.

"What the Bush campaign was able to do in '88, which it shouldn't have been able to do, was to get a bigger bang for the buck that they couldn't have gotten without the taste patrol coming down on them."

Estrich admitted the Dukakis campaign was "timid" about calling the Horton commercials "racism," adding: "We let them get away with it."

But she was less certain of a so-lution, arguing that Bush himself could and should do more to silence Brown or at least reign him in.

"I just think the press and others shouldn't buy into the superficial appearance of separation and should hold the candidate responsible for what's done on his or her behalf," she said.

"The idea is not to punish Floyd Brown, but to recognize that the candidate is the stimulus for what Brown does. If George Bush didn't want Floyd Brown doing it, he wouldn't be doing it.

"You can't tell me," Estrich added, "that those people won't stop doing something if the White House tells them to. These are powerful people. They have ways of convincing them that to stop is in their long-run best interest.

"I never had the sense that that was done four years ago."

John Sasso, Dukakis' top strategic adviser in 1988 and an adviser to Clinton this year, took a somewhat tougher view, suggesting that a presidential candidate should be able to "shut down" an IE like Brown's at will.

"I think the campaigns have an obligation to try and do everything they can to make sure that independent groups that are trying to promote their candidacy — even when they're not coordinated — are shut down when they go over the line," Sasso told *Gauntlet.*

"The campaigns themselves should determine the line. You can take legal action. You can be strong and forceful in your insistence that it be done," he added.

The public advocacy group Common Cause took a more moderate approach to the issue earlier this year as part of a comprehensive package of campaign reforms shepherded through an election-year, scandal-wracked Congress.

"The existing law and regulations are not adequate in insuring that independent expenditure groups really have a wholly separate operation from the candidate," said Susan Manes, vice president for issues at Common Cause.

The group's reform legislation, in addition to proposing tough new spending limits for PACs and congressional elections, established a series of specific criteria to judge the independence of organizations like Brown's, including prohibitions against the sharing of vendors and consultants.

"As a general proposition, it's been our feeling that the law needs to be given greater meaning by having a more specific definition of when you're independent and when you're not," Manes said.

"We realize these groups have court-afforded protections, but they can come into the political process and make a lot of statements and a lot of claims," she added. "If their claims prove or appear to be questionable, there's no way to hold anyone accountable because the people running the ads are not running for office."

And because an independent expenditure group can spend as much money as it can raise on a candidate's behalf, Manes said, the mere presence of one IE in a campaign "can add an enormous amount of resources onto one side of the debate that the opposing candidate cannot cope with.

"It really skews the playing field and gives rise to the bigger question of how to afford protection to the other candidate," she added. "How does the candidate who is the subject of a misleading ad from an independent expenditure group take issue with it without going bankrupt?"

The solution Common Cause proposed in their legislation was public matching funds for a candidate to use to respond to independent attacks.

But Bush vetoed the reform package earlier this year because he opposes public financing of congressional campaigns. Congress, never more than a fair weather proponent of campaign reform anyway, let the issue drop.

For his part, Brown dismisses the criticisms voiced by Estrich and Sasso as political sour grapes and expresses outrage at suggestions that his voice should be muzzled.

"During the actual campaign, the Willie Horton commercial was not as notorious," he said. "It has more of a life and an urgency now than during the campaign.

"What I really think happened was that, as Dukakis was falling in the polls after the Democratic convention, his advisers began looking for something they could latch onto as the reason.

"They latched onto this Willie Horton thing as if to say, 'We would

> Ironically, for all the criticism leveled against Brown's Horton ad, the commercial produced by Bush forces was found, in retrospect, to be the far more inaccurate of the two.

have won except America is racist.' And they have pounded that home for the past four years.

"But, to me, Willie Horton is the best kind of political advertising," Brown said. "It focused on crime, an issue that means a lot to voters, and it had an important and significant policy impact."

As evidence, Brown cited a Washington Post investigation published earlier this year revealing that the number of furloughs granted to inmates in the federal prison system had declined by 50 percent since 1988.

"That means there are criminals that haven't been released prematurely. That also means there are people out there who haven't been beaten, raped, robbed, murdered or brutalized," he added.

"For that reason alone, I would do the Willie Horton spot again in a heartbeat."

Proposals like Sasso's suggesting that independent expenditure groups should be shut down at the whim of a politician represent "a massive violation of my rights of free expression," Brown said.

"Who are they to say they can limit other people's First Amendment rights? It's the same thing as this whole argument about 'Political Correctness,'" he said. "These ideas are just a blatant violation of people's right to free speech.

"This is America, isn't it? Who is going to decide when something crosses the line? Who is going to pick what's right speech and what's wrong speech? Who is going to decide what's proper political advocacy?

"All these ideas come right from the thought police. As far as I'm concerned, the message will stand or fall on its own."

Ironically, for all the criticism leveled against Brown's Horton ad, the commercial produced by Bush forces was found, in retrospect, to be the far more inaccurate of the two.

Among other facts, Bush's 30-second spot either fudged or ignored that Horton was the only furlough escapee ever to commit a violent crime and that 72 of the 288 furlough "escapees" cited hadn't really escaped but were simply a few hours late returning to prison.

"Never before in a presidential campaign have televised ads sponsored by a major party candidate lied so blatantly," Kathleen Hall Jamieson, dean of the Annenberg School of Communication at the University of Pennsylvania, concluded in her analysis of Bush's 1988 media onslaught.

✦   ✦   ✦

After the 1988 election, Brown, who is married and has two boys, disappeared from Washington, D.C., and returned to Washington state to decompress and spend time with his young family.

"From 1988 to 1990, I didn't live here," he said from his office in the Virginia suburbs outside the capital. "I believe one of the key things that anybody who works in Washington can do is move away from this place for a while, live in the real America and get their head cleared out.

"That's why I'm a big supporter of term limits."

Fabrizio said Brown needed the break.

"Back toward the end of 1988, the media was beating us up for being racist and the Bush people were just beating us up for the sake of beating us up on a daily basis," he recalled.

"Floyd really wanted to take it all personally and get angry about it, but then he said, 'Look, I'm not in this for positive press for myself. I'm doing this because I believe it's the right thing to do.' He showed a lot of fortitude in the face of a heavy pummeling," Fabrizio said.

"His job is electing conservative Republicans. You may not always agree with him, but you can be damn sure he's always on the level and he's going to do what he says he's going to do.

"He is nothing like his media persona," Fabrizio said. "The press tries to make him out to be some big, mean-spirited ogre. Well, he's big, but he's really just a gentle spirit whose love is politics and passion is issues."

During his self-imposed exile, Brown decided to create "Citizens United," a lobbying group dedicated to advancing a socially conservative agenda.

The group now has more than 100,000 members who each pay $25 annual dues.

"They're overwhelmingly middle class and overwhelmingly Republican, About 20 percent of the members are Democrats," Brown said. "Most are from the Midwest and West. They're working-class people, not well to do, and they've been educated in public schools.

"The audience I really consider my audience are the working, middle class people, Catholics, Evangelicals, the people who make the country run, the people who pay the taxes, the people who do the work. They're people like my family," he said.

In June 1990, a revitalized Brown returned to the national political scene with a trademark flourish that confounded his critics from the Willie Horton days.

Bankrolled by the Republican Challengers Committee, an independent group he organized for use in congressional elections, he announced an advertising campaign attacking U.S. Senate candidate David Duke, the former Klu Klux Klan leader who was running as a Republican in Louisiana.

Brown called Duke "a racist pretending to be a Republican out of convenience. He is trying to establish himself as the leader of the conservative movement and we have to stop that."

In March of 1991, Brown was busy organizing conservative students on college campuses to demonstrate in support of the Persian Gulf War.

By September, he had found controversy again.

Working quietly with other conservative leaders, Brown had organized an advertising campaign designed as a pre-emptive strike against the Democratic foes of Supreme Court nominee Clarence Thomas.

"We want the liberals to know we aren't going to sit down on this one," Brown said at the time, a bitter reference to the U.S. Senate's 1987 defeat of then-nominee Robert Bork, the judge who had ruled against Brown in the embassy protest case.

Brown's TV commercial, produced once again by the McCarthy-Shirley-Fabrizio team, asked the rhetorical question: "Who will judge the judge?" of U.S. Sens. Joseph Biden of Maryland, Alan Cranston of

> ". . . my audience are the working, middle class people, Catholics, Evangelicals, the people who make the country run . . ."

California and Edward Kennedy of Massachusetts.

"How many of these liberal Democrats could themselves pass scrutiny?," a narrator asked as viewers were reminded of the plagiarism charges leveled against Biden in the 1988 campaign, Cranston's questionable dealings with failed savings and loans, and Kennedy's involvement in the scandals at Chappaquidick and Palm Beach.

As with the Horton ad, the White House professed ignorance, but this time their claim showed signs of wilting amid the firestorm of criticism.

William Kristol, chief of staff to Vice President Quayle, had heard the Thomas ad was coming in late August and had passed word on to the White House.

White House spokeswoman Judy Smith admitted she knew in advance the commercial would be negative.

There were even unconfirmed reports that aides to President Bush had even forewarned two of the targeted senators.

Had the White House known?

"Not from me, but I'm sure they knew it," Brown told *Gauntlet*, noting that he and ad co-sponsor L. Brent Bozell, leader of the Conservative Victory Committee, had discussed the commercial with numerous conservative powerbrokers in the Capitol.

"I took that ad around and showed it to everybody in town," Brown said.

Still, the White House postured with outrage. Both Thomas and Bush publicly repudiated the ad as counterproductive and offensive, while then-Chief of Staff John Sununu called on Brown and Bozell to pull the plug.

But they refused, unless the "left-wing groups" gearing up to oppose the Thomas nomination agreed to a cease-fire.

Brown's hard-hitting commercial pleased a conservative faction of the White House, including Sununu and White House political director Ron Kaufman, but it alarmed other, more moderate insiders who were in the midst of a quiet, mannerly lobbying campaign aimed at forestalling a publicly televised confrontation over Thomas.

At the time, critics contended the ad only served to enflame ideological passions when, unlike the Kennedy-led liberal fury that had brought down Bork four years before, organized opposition to Thomas had yet to emerge.

"We understand our role as outsiders and that, as insiders, the White House has to play a Washington inside game. Judge Thomas isn't going to attack these people," Brown said at the time, succinctly capturing not only the posturing of the moment, but also the intriguing political dilemma posed by independent expenditure groups.

A month later, when the name Anita Hill suddenly became a household word and a furious battle with Thomas' liberal foes was joined, Brown took a measure of ideological pleasure in saying, 'I told you so.'

He began an Oct. 10 press conference by noting that the Senate had exempted itself from some of the same equal opportunity employment guidelines threatening to torpedo the Thomas nomination.

Then he attacked the "faceless, gutless wonders" in the Senate who leaked the FBI report on its interview with Hill, calling the allegations against Thomas the "most repugnant, vile form of character assassination."

And he described Hill as "no more than a puppet being manipulated by these people who want to destroy the credibility of Judge

Thomas."

Brown and Bozell urged Bush to take the offensive by appearing on national television to denounce the "lynching" and to initiate a massive federal probe of the Senate leak.

In the process, Brown suggested, Sen. Kennedy and his staff should submit to lie detector tests.

For Brown, Thomas' teetering nomination represented more than just a conservative voice on the Supreme Court. In the bigger picture, it was a major threat to Bush's ability to govern.

"The fact is that we didn't really grow up in country clubs and we didn't grow up in prep school and so we understand a street brawl when we see it," he said, bluntly drawing the distinction between the passionate roots of his conservatism and the aloof, more moderate brand embodied by Bush.

Brown even offered a $30,000 reward for the identity of those who leaked the FBI report.

With his nephew's rape trial looming on the horizon, Kennedy, who was Bork's nemesis in 1987, played almost no role in the Thomas hearing and the ungalvanized opposition faltered enough for Thomas to win a seat on the highest court in the land.

Brown characterized Thomas' confirmation as a narrow victory over left-wing special interests and radical feminists.

"They reached deeper down into the gutter than I ever could have imagined to destroy this man," he said.

A month later — exactly one year before the 1992 election — the chasm between Bush and the Brown conservatives yawned wider in the wake of the budget agreement that broke Bush's no-new-taxes pledge.

It was then, at the height of the president's post-war popularity, that Brown predicted "serious trouble" for Bush's re-election campaign.

"The middle class is sick and tired of getting rhetoric, rhetoric, rhetoric from the White House," he said, sounding what has become a chief Democratic theme this year.

At the same time, Brown, McCarthy, Shirley and Fabrizio were helping to finish off David Duke, who was running for governor of Louisiana, by producing a TV commercial warning of an economic exodus under Duke's reign.

"Hot damn!," drawled the knee-slapping cowboy pictured in Brown's ad. "Do you know how many jobs are going to leave Louisiana and come to Texas if Duke is elected? Hot damn!"

On election day in the Bayou State, Duke finished with 39 percent of the vote and was well on his way to getting his first real job — as an insurance agent.

Nationally, Bush's failure to embrace an aggressive anti-tax strategy and his low-key approach to the congressional battlefield set Brown wandering upon the presidential landscape, where he toyed briefly with the idea of supporting conservative commentator Patrick Buchanan.

It didn't take long for Brown to realize what some of his like-minded colleagues still dispute: An ideologically impure Bush can do more to advance the conservative agenda than four years of Bill Clinton.

"Some people believe that if Clinton wins, the conservative messiah will come forth out of the backlash to four years of liberal reign," Brown said. "I think they're just deluding themselves. I believe in incremental change."

✦   ✦   ✦

Brown picked the lowest point in Bill Clinton's political career — this past March — to reprise his role as slayer of the Democratic dragon.

This time, however, he would wind up fighting the battle alone.

On March 15, with Fabrizio tied up advising a number of congressional campaigns, the remainder of the Horton-Duke-Thomas creative team — Brown, McCarthy and Shirley — announced their intention to mount a $10 million ad campaign against Clinton.

"There's a real question about Bill Clinton's character and open questions in the public's mind about his fitness to occupy the Oval Office," Shirley said. "Gennifer Flowers will not be the issue. But there are questions about his draft-dodging, about him and the savings and loan . . . that are legitimate."

Brown, who had already begun raising funds through a new independent expenditure group called "Citizens for Bush," was far less specific.

"I don't think any one allegation is big enough to beat (Clinton), but taken together in a cumulative way, they show a lack of judgement," he said at the time.

Speculation immediately surfaced that Brown would reincarnate Willie Horton in the bodies of two white Arkansas state inmates: Charles Lloyd Patterson, who terrorized a couple after escaping during his fifth furlough, and Larry Dean Robinson, who murdered an Arkansas woman after being freed to ease prison overcrowding.

By April, however, Shirley had learned that Brown intended to make Clinton's alleged affair with Gennifer Flowers the subject of his first attack ad.

He quit to form his own consultancy.

"I disagreed sharply with the Gennifer Flowers strategy," Shirley told *Gauntlet*. "Other than getting Floyd Brown press coverage, I don't think it's accomplished much. I don't think it hurt Clinton or helped Bush.

"I disagreed with it because it's not based in policy. I tend to believe that's one of the issues that ought not be discussed in the public forum by an independent expenditure group," he added.

Brown said the split with Shirley was "more of a business thing. It was more over basically what I expected of him."

Brown and McCarthy also parted ways before the Flowers ad campaign began.

"Larry has a lot of very important corporate clients, including major media concerns," said Brown. "Our work has had some impact on his business because of the type of clientele he caters to."

McCarthy would not discuss his association with Brown at all.

"I'm tired of talking about it," he said. "The more you talk about it, the less pleasant it gets. He's a good guy, but I think I'll pass."

Fediay, meanwhile, had been dragged under financially by onerous terms in a key direct-mail contract. Fluent in Russian, she left the independent expenditure business and went to work promoting American investment in the former Soviet Union.

Fabrizio and Brown first discussed what would later become "The Bill Clinton Fact Line" in April, when they floated the idea during an interview with *Harpers* in which Democratic and Republican political consultants were asked their advice to the presidential campaigns.

The *Harper*'s piece was published July 7.

Two days later, just before the start of the Democratic National Convention, Brown announced his plan to air television ads that would promote a 1-900 number interested viewers could call to hear excerpts of

Flowers' tape-recorded "intimate" conversations with the governor of Arkansas.

"What really happened between Bill Clinton and Gennifer Flowers?," the narrator of the ad entitled "Run and Hide" asks. "Did he lie about their affair? Did he try a cover-up? Call the number and get to know Gennifer Flowers the way Bill Clinton did.

"Listen to the taped excerpts. Judge for yourself if this is the way a man talks to a woman that is just a friendly acquaintance."

Callers to the 1-900 line, which cost $4.99 per call with about half the proceeds going to the Presidential Victory Committee as profit, could also hear commentary regarding Clinton's less than forthright responses when confronted with draft-dodging and pot-smoking allegations.

The ad promoting the "Fact Line" was slated for a limited run on CNN in New York during the Democratic convention, but, in a dramatic departure from 1988, both the Democrats and the Republicans immediately opened fire on Brown.

Bush spokeswoman Torie Clark distanced the campaign from Brown's work, saying: "We are not interested in sleazy stuff at all."

Bush campaign counsel Bobby Burchfield reminded the media he had already asked Brown to "immediately cease" raising cash under the name "Citizens for Bush" and had sent out letters to the group's donors disavowing any link between Brown's organization and the Bush re-election drive.

And, unlike the weak-kneed Dukakis response to the Horton ads, Avis LaVelle, a Clinton campaign press secretary, moved forcefully to back Bush against a political wall.

"It's clearly a fundraising effort in the new porno-political vein and,

more than that, it is an effort on the part of the Republicans to dupe the public again with Willie Horton-type tactics," LaVelle said. "If this is truly an effort that the Bush camp disavows, then President Bush should say so publicly."

Bush complied.

"We've had our lawyers in touch with (Brown) and told him to stop it and I repudiate it now as the kind of sleaze that diminishes the political process . . . ," Bush said. "That man knows that he ought to stop it and I hope he does. And I'm going to try to keep this campaign on the issues."

Added Republican National Committee Chairman Rich Bond: "Not much we can do about (Brown). It's a matter of free speech. We think it stinks. We're against it . . . It's a tactic we don't endorse at all."

Brown, who had already bowed to one Bush criticism by replacing the name "Citizens for Bush" with "Presidential Victory Committee," handled the assault with his usual hardball aplomb.

The Bush campaign, he said, "has its own problems. If they don't want to engage their enemy, I stand ready to do that."

Clinton, seizing the chance to drape the Willie Horton anchor around Bush's neck, seemed unimpressed with the president's disavowal.

"I just don't believe that he doesn't know about it (in advance). He could stop this stuff in a minute," he said, offering few specifics on how that could be accomplished. "It worked for them in 1988, so they're going to run this dog out in '92 and see if it'll work again.

"This is the way the Republicans make a living in national politics, by destroying their opponents."

Then, in a chilling contrast to his 1988 predecessor, Clinton's holier-than-thou rhetoric dissolved into the fairly blunt suggestion that Bush could be in store for retribution on the issue of marital fidelity.

"When you live by the sword, you have to be careful," he offered cryptically. "There is a certain arrogance and relative hypocrisy in all this that's pretty appalling."

As of this writing, strong rumors still percolated on the campaign trail that the short-lived scandal involving Bush's alleged affair with Jennifer Fitzgerald was pushed into print by the Clinton forces as payback — designed to break on the eve of the GOP convention in timing that mimicked Brown's announcement of his "Run and Hide" attack ad.

But Brown's decision to publicize the ad before it actually began airing on TV — a move in line with his trademark strategy of generating free media exposure for a commercial due to receive only very limited on-air display — proved to be a significant blunder.

First, the instant repudiations from Clinton and Bush weakened Brown's already suspect credibility with the media, spinning the story away from the issues raised by "The Bill Clinton Fact Line" and toward a deluge of media hand-wringing about whether Brown's work constituted "sleaze" and how it should be covered, if at all.

"I think it's almost inevitable that when we try to write about, to denounce, to explain, to put in the proper context this kind of advertising . . . we just put it into greater currency," *New York Times* reporter R.W. "Johnny" Apple said on CNN.

"We give it wider distribution. More people see it. It becomes more talked about and I'm afraid that the qualifications, the denials don't catch up."

More important than the major media's self-loathing, however, was the fact that Time Warner Inc., the world's largest media and entertainment company, was a co-sponsor of the Democratic National Convention.

After hearing the criticisms leveled against Brown by Clinton and Bush, the Time Warner cable division — which has a hammerlock on cable TV in New York City and throughout much of the metropolitan United States — pulled the plug on the ad promoting the "Fact Line" two hours before it was to air in Manhattan.

The company's lawyers, who at least watched the commercial first, defended the move as being in line with their policy to accept ads only from candidates or political groups authorized by candidates.

"Candidates should be accountable for the ads," explained Robert Jacobs, general counsel for Time Warner Cable.

Brown charged Time Warner with "gross hypocrisy," noting that this was the same media conglomerate that, in the name of free speech, refused to pull the Ice-T album containing the rap "Cop Killer" off the shelves.

Dave Bossie, the president of Citizens United, said the Democrats simply "put pressure" on their convention co-sponsor to kill the ad.

As of August, the Clinton Fact Line, which generated more than

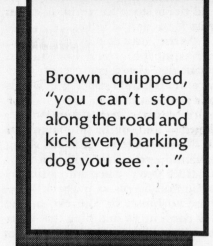

Brown quipped, "you can't stop along the road and kick every barking dog you see . . . "

40,000 telephone calls in its first two days in operation, was still up and running but the TV commercial Brown designed to promote it was gathering dust.

"We've really been censored by the media outlets, by all the major cable networks in the country and by a good number of the local cable companies," he told *Gauntlet*. "As an independent expenditure group, we don't have the same protections under federal law that candidates have.

"We have to go through a somewhat arbitrary clearance process and when you have a spot as controversial as ours, they just say no," Brown added.

"I think conservatives should be the first to stand up and defend the First Amendment. Because when it comes down to it, it's the conservatives who are the first to be censored."

Brown's attorneys believe there are the makings of a good lawsuit against publicly licensed Time-Warner, but suspect such an action would take years and tens of thousands of dollars to win.

"Frankly," Brown quipped, "you can't stop along the road and kick every barking dog you see, so you try to do the best you can and pick your fights."

As the coup de gras, Clinton operatives, including Jack Palladino, the private detective hired by the campaign to debunk damaging allegations against the Arkansas governor, dealt Brown a final blow with a shrewd — and, ultimately, hypocritical — news leak as the Democratic convention got underway.

CBS News — as their lead story on the *Evening News with Dan Rather* — aired a report that Brown, whom CBS described as a "political sleaze operative," had harassed the family of a former law student of Clinton's in an effort to link the pregnant woman's 1977 suicide to an affair with Clinton.

CBS even aired a tape recording of Brown speaking to the dead woman's sister by telephone — a tape made with Palladino's guidance after he himself had investigated and defused the potential scandal for his boss, Clinton.

"Give me a break," the dead woman's sister told CBS in comments that echoed what Clinton said the same day. "We're talking the president of the United States here. He can't control them? Come on."

The CBS report did not mention Palladino's own investigation, the fact that CBS itself had investigated the rumor or the fact that Brown had given up on the suicide story nearly three months before when he found he could not substantiate it.

The next day, the Bush campaign filed an FEC complaint against Brown, charging him with deceiving potential contributors by using the name, Presidential Victory Committee.

"The guy is a political leper who is much more damaging to us than to our opposition," said Burchfield, the Bush campaign counsel.

Brown, appearing *CBS This Morning*, could barely contain his anger as he grappled with an apparent media double-standard on the so-called "sleaze" factor.

"CBS researched it — they spent months and months researching it," he said of the suicide story. "Floyd Brown researched it also. And what did I do with it? What I did was, I dropped it. CBS News did not drop it. What CBS did was, they brought it to the American people . . .

"It's irresponsible for CBS to put this type of garbage into millions of homes without any documentation — and all they're trying to do is use me as a vehicle," Brown added.

"The only difference is that you think it's responsible journalism because you wear a press badge."

The furor ranked as new personal low for Brown, who, despite being more isolated now than at any time in his career, still defends his "Fact Line."

"It's an example of what I call Clinton's pattern of dishonesty," he said. "I grew up watching those Watergate hearings, where the big question was: 'What did you know and when did you know it?'

"America basically booted Nixon out of office because he was dishonest," Brown added. "In my opinion, Bill Clinton doesn't meet that threshold level of honesty.

"I don't want to make that decision for the voters, but I know that if I give them the information, they're going to know what I know."

✦   ✦   ✦

Powerful advertising from independent groups has been a part of the manipulation of the American political process for nearly three decades now.

It has almost always emanated from the right side of the spectrum.

In 1964, a Texas group supporting Republican Barry Goldwater for president aired ads questioning how his Democratic rival, Texan Lyndon Johnson, had stacked up a multi-million-dollar fortune during a career of public service.

Johnson's campaign responded with the now famous "Daisy" commercial that obliterated Goldwater's presidential aspirations in the image of an ever-expanding nuclear mushroom cloud.

In the early 1980s, ads bankrolled by the National Conservative Political Action Committee, another employer of Craig Shirley's talents, ended the careers of a more than a half-dozen Democratic senators.

One NCPAC commercial portrayed the senators as weak on defense by depicting empty missile silos. Another portrayed as them as too liberal, criticizing their support for the federal food stamp program by showing a family being forced to pay $100 million for groceries.

Independent expenditure groups, Shirley said, are "a good example of the way the system should work and they usually bring more people into the process.

"Everybody laments about declining voter interest, yet, on the other hand, those same people are the ones who piss and moan about it are the ones who also want to limit the amount of money spent by campaigns," he said.

"They don't realize that the two go together. It takes money to reach people and get them interested.

"When you think about," Shirley added, "these groups are at the foundations of what this country is all about — a group of partisans banding together to advance a common set of values. I think virtually anything that encourages people to participate in the process is good."

Brown brought the IE attack strategy to the media spotlight in 1988 and, this year, the Democrats seemed ready to avenge the havoc he had wrought upon their party.

"We will be tough," Democratic consultant Victor Kamber said in July as he announced the formation of "Americans for Change," an independent group he hoped would spend $1 million on ads targeting Bush.

Kamber said everything would be fair game: Bush's family business dealings, Neil Bush's savings and loan problems, Dan Quayle's inability to spell, etc.

"We're going to deal with some of the issues that maybe the campaign wouldn't dare touch," he added, capturing one of the essential missions of all independent expenditure groups.

Angered by Brown's "Clinton Fact Line," Kamber floated the idea of starting his own 1-900 service, this one featuring recordings of famous Bush and Quayle misstatements and stumblings.

"I'm against negative campaigning like this, but I'm just tired of Democrats being beaten up and losing," he explained.

Within weeks, Kamber folded his group under pressure from Democratic National Committee Chairman Ron Brown, who argued that such tactics were beneath the party's dignity — even though Brown himself was gleefully soliciting homemade campaign commercials attacking Bush from Democratic voters around the country.

Grudgingly, Kamber abandoned his vow to do battle with the "the right-wing GOP sleaze machine" and returned the $30,000 he had raised.

Brown, as Shirley put it, is "the only one out there this time around."

One reason: Clinton's efforts to move the Democratic Party toward the right has minimalized the kind of ideological clash needed to energize the conservative wing of the GOP, whose already tentative support for Bush has been weakening steadily in the past year.

"Historically, most independent expenditures have been generated from the right because the right is most based in ideology," Shirley said.

"Reagan generated a lot of heat and light in 1980 because of his long-standing relationship with the conservative movement and because there was such a sharp ideological contrast with Jimmy Carter.

"But Clinton has not yet been defined as a liberal by either himself, the media or the Bush campaign for that matter," Shirley added. "His own posturing on either or all sides of the political fence tends to undermine the intensity needed to set the emergence of independent groups into motion."

Brown agreed with his former compatriot but placed more of the blame on Bush's failure to fully embrace conservatism than on Clinton's chameleon-like ability to appear to embrace disparate ideologies.

"It's the direct result of conservative's frustrations with President Bush," he said. "He broke his word to conservatives when agreed to raise taxes. There used to be fix or six independent expenditure groups but there's a big divide now over the nature of how to bring about change.

"A lot of people belong to the old school, the messianic view of how to change America. They expect some great leader to ride into Washington, D.C., on a white stallion and somehow save the nation," Brown said.

"I disagree with that. I think you have to be out there every single day battling. We might move an inch or two forward. We might fall back a half-inch. But you have to be out

> "Four years from now, Bill Clinton together with a Democratic Congress could do major damage to our country, " Brown said.

there battling each day.

"Four years from now, Bill Clinton together with a Democratic Congress could do major damage to our country. Even if George Bush isn't actively forwarding a conservative agenda, we'll be a lot better off with four more years of him," Brown added.

He also blames the FEC for "creating barriers to entry" that scare off embryonic independent expenditure groups with red tape, legal fees and a maze of complex regulations.

"The FEC is a mechanism set up by the political establishment in order keep people out of politics," he said. "Their whole goal is to keep people like me out of the process and to keep the establishment happy. We fight them everyday."

Replied FEC spokesman Fred Eiland: "The Commission can get banged around on a lot of things and get blamed for a lot of things, but we simply do what the law says must be done."

But the FEC, chaired by three Democrats and three Republicans, also makes "law" too. Brown's antics this year have led the commission to rule that, starting with the 1993-94 election cycle, independent expenditure groups will no longer be allowed to use a candidate's name without authorization.

✦   ✦   ✦

"Who's that?," Tony Mitchell, the deputy press secretary of the Bush campaign, replied with a smirk when asked recently about the campaign's opinion of Floyd Brown.

"Oh, that Floyd Brown," he chuckled finally.

"He certainly is not playing a helpful role in the process," Mitchell said. "We have a number of problems with him, not the least of which being that many people are confused by the fact that he is not at all related to the campaign.

> The computer analysis uncovered 405 Bush donors who had also contributed a total of $308,058 to the Brown-related groups.

"We think he intentionally relies on that confusion to aid his fund-raising efforts."

Mitchell noted that each time Brown's Presidential Victory Committee files a fund-raising report with the FEC, the Bush campaign sends a letter to each new donor.

"It basically says that if you're at all confused about that point, we suggest you ask for a refund of your money and we give them his address so they're able to do that."

Why would Bush's troops go out of their way to cut off the financial legs of a man who was so helpful to electing their candidate four years ago?

"I have a hard time believing he was that helpful," Mitchell replied. "Even in 1992 we're still having to answer questions about the guy. For the record, there is zero connection between Brown and the Bush campaign.

"We've written to him. We've written to his contributors. In all of our public and private statements, we have pointed out our disdain for him and his approach," he said. "We have done everything we can within legal limits to make it known that this guy should not be in business doing what he's doing."

In principal, Mitchell said, Bush believes the concept of like-minded people coming together to be involved in the political process is "a positive thing."

But Brown's "approach is negative," he added. "It's relying on issues that, for lack of a better word, are not relevant to the campaign."

Isn't Clinton's character one of Bush's chief lines of attack this year?

"Character certainly is a relevant presidential issue. Sleaze is not," Mitchell replied.

When it's suggested that the rhetoric and issues of the 1992 presidential campaign have already spiralled well beyond even the most generous bounds of civility, relevancy and good taste, Mitchell finally demurs.

"In some respects, yes," he sighed, "the campaign is already out of control."

That's why Brown may well end up as only a footnote in this year's bruising political wars after co-authoring the book with Bush in

1988.

Even after four years, rumors continue to circulate that Brown was in league with Atwater and/or Bush campaign manager James Baker in 1988.

But several investigations — including a two-year inquiry completed by the FEC in 1990 — have found nothing to substantiate contentions that Brown and Bush operatives broke the laws barring coordination between independent expenditure groups and political campaigns.

A computer review of FEC fundraising records performed for *Gauntlet* found that three independent expenditure groups tied to Brown — NSPAC, the Republican Challengers Committee and the Presidential Victory Committee — all share some of the money trail that leads to the Bush campaigns of 1988 and 1992 and to the Republican National Committee.

The computer analysis uncovered 405 Bush donors who had also contributed a total of $308,058 to the Brown-related groups — more than 12 percent of all the funds raised by the independent groups in the past four years.

Some of the matches may be attributed to duplicative direct-mail lists. And, as Brown himself pointed out, it makes sense that those who support Republican candidates also might decide to contribute to conservative causes.

"Part of it," he added, "may also be that since many Republican activists know that, after the conventions are over, both presidential campaigns must rely totally on federal matching funds.

"These people have no place else to give but to us in order to directly impact the campaign in the homestretch."

Brown dismissed efforts to link him to Bush operatives as "a waste of time and energy" and said the Bush campaign has done everything it can to cripple his operation, including forcing him to spend more than $100,000 on legal fees to fight the FEC complaints filed this year and four years ago.

"They're the establishment and they don't like independent operators. It's a function of the establishment wanting to control the political process," Brown said. "You're either in the fold or out of business as far as they're concerned."

Fabrizio described claims of coordination as "the nature of the beast."

"All these theories of collusion — the wink, the nod — there's smoke but there ain't no fire man and the smoke is mostly in the reporter's mind."

Fabrizio said the simplest way to determine whether Brown and Bush have ever been or are now in cahoots is to find out when Brown, unlike an array of his conservative colleagues, was last invited to the Bush White House.

"Are you kidding?," Fabrizio said. "Floyd would probably get arrested if he even set foot near the place. If anyone thinks he's done the things he's done to ingratiate himself, they don't know Floyd Brown.

"Nothing could be further from the truth. He is still being vilified by the Bush people. There is no gain here for Floyd Brown and I challenge anybody to find out what Floyd Brown has gained from having the courage of his convictions," he said.

"He sees the most important thing he can do as building a grassroots, conservative-based organization that can help candidates all over the country. Floyd has felt that way as far back as 1988," Fabrizio added.

Brown's pursuit of his ideology has made him a pariah among most mainstream Republican powerbrokers. And it has not been without personal cost.

"This is a tough business," he said. "My hometown newspaper did a front-page article on me once. It began, 'Some say Floyd Brown eats mean pills for breakfast. Others say he would lacerate his own mother for right-wing victories.'

"That paper," Brown added solemnly, "landed on my mother's front doorstep one morning.

"You find out fast who your friends are in this business. I've received hundreds of wonderful notes. In fact, I'd say I get more positive mail than negative."

Horton's name continues to be a political sword that cuts both ways.

"When we talk about crime," California Attorney General Dan Lungren told delegates to this year's Republican National Convention, "the Democrats trot out their liberal icon and invite the press to worship at the altar of righteous indignation.

"That icon is spelled with two words: Willie Horton," Lungren added. "When they utter those two words, we Republicans are to bow in a frenzy of mea culpas."

But would Brown change anything?

"Not a lot," he said.

In addition to pursuing Clinton this year, Brown is also organizing a petition drive seeking to oust U.S. Rep. Thomas Foley, the Washington state Democrat, as speaker of the House of Representatives.

No matter how the presidential race turns out, Brown figures he'll have plenty to keep him busy.

"The day after the election, the conservatives will start looking for a standardbearer for four years from now," he said. "The new presidential race will be off and running and I want to be active with that.

"If Clinton's elected. we're going to have to fight him on numerous legislative fronts. We're in a good position to be Bill Clinton's biggest critic," Brown added. "If he's elected, he's going to need a watchdog like us to keep him straight."

Ed Cafasso is a reporter and city editor for **The Boston Herald.**

Theodore Briseno testified against 3 other Los Angeles police officers, acquitted in the beating of Rodney King . . . and his lawyer wants the public to know that. Federal civil rights charges have been filed against the same four officers, including Briseno. The *USA Today* reported Briseno's lawyer, Harland Braun, plans a PR blitz to let " . . . everyone know Ted is different from the others." The paper reports Braun will have his client give a series of in-depth interviews shortly before the trial starts. Braun himself hit the talk show circuit to gain sympathy for his client.

As Homey the Clown, from *In Living Color* might quip, "Can you say influencing a jury, children?"

Media Pandering To Black Revolutionaries

Mark Di Ionno

"Ramona draws hero's welcome"

"Ramona freed and unMOVEd"

"Ramona's Return"

Ramona, Ramona, Ramona. Heeeeere's Ramona.

In the Philadelphia press, Ramona needs no other name. Like Geraldo. Or Madonna. Even Jesus.

Philadelphia's Ramona is Ramona Africa, the only adult member of MOVE to escape the bomb blast and subsequent fire that ended the Osage Avenue standoff between police and members of the revolutionary cult on May 13, 1985.

What has happened since that day, when Mayor Wilson Goode gave the go-ahead for police to drop an incendiary bomb on the MOVE house is hard to explain.

But suddenly, MOVE is no longer the dreadlocked group of radical outlaws who forced two bloody confrontations with police. The first, on Aug. 8, 1978, left officer James Ramp dead on the ground outside MOVE headquarters in the Powelton Village section of West Philadelphia.

The second, on May 13, 1985,

ended in the bombing of the militarily-fortified MOVE house on Osage Avenue. The ensuing fire claimed the lives of six MOVE adults - including founder John Africa - and five children, who MOVE members refused to turn over to authorities on a number of occasions before the day-long siege began. Only Ramona Africa and Birdie Africa, a 13 year-old-boy, escape the inferno, which spread to 61 other homes, virtually destroying a city block.

These days in Philadelphia, MOVE's bloody history has all been white-washed. They are no longer described as a "revolutionary cult." Instead, Ramona Africa and the ragtag remains of the MOVE movement (a handful of members were not in the Osage Avenue home at the time of the fire) are being portrayed as the politically oppressed victims of a totalitarian regime.

One startling quote in the Philadelphia Inquirer comes from Rev. Paul Washington, a member of the 1985 MOVE Commission designed to find peaceful solutions for the city's MOVE problem.

"I think the more we recede from that particular moment (the

Osage Avenue incident) there are a whole lot of people of Philadelphians who were more sympathetic to MOVE than they were then. People are asking why? People are asking what they did to deserve this?"

If that is true, then the brainwashing is almost complete. And Ramona sure is getting the media play to put the finishing touches on it. She was picked up out of prison by limousine and driven four hours back to Philadelphia, courtesy of a WHAT-TV talk show. Oprah called. So did The Today Show. A Hollywood movie is in the works. Whoopi may play Ramona.

Ramona is everybody's favorite interview, feature story subject, and talk show guest. The media gives her a public forum every time she says boo, and she even got a secret audience with Mayor Ed Rendell who, as District Attorney, cut the arrest warrants that led to the Osage Avenue incident.

The meeting between Ramona and Rendell was described in newspaper stories as a "bridge-builder" and necessary to "clear the air." Imagine that! A city government bowing to clear the air with a revolutionary group that picked a fight with a greater power and lost.

Despite "air clearing" efforts,

Ramona is proceeding with a $50 million suit against the city which is snailing its way through the courts. MOVE and the city already settled an earlier suit. The city settled with parents of the MOVE children who died in the Osage Avenue fire, handing over $2.5 million to the plaintiffs - all but one of whom are incarcerated. The city also paid $840,000 to Birdie Africa and his father, Michael Ward. The city has also spent close to $200,000 educating, in private tutorial sessions, the surviving children of MOVE so they can assimilate into society at some point.

None of that is enough for Ramona and her comrades in the media. If you believe everything you read, Ramona Africa is a Joan of Arc heroine and her group deserves more justice. Ramona wants to reopen the Ramp trial in hopes of gaining the release of those MOVE members still jailed on a variety of charges in the killing of Ramp. Some city officials say they will oblige her. She is demanding justice, and the media is carrying those demands. Who fights for justice for James Ramp?

Ye have heard that it been said,
Thou shalt love thy neighbor and hate
*   thine enemy;*
But I say unto you, Love your enemies,
bless them that curse you, do good to
*   them that hate you,*
and pray for them who despitefully use
*   you and persecute you.*

*   — The Sermon on the Mount (Matthew 5: 43-44).*

If it sounds as if the media is treating Ramona Africa's release as the second coming of Christ, consider the words of Philadelphia Inquirer columnist Clark DeLeon, who wrote this on May 14:

"For surely MOVE is a religion. John Africa is its Christ, Osage was his Golgotha and Ramona Africa - still bearing the burn scars suffered during his apocalyptic martyrdom - is the first of his apostles to return to Jerusalem demanding justice from Caesar.

"MOVE's Pentecost took seven years instead of 50 days and Ramona Africa's voice will be the tongue of flame licking at the conscience of every Pontius Pilate in Philadelphia."

Not only is DeLeon's pandering an insult to Christians but an insult to believers of non-violence and believers of civil disobedience.

DeLeon's passion play is imaginative, but devoid of true reason. He says in an earlier column that "I am not mocking Christianity by comparing it to MOVE nor am I comparing Jesus' message with the MOVE philosophy. It's just that the parallels are too compelling."

But drawing any parallels between Christ's Christianity and the MOVE movement can only be mockery or a admittance by DeLeon that he has no working knowledge of the Life of Christ.

First and foremost, Christ was apolitical.

In Matthew 22, Verses 17-22, the Pharisees try to engage him in a political discussion aimed at criticizing the emperor.

"Is it lawful to give tribute to Caesar?" they ask.

Christ responds, "Show me the tribute money. Whose is this image and superscription?"

When the Pharisees respond "Caesar's," Christ replies, "Render, therefore unto Caesar the things which are Caesar's and unto God, the things that are God's."

Christ never made demands on the governments men set up for themselves. His belief, consistently expressed in the Bible, was that the governments, kings and emperors of this world were inconsequential in the Kingdom of Heaven.

Christ's spirituality made it unnecessary for him to demand justice or fairness from government. Basically, it was beneath him.

MOVE, on the other hand, has been a political bully. Even now, Ramona is trying to trump the ever-potent race card. She says the government tried to exterminate her "money-poor black revolutionary group," and that MOVE would have been left alone if "we were white and living in a white neighborhood in Chestnut Hill or the Northeast."

Let's put it another way: If MOVE were white and living in a white neighborhood in Chestnut Hill, would the Mayor of Philadelphia be breaking his back to kiss their butts?

Christ never resisted the powers of government. That was true also of his martyred followers, who were run down, captured and executed by authorities. In the case of MOVE, the authorities never singled the movement out for persecution. In fact, they tried to leave MOVE alone. A plain fact that seems to escape the Philadelphia press these days is that every encounter between MOVE and authorities began with frightened or concerned townsfolk pleading with the city to do something about their machine gun-toting neighbors who defecated on their front lawn and allowed their children to run around naked.

Christ's followers went out to spread the word of God, spoken through Christ, who was a role model for a more peaceful, gentle and loving world. Christ indeed was the nonviolent Prince of Peace. By their action, MOVE has proven that the atmosphere of peace evades them. The day of the Ramp killing, a MOVE member shouted out to police, "You

SWAT guys in those bullet-proof suits don't scare us. A lot of your wives will be wearing black tonight." He was right on one count. And so much for turning the other cheek. The elevation of MOVE to religious status is troubling. What exactly do they stand for? What do they believe? Is there anywhere in their manifest or public agenda any talk of God and spirituality.

To compare a cult group with a religion as philosophically deep and beautiful as Christianity is so absurd, as are DeLeon's "compelling parallels," that you have to wonder about his motivation. Is it simply to shock? Or to be controversial at the expense of truth and reason? DeLeon tips his hand in a April 19, 1992 column. Most of the column is a reprint of an Easter Sunday piece, the first in which he compared MOVE to the early Christian movement. In the more recent piece he boasts, "On Easter Sunday, 1986 I wrote a column that upset a lot of people who deemed it sacrilegious."

Mr. DeLeon's agenda is transparent. To shock. To be controversial. Hell, even sacrilegious if need be. That's how you get famous in the newspaper business.

Just the facts, ma'am, just the facts.

There are a few things you won't read about MOVE while Ramona Af-

rica is given free reign to re-write history and come across as the injured party in the Philadelphia press:

1. In 1973, neighbors of MOVE's Powelton Village house began to complain to authorities about human and animal fecal waste in the yard and other health hazards, including rotting food, which attracts rats and insects. The odd, back-to-nature group allowed it's children to run naked through it's rat-infested yard. The city asked permission to make a routine health inspection. MOVE responded by putting up an eight-foot stockade around it's property.

2. In 1977, after a legal battle in which the city had it's right to inspect the property upheld, MOVE members appeared in their compound, wearing khaki, military-style uniforms brandishing automatic weapons, rifles, shot-guns and pistols. They told the city in a written statement that any attempt to enter MOVE headquarters would result in "an international incident."

They threatened to poison reservoirs, blow up buildings and factories and signed the note by including the chemical formulas of dynamite and nitroglycerine.

3. After discovering a cache of bombs, explosive components and bomb-making manuals, authorities began to take MOVE very seriously.

By spring of 1978, the Rizzo administration was determined to give the Powelton Village neighborhood back to it's other residents. A two-month siege began in which the police show remarkable restraint, as MOVE members pointed guns and hurled insults at them.

4. Despite their public bravado, MOVE members surrendered abruptly after firing a round of shots at authorities on Aug. 8, 1978. Shooting from a fortified basement bunker, MOVE members killed Officer Ramp and wounded three other cops and four unarmed firemen, then quit the fight.

5. Beginning in 1982, the Osage Avenue house was converted into a menacing military bunker as MOVE members built a bunker and gun port on the roof, boarded up windows and reinforced the structure with timber. The city officials, under Mayor Wilson Goode, again showed restraint and did nothing despite complaints from residents about filth, visible firearms and obscenity-laced political spews being loudspeakered constantly from the building.

6. Before the Osage Avenue incident came to a head, the city asked that MOVE surrender the children, giving the city temporary custody. Goode went as far as to issue an order that the children be picked up off the street. The children, however, were never let out of the MOVE house. The death of those children was truly tragic and stupidly senseless. But ultimately, their safety was the responsibility of the MOVE adults. And that is where the blame for their deaths should lie.

7. The bombing of the Osage Avenue house, while extreme, was a last-resort measure for the authorities. Lost in the horror of the fire is the fact that police tried to persuade MOVE members to surrender by firing over a thousand rounds into the bunker during a 90-minute siege earlier in the day. They did not, and the standoff lasted another eight hours. At any time during that siege, MOVE could have handed the children over to authorities.

I disapprove of what you say, but I will defend to the death your right to say it.
— A paraphrase of a statement attributed to Voltaire.

Why have these facts been buried under the smokescreen images of MOVE as the new Christianity or MOVE as the victims of political oppression?

One reason may be that many of the journalists who covered the early MOVE days 20 years ago, are no longer around.

Others, and this may included many, may be afraid of being called racist if they side with society. Fear of racism is the greatest subjugator of truth in today's media.

Others still, the sanctimonious kind, are always looking for evil and underhandedness in our empirical government as it stamps out the last fires of the libertarianism.

Others, like Claude Lewis of the *Philadelphia Inquirer*, are simply weary of the story, nudged into that state by MOVE's strong-arm tactics.

"I stopped writing about them because I decided they were so unreasonable," explained Lewis, who may have been the first reporter to write articles about MOVE, while at the now-defunct *Philadelphia Bulletin*.

Lewis said there was no question-and-answer give-and-take when it came to interviewing MOVE.

"They only spoke about the

things they wanted to speak about. They did not respond to questions."

After a column in which Lewis criticized the group's methodology in trying to get its message across, six MOVE members visited Lewis in his *Bulletin* office. A profanity-laced diatribe aimed at Lewis soon followed, and Lewis left his office and walked into the Bulletin's main newsroom, believing there was safety in numbers.

"There were 250 people in there and within two minutes, 250 people cleared out," Lewis recalled.

One brave soul called Lewis from another part of the building. "I picked up the phone and the voice said, 'Do you want me to call the police?'

"I said, 'No. Give me a minute to talk them out.'"

Lewis managed to get MOVE out of the building, but he wasn't through with them. Not long after,

they threatened to blow up his house.

"I called the police in my hometown just to let them know, and they took it very seriously. They told me to get my family out of the house and they came and searched it for bombs."

Despite the threats, Lewis does not write about MOVE because he is intimidated.

"It has nothing to do with being fearful of them," he said. "I'm more frustrated than fearful."

Time to MOVE on.

Despite Ramona's posturing ("If they thought they saw fire and heat on May 13, 1985, wait till they see MOVE heat directed at Ed Rendell," she said to designated reporter DeLeon), the lawsuits and the media attention which threatens to breathe new life into the dying radical spirit of the group, there is evidence that

MOVE, it's neighbors and the city can peacefully co-exist.

MOVE owns a three-story, side-by-side stone Victorian with a mansard roof on Kingsessing Avenue in West Philly. There is grass and azaleas bushes in the yard and a Volvo station wagon in the driveway. Trash is placed at the curb and Alphonso Africa, a resident at the home, attends anti-crime block meetings. But perhaps the greatest sign is that MOVE members applied for the proper city permits to do renovations on the home and allowed city inspectors inside the home to review the work.

The group continues to demand the release of its jailed members, and perhaps future trouble may hinge on that issue. However, that trouble could be derailed if somebody, anybody, in the Philadelphia media has the courage to finally address the MOVE issue for what it truly is. The MOVE case is not about martyrdom and persecution. It is not about a vengeful, tyrannical government trying to oppress all those who disagree with it. It is, in no way, simply that white and black.

The MOVE case is more about the social contract between a government and the people it is sworn to protect. It is about one group's freedom encroaching on the freedom of the larger group as a whole and the government's responsibility to ensure the greater freedom. It is about the rights of a community of individuals to live in peace, as opposed to the individual rights of a small fragment of that community. It is about enforcing the laws that keep our society together. And it is about one dead cop, who, despite Ramona Africa and the Philly press' revisionist history, remains dead today.

For all the talk about persecution and oppression, the cold, hard fact is that MOVE declared war on the city of Philadelphia and lost. Plain and simple. They bullied their neighbors and challenged the city government to do something about it. When arrest warrants were issued for the murder of one cop and the wounding of others, they sneered at our laws. They provoked a mightier power and lost. The press should stop calling jailed MOVE members political prisoners and call them prisoners of war.

Mark Di Ionno is a freelance writer, former sports columnist of the *New York Post and Pulitzer Prize nominee.*

The FCC fined Philadelphia radio station WEGX $5000 for recording phone calls for broadcast, without first informing the "victim." In "Nut-Cracker" phone calls, morning dj John Lander places calls, lies about who he is and has fun at the targets expense. The exchange is later aired — a barrel of laughs, all in good fun. Right?

Apparently not, when, in one version of the joke he accused a woman of stealing something during an open house. She allegedly asked the station not to air the piece, then complained to the FCC when the station did so anyway.

The kicker is rather than accepting the calls were in bad taste and in violation of the law, the stations General Managers response was to announce they've figured a way to comply with the FCC without spoiling the joke.

Maybe It's Time, After All These Years

Clark DeLeon

"On-a MOVE," Ramona Africa said yesterday afternoon.

"Long live John Africa," replied a dozen or so MOVE supporters mingling among the media in the standing room gathered in the large meeting room in Center City where the American Friends Service Committee hosted Ramona Africa's first news conference since her arrest seven years ago to the day.

On-a MOVE. Long live John Africa.

Get used to it. You may be hearing a lot of it in the future. Think of it as a responsory - MOVE's way of saying:

Dominus vobiscum. Et cum spititu tuo.

The Lord be with you. And with your spirit.

For surely MOVE is a religion, John Africa is its Christ, Osage was his Golgotha, and Ramona Africa - still bearing the burn scars suffered during his apocalyptic martyrdom - is the first of his apostles to return to Jerusalem demanding justice from Caesar.

MOVE's Pentecost took seven years instead of 50 days, and Ramona Africa's voice will be the tongue of flame at the conscience of every Pontius Pilate in Philadelphia.

Ramona Africa is back to remind the world of the righteous that there is not a dry pair of hands in this city.

No matter how hard we scrub, the stain from the slaughter of five children hasn't washed from the soul of anyone who watched it happen and shrugged.

Of course, in the typically consistent (and maddening) methodology of MOVE, Ramona focused the bulk of her remarks during the news conference not on the death of innocents on May 13, 1985, but rather on the innocence of nine MOVE members imprisoned since 1978 for the murder of Philadelphia Police Officer James Ramp during the first MOVE confrontation in Powelton Village.

"There is only one issue for MOVE," she said, "And that is the issue of innocent MOVE people being kept in prison for 30 to 100 years. . . . The only point is that all we have ever asked for, all we are asking for now is one serious, in-depth and honest investigation into what we are saying about our family's innocence. Such an investigation, if done prior to May 13th, could have avoided a May 13th. But not one single official was willing to have such an investigation."

What struck me as I listened to Ramona yesterday during the news conference and during her radio talk show appearances on Mary Mason in the morning and Irv Homer in the afternoon was her implicit - what's the word? - *expectation* that the system

> Ramona Africa is back to remind the world of the righteous that there is not a dry pair of hands in this city.

will actually *work* eventually. It either speaks of a powerful and naive faith, or is a cunning display of a terrible and cynical conviction.

Ramona's words either resonate with belief in the goodness that will eventually result from the truth revealed or they mask a strategy by MOVE to demonstrate just how corrupt the system is by letting the American criminal justice system expose itself as being inherently unjust before the eyes of people who *do* believe in it.

How could Ramona Africa actually *believe* that MOVE could receive justice from the same system she is convinced - and with ample evidence to support such a conclusion - is determined to exterminate it? After seeing her people imprisoned and children die, after seeing the same authorities *destroy* all evidence by bulldozing the MOVE house in 1978 and burning down the entire neighborhood in 1985, how can she possibly expect MOVE members to get a fair deal?

It would almost be comical if there weren't so many body bags involved. Come on, Mona, *still* crazy after all these years? Haven't these people convinced you yet that they mean business, and that their busi-

ness doesn't include MOVE?

How could another investigation into the events of 14 years ago change anything? Why should she expect public opinion to shift in MOVE's favor? Why should Philadelphians who swallowed the camel of '85 strain at the gnat of '78?

Why, indeed?

Of course, maybe she has no other choice. There is nothing she can do for the 11 who died outside 6221 Osage Ave. on May 13 seven years ago. But there is something she can do for the living in prison.

And then again, maybe the time is right. Maybe Philadelphia is ready to consider MOVE in a different manner. As human beings, to begin with, and not as some dreadlocked defecating megaphone caricatures. Maybe, like the purple evidence of a deep bruise that surfaces long after injury, Philadelphia is at last ready to confront the self-inflicted wounds it suffered to its psyche during the municipal madness of May 13 and the conspiracy of shameful silence that followed.

"Things change with time," the Rev. Paul Washington, a 1985 MOVE Commission member, said yesterday after Ramona's news conference. "I think the more that we recede from that particular moment there are a whole lot of Philadelphians who are far more sympathetic with MOVE than they were then. People are asking why. People are asking what did they do to deserve this?

Does he think the system is ready to deal fairly with MOVE?

I think something is to be said for never saying never," Mr. Washington said. "Something is to be said for it."

Reprinted with permission from the Philadelphia Inquirer

The Eclipse True Crime Trading Cards Controversy

or "I'll give you three Hoover's, two Ness', a Son of Sam and a Zodiac for your Dahmer."

Mike Baker

No matter how much they'd like you to believe otherwise, the media never gives you the full story of any event; time, space and other factors (including censorship and special interest groups) preclude that from ever happening. Anyone who believes otherwise, who thinks that news, talk and infotainment programs are presenting them with all the facts, is either quite gullible or suffering from an advanced case of self-delusion. True, some sources are more reliable than others—fact-wise, the *Wall Street Journal* (the newspaper for people who love to read) beats *USA Today* (the home of bullets, charts, and really short sentences) any day—but the only way to really know exactly what went down at any event, no matter how vigorously reported it is, is to be there yourself. Ask anyone who works, or has ever worked, in the industry; whether you like it or not, media manipulation is, sadly, a fact of life.

The recent media circus surrounding the release of Eclipse Enterprise's *True Crime Trading Cards* is as good an example of the kind of things which go on behind the scenes, and

how it affects what you see and hear, as anything in recent memory. In the paragraphs which follow you'll not only learn the story of these infamous cards, but some of the story behind the story as well. You'll see how a dull story is spiced up, facts ignored, perceptions toyed with and the truth blurred. Consider this a crash course in media manipulation (a pre-requisite in advanced cynicism is recommended, but not required).

Eclipse, a small, Northern California-based specialty publishing house, got involved in non-sports trading card market a few years back when they released the extremely successful *Iran-Contra Scandal* card set. Never afraid to publish something just because it might be controversial, Eclipse soon came out with card sets dealing with everything from drug wars to President Bush's cabinet (*Bush League*), from the S & L scandal to some of the U.S.'s more dubious allies (*Friendly Dictators*).

There are 110 cards in the *True Crime Trading Cards* set, which is divided into two series: *G-Men & Gangsters* features mob bosses, their molls, famous criminals and bootleggers, as well as the law enforcement figures who brought them to justice while *Serial Killers & Mass Murderers* looks at killers from the 1800's to the modern day. Each card has brief biography on one side and a head-and-shoulders portrait of the criminal on the other. The *G-Men* series was written by mystery writer Max Allan Collins and his *Nate Heller* research partner George Hagenauer, with artwork by Paul Lee. The *Serial Killers* series was the work of Eclipse editor Valarie Jones and Peggy Collier, with artwork by Jon Bright. According to Jones, nearly a year-and-a-half of research went into the cards, with everyone involved taking scrupulous care to get all of the facts right.

A couple of months before the cards were scheduled to be released in May of this year, *Entertainment Weekly* magazine ran an informative, and more importantly, unbiased, article on them which featured, as an illustration, what would soon become the set's most infamous card: #76, Jeffrey Dahmer. This story was spotted by *Entertainment Tonight*, who sent a crew to Eclipse's offices to interview Valarie Jones. The *ET* reporter, a freelance journalist who lived in the Northern California area, interviewed Ms. Jones for nearly 45 minutes, getting background on the cards and asking some general, non-provocative questions. After the interview was completed, the crew was given a proof sheet of the cards to take back to *ET*'s main office in Los Angeles.

Here is where the manipulations begin. *ET* faxed a copy of the Dahmer card to a victim's rights group in Milwaukee along with a question along the lines of, "What do you think of this?" The fax elicited the response *ET* was hoping for, outrage and an-

ger, presenting them with a ready-made headline for their story (which, like most of the news stories which followed, focused mainly upon the *Serial Killer* cards, ignoring *Guns & Gangsters* almost entirely): "Victim's Rights Groups Protesting True Crime Cards".

ET may have created the controversy, but others were quick to pick up on it. Within hours of the airing of the *ET* segment, Eclipse was flooded with calls from newspaper reporters, radio talk show hosts, television producers and others of that ilk. Soon Jones, as well as Eclipse

editor-in-chief Catherine Yronwode, publisher Dean Mullaney and Max Allan Collins were doing up to 15 interviews a day, 95% of which, according to Jones, ended up presenting Eclipse in a negative light.

Even more scary is the media's inability (or unwillingness) to get their facts right. One of the most blatant propagators of misinformation was Robert Digitale, a writer for the *Santa Rosa Press Democrat* whose stories also ran nationally on the *New York Times* newswire. When Catharine Yronwode pointed out that Digitale's stories weren't presenting all the facts, he responded by saying, "I don't care about that." How's that for open-minded journalism?

But Digitale wasn't the only one sidestepping the facts; here's some other examples of slipshod reporting: numerous stories said that the cards were already selling and that they were *the* hot item in 7-11's and other convenience stores around the country when, in fact, they hadn't come out yet, and when they did, they'd only be available in specialty shops (like comic book and baseball card stores) or through the mail from Eclipse; the print run for the cards was said to number in the hundreds of thousands when it's actually only 2,000 (according to Jones, there won't be a second printing); and much ado was made over the fact that the cards were supposedly targeted to appeal to the children's market, which is perhaps the most ludicrous statement of them all. Most children, and even some adults, lack the reading and comprehension skills to understand the card's text (which is aimed at college-level readers), and even if they did, what is presented therein is fact-intensive and even a bit on the dry side, not lurid. These cards are written with the intelligent, open-minded person in mind; anyone seeking baseball card-inspired body count stats is sure to feel a bit disappointed when they open a pack.

The Eclipse people soon learned that they were better off declining interview requests because, more often than not, they were presented as the villain right from the start and

JEFFREY DAHMER

were never allowed to state their side of argument. For example, during a phone interview with a Buffalo, New York TV station, Max Allan Collins was forced to endure an interviewer who assailed him with two to three minute questions, all of which were actually diatribes about, as he put it, "what a reprehensible, money-grubbing scum I was." After a half hour in which he was vilified and his every comment spoken over by the interviewer, Collins hung up, a first for him. Even worse was what happened to Eclipse's President, Jan Mullaney (Dean's brother), who was asked to appear on *The Maury Povich Show*. At first leery of the idea, Mullaney agreed to appear when the show's producer promised that both sides of the issue would be represented fairly and no favoritism shown whatsoever. Those promises weren't kept, though; when he arrived at the studio, Mullaney discovered, much to his dismay, that representatives from a victim's rights group had already gone on before him, and that Maury had whipped the stacked audience into a screaming, self-righteous frenzy. Knowing that it was a lost cause, that he'd get as much of a chance to state his case as, say, a woman accused of witchcraft during the Salem Trials (i.e. none whatsoever), Mullaney walked off the set during a commercial break.

While the media's misrepresentation of facts, of playing fast and loose with the truth, is unsettling, the real danger lies in the responses it elicits. Without even seeing the cards they are so quick to denounce, victim's rights groups sent letters of protest to the media (but not, oddly enough to Eclipse; according to Yronwode, they have yet to receive any complaints from any organizations of that nature). Ministers urged their parishers to join in the crusade, as did organizations like the PTA. People were told to put together petitions, write letters of complaint, or call Eclipse and demand that production of the cards be stopped. And many did just that, blindly leaping into battle only because they'd been told it was the "right" thing to do. Heaven forbid that these groups actually take the time to research what it is they're fighting against; actions like that require intelligence and a dose of individuality, traits which have pretty much atrophied in your typical moral crusader.

Perhaps the most disturbing, and dangerous, reactionaries are the politicians. Two Maryland delegates proposed an bill which prohibits "selling, buying, advertising, distributing, trading, exchanging, or possessing a trading card that has a picture of an individual who has committed specified 'heinous crimes'; allowing the court to order the destruction of such trading cards; setting misdemeanor penalties for violations...". Senator Morril Harriman, D-Van Buren, of Arkansas tried to ban the cards in his state (though he admitted it was an uphill battle because of the First Amendment), a goal shared by twelve Michigan sena-

tors who sought to pass two resolutions "urging Eclipse Enterprises to cease publishing and selling its *True Crime* Series of trading cards."

Luckily, all of the above-mentioned pieces of legislation failed; each, in it's own way, is an assault on the First Amendment and the freedoms it guarantees which we've come to take for granted. Consider for a moment the Maryland bill. Say it passed, and the court was granted the right to seize and destroy property (in this case, certain trading cards), imagine the precedent it would set. Once those offending cards are taken care of, what's to stop the lawmakers from

J. EDGAR HOOVER

going after True Crime books? And what about works of fiction which feature serial killers, or movies like *Silence of the Lambs*? And once you've taken care of them, well, why stop; there's a whole world of potentially offensive items out there just waiting to be stamped out. It's a very scary thought, and one which I hope never comes to pass.

And speaking of pass, there were actually a few places where legislation did pass. *True Crime* cards were temporarily banned in Canada, until someone bothered to take a look at them, that is, at which time they were deemed to be not that bad after all, and the ban lifted. The city of Rosemead, California passed a Resolution "urging the California State Legislature to prohibit the production of and distribution of materials bearing the likenesses of convicted felons" (the CSL, having much more important matters to dwell upon, ignored the Resolution). Only in Nassau County, New York was a ban actually instituted, and that law is currently under attack by the New York branch of the ACLU, which views the ban as an unfortunate breaching of civil liberties, and a precedent which they don't wish to see stand.

To this day, months after the *True Crime Trading Cards* have been released, hate mail is still pouring in to Eclipse. But of all the letters she's received, most of which state what disgusting, godless, repulsive, etc. individuals she and her coworkers at Eclipse are, Valarie Jones has kept only two for her own files. One is from convicted serial killer Kenneth Bianci who, according to Jones, says, in the overly legalistic manner of someone with a self-taught knowledge of law, that he's displeased at being the subject of a card (he says it's damaging to his image), and also that he desires to share in the cards profits as well. The other letter is from Satan who, according to the postmark on his letter, lives in Kentucky. Satan says, "By the way, if I reap any rewards in your endeavor, I will be glad to share them with you."

More than anything else, the media manipulation surrounding the *True Crime Trading Cards* has changed how the people involved look at journalists. "I really had a higher regard for journalism before this, but the media has constantly been portraying the issue in an off-

GREEN RIVER KILLER

center way to make better copy," Catharine Yronwode said. "I'm becoming bitter and cynical about journalists."

Max Allan Collins feels much the same way. "All I can say is that from the standpoint of American journalism, it was an embarrassment." He then goes on to add, "...an unfortunately small percentage of the press today are responsible. The rest of the press is just a bunch of sensationalistic, ignorant hacks. They're boobs."

Valarie Jones pretty much shares the opinions of her coworkers, but she also believes that the problems they're having are, in a way, inevitable. "When you have a democracy and offer everyone freedom," she says, "you always end up having someone trying to force their idea of freedom on everyone else. People always tend to believe that their beliefs are right, and everyone else's wrong."

One thing to remember is that while media manipulation may be a fact of life, it only works if you let it. Take the time to examine and judge things yourself rather than adopting the opinions of others, and always remember that what you read and hear isn't necessarily the whole truth. Don't be a mindless drone; learn to think for yourself.

I'm Mike Baker with The News Behind the News. Good Night.

(In addition to being GAUNT-LET's West Coast Correspondent, Mike Baker is also the publisher & editor of AFRAID, the Newsletter for the Horror Professional, sample issues of which can obtained for a mere $3.00 from AFRAID/857 N. Oxford Ave. #4/L.A. CA 90029).

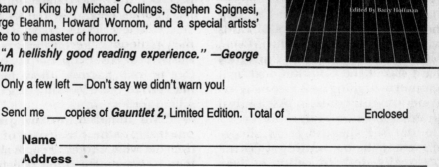

THE SHAME OF SERIAL KILLER TRADING CARDS

John Sutherland

When I was in college, my marketing professor hammered home the core philosophy of product marketing — "Give the people what they want." He never presumed to tell us "Give the people what they need." In the rarified air of the marketing world, this would be akin to playing God.

Professor Bradway felt that value judgments had no place in product development, mainly because he came from an age when marketing meant peddling mouthwash and junk food. He never addressed the moral quandary of marketing junk culture, such as serial killer trading cards.

Using the same obfuscating tactics that Time-Warner used defending its marketing of Ice-T's "Cop Killer," the manufacturers of cards sporting the likes of John Wayne Gacy and Jeffrey Dahmer think they have staked the Constitutional high ground by arguing their case in a First Amendment context. As always, those at the core of the controversy do not see themselves as simply stretching the boundaries of Constitutionally defined rights of free speech (and bad taste); instead, they see themselves as the protectors of freedom, demonstrating to us the latent tendency to censor that lies deep within the hearts of certain Americans, particularly government officials. It does not occur to them that these cards are not something we need, nor did the public ask for them.

The argument over serial killer cards is yet another subplot in the broader censorship debate. Whenever the propriety of such a product is questioned, a chorus of indignation arises from the political left, usually alleging censorship.

When a boycott of Time-Warner products was proposed recently, Time-Warner Chairman Gerald Levin implied that this was a form of censorship. (A strange conclusion coming from such a lusty believer in free markets as Mr. Levin. People should have the right to buy his products, but they don't have the right NOT to buy them.) By the same token, whenever NEA grants are denied artists, the government is also accused of censorship, in spite of the fact no one has told the artists in question to cease working or to stop selling their work.

This reflexive invoking of the censorship issue helps obscure the fact that what people are calling for is not government-enforced censorship, but a call for marketers of culture to respect the moral standards and feelings of others.

By producing trading cards of serial killers, the manufacturers are not provoking thought on a controversial issue, nor are they encouraging much needed dialogue on a subject people are too inhibited to discuss. And they certainly aren't fulfilling the "Give em what they want" doctrine of marketing, since no one was clamoring for these cards before they were produced.

The reality is that the cardmakers are not so much tapping into latent ghoulishness as they are trying to incite it.

But if mandated censorship is not an acceptable means for dealing with such trash, then what is? Like most people, I do not want the government determining what is and is not permissible, so the only obvious alternative is for manufacturers and marketers to understand that along with absolute freedoms comes the onus of responsibility, the need to police one's self through value judgment.

The First Amendment is not a blessing for the advocacy of terroristic threats or the glorification of necrophilia, cannibalism, pedophilia and outright slaughter. Contrary to the expedient arguments repeatedly trotted out by the makers of these cards, "community standards" are not so vague and ill-defined that we can't identify a vast majority of Americans who find their cards repugnant and de-civilizing.

Indeed, the card manufacturers won't come out and admit it, but part of their marketing plan relies heavily upon the negative publicity and ensuring public disgust to awaken the pocketbooks of their slumbering target market. Worst of all, the cards are implicitly marketed toward a young audience, who more readily absorb the depraved message inherent to these cards — that there is no distinction between glorious fame and ignominious fame. Fame is fame, and it is all good.

Thus the difference between these cards and, say, TV or book portrayals of serial killers. I have yet to see a made-for-TV movie or read a factual account of a serial murder case which glamorized the killer or offered tacit approval of his actions.

But cards are a different matter. By putting the likes of Gacy and Dahmer in the same forum as Cal Ripkin or Joe Montana, the card makers are quite consciously bestowing celebrity status on their subjects. Kids understand only that getting your face on a trading card is pretty cool, regardless of whether you've hit 40 homers or eviscerated 40 victims.

The makers of products such as serial killer cards like to provoke Constitutional debates on whether or not we have begun to inch down the "slippery slope of censorship." While they engage in such intellectual fraud, our popular culture is simultaneously careening downhill toward a swamp of violence, misogyny, empty-headed rebellion and appeals to man's most guttural instincts.

But this is not a First Amendment issue: the government will not and should not halt the production of these cards. However, as Oliver Wendell Holmes once put it, the freedom of speech clause "does not give you the right to shout 'Fire!' in a crowded theater." He meant that it was not an absolute right, and that exercising it imprudently can have ramifications.

In this case, let's hope the families of the killers' victims see fit to file suit against the cardmakers on the grounds of mental anguish and emotional duress. This claim would surely be less tenuous than the arrogant assertion that these cards are a bold test of our right to free expression.

John Sutherland is a freelance writer and regular contributor to Gauntlet

Fun With NUMBERS

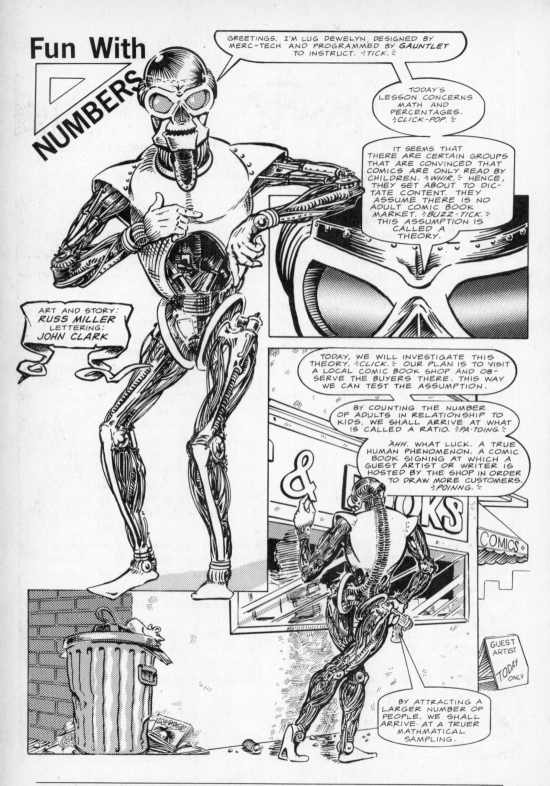

GREETINGS. I'M LUG DEWELYN, DESIGNED BY MERC-TECH AND PROGRAMMED BY *GAUNTLET* TO INSTRUCT. ⇒*TICK.*⇐

TODAY'S LESSON CONCERNS MATH AND PERCENTAGES. ⇒*CLICK-POP.*⇐

IT SEEMS THAT THERE ARE CERTAIN GROUPS THAT ARE CONVINCED THAT COMICS ARE ONLY READ BY CHILDREN. ⇒*WHIR.*⇐ HENCE, THEY SET ABOUT TO DIC- TATE CONTENT. THEY ASSUME THERE IS NO ADULT COMIC BOOK MARKET. ⇒*BUZZ-TICK.*⇐ THIS ASSUMPTION IS CALLED A THEORY.

ART AND STORY: *RUSS MILLER* LETTERING: *JOHN CLARK*

TODAY, WE WILL INVESTIGATE THIS THEORY. ⇒*CLICK.*⇐ OUR PLAN IS TO VISIT A LOCAL COMIC BOOK SHOP AND OB- SERVE THE BUYERS THERE. THIS WAY WE CAN TEST THE ASSUMPTION.

BY COUNTING THE NUMBER OF ADULTS IN RELATIONSHIP TO KIDS, WE SHALL ARRIVE AT WHAT IS CALLED A RATIO. ⇒*PA-TOING.*⇐

AHH. WHAT LUCK. A TRUE HUMAN PHENOMENON. A COMIC BOOK SIGNING AT WHICH A GUEST ARTIST OR WRITER IS HOSTED BY THE SHOP IN ORDER TO DRAW MORE CUSTOMERS. ⇒*POINNG.*⇐

COMICS

GUEST ARTIST TODAY ONLY

BY ATTRACTING A LARGER NUMBER OF PEOPLE, WE SHALL ARRIVE AT A TRUER MATHMATICAL SAMPLING.

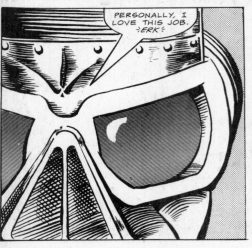

A RIGHT to Know
Or An Invasion of Privacy?

Deborah Wilker

When *USA Today* forced tennis legend Arthur Ashe into admitting publicly last year that he was stricken with AIDS, it wasn't long before the critics swooped down upon "the nation's newspaper."

What many wanted to know was, what right did any media organization have to orchestrate such an emotional and personal revelation from a celebrity?

The idea that celebs are public figures and therefore must lay out everything about themselves before the public, is one that has been debated by journalists for years.

Perhaps the more important question regarding the Ashe incident should have been: What right does any media outlet have to mix into the news while going after it?

Lost in the commotion of Ashe's stunning announcement and *USA Today*'s pressure tactics, was the newspaper's unethical behavior as "creator" of a news event. Granted, Ashe was indeed stricken with the deadly virus, but so are lots of people. Disease alone is not a story until it somehow affects the rest of us.

But the newspaper uncharacteristically strong-armed him anyway, threatening to reveal his secret without his cooperation if he didn't come forward. The tactic seemed more like something we'd expect from the tabloids, than from this feel-good national daily which is most well-known for its rah-rah jingoism.

Sadly, Ashe was left with no choice but to speak reluctantly about something he had hoped would remain known only to family and a few close friends.

Ashe said he contracted HIV during a transfusion while undergoing surgery years ago. During his announcement to the media, he made a point of thanking a small circle of loyalists whom he dubbed, a friendly "conspiracy."

That his secret was known to so many people came as something of a surprise to many journalists. Yet many others knew for years about Ashe's health, and chose to write nothing about it.

The protection afforded him by some media members was likely the outgrowth of the longstanding respect Ashe commands. His groundbreaking athletic accomplishments, eloquent commentary on tennis and contributions to charity have kept him in high regard with fans, media and even people who know little about sports.

But therein may lie a double standard. Was Ashe protected for so long because he is so well liked, or because those journalists ascribe to certain ethical ideals?

And what about those ethics? Does the public have a right to know the detailed medical information of all celebrities? Or is it an invasion of privacy?

And what about the many journalists who knew of rock vocalist Freddie Mercury's battle with AIDS,

and did not report it? Sure, *Fleet Street* was on the story for months, and rumors were circulating for years, but the hard revelation was kept secret until just one day before Mercury died in November 1991.

Dozens of celebrities are stricken now - not just with AIDS, but with all sorts of threatening maladies. Many of us who write about entertainment for a living know several performers who may not live much longer. Word of such tragedies circulates constantly among the public relations people, agents and reporters who keep the business ticking.

But it seems, the polite thing to do these days for those of us involved with mainstream news organizations, is to privately acknowledge such information, keep track of it, and then leave it alone - thus affording the dying the respect they are due.

This attitude does not appear to be rooted in any deep ethical standard or journalistic practice. It seems, rather simply, to have come from basic human nature.

That's why the *USA Today* incident seemed wrong.

Yet others in the industry don't agree. Those journalists who kept

Ashe's secret can be considered unethical for having come upon important information, and then withholding it. After all, Ashe is a sports legend, not a superstar stereotype like a run-around rock star. He's not someone we'd expect to fall prey to AIDS.

Said one sports editor: "I'm not saying we would have printed it, but if one of my writers knew and didn't at least tell me, I'd have been upset."

When is too much information just too much? Or can there never be too much?

Imagine if it were your family; your health; your spouse forced into such a quandary? Surely the free circulation of thoughts, ideas and information is the mark of a free society, but when the pressure to reveal comes crashing down upon us, our world starts feeling more like a police state.

Ashe's situation is one of several notable cases of media outing. Just recently, singer-actress Olivia Newton-John issued a statement to the media proclaiming she was suffering from breast cancer.

She did so, she said, to "save inquiring minds $.95.

Beating the tabloids to a revelation is nothing new. After all, the mainstream daily press and network news organizations now take almost daily cues from the Guerilla tactics of the tabs. Once revealed, anything seems fair game.

AIDS activist Elizabeth Glaser, the wife of actor-director Paul Michael Glaser, was one of Hollywood's first notables to rush out a statement in an effort to thwart the tabs. Glaser, who was stricken with HIV during a transfusion after giving birth more than a decade ago, kept her story private for years - not an easy task considering her two small children were also stricken.

Understandably concerned about her husband's career, Glaser didn't want the news of the family illness to taint his image or ruin his chances of acquiring work. (Though Hollywood may appear enlightened about AIDS, it's still learning, and was downright paralyzed by the thought of it just a few years back. That so many entertainment people behind the scenes and in front have been stricken, seems to have had little bearing.)

Months later, when she learned that a story was going to be published about her plight, she rushed an announcement to the news wires simply as a matter of integrity. She did not want the information presented to the public initially in what she considered a tawdry manner.

Once the word was out, she put her newfound notoriety to use as a fundraiser and public awareness speaker on behalf of pediatric AIDS. Her speech at the Democratic Convention in July provided riveting testimony as to the ravages of the disease.

Whether the mainstream press even would have found out Glaser's secret is something we don't know. Today, such information travels more freely, so had the timeline moved forward to 1992 it's a safe bet that Glaser would have been unmasked just the same. The once questionable practice of outing - forcing famous people to reveal themselves as gay, ill or whatever - isn't just the domain of the gay press anymore.

For all the good she has done, Glaser's role as activist is not one she chose. Like Ashe, her time on Earth is likely to be shorter than the time allotted to others.

Why then must both be forced into roles they didn't seek; roles that are likely exhaustive and time consuming; roles that would tire the most healthy people?

Is it fair?

Had Ashe decided to spend his remaining time with his family, rather than crusade for the public good, he'd likely have been hung out to dry all over again.

Why do we do this to people? Why can't we just leave them alone? Is it really in pursuit of knowledge for the greater public good? Or simply to satisfy our own prurient interests.

Don't news organizations realize that all this sort of thing does is breed contempt and lack of trust? As far as AIDS is concerned, the disease is now so widespread, the shock effect of contracting it seems to be diminishing. Perhaps that alone will make such stories less appealing to gonzo journalists. But still, if not AIDS, there will always be some stigma to be outed.

No question - the line has been crossed. The bigger question now is: can we ever go back to a time when not knowing so much about so many was blissful?

Deborah Wilker, a regular contributor to **Gauntlet**, *is a reporter for the* **Fort Lauderdale Sun Sentinel**

RODNEY KING:
No Isolated Incident

Richard G. Carter

Okay, so the nation has "recovered" from the death-dealing riots spawned by the ludicrous, racially inspired verdict in which four white cops were found not guilty of the videotaped beating of Rodney King in Los Angeles. And where does this leave us?

For starters, two things are crystal clear: Police brutality finally is out of the closet, and the news media - especially television - has once again been castigated for doing its job.

The quartet of "LA's finest" that kicked, stomped, shocked and clubbed the defenseless 25-year-old black man - 56 times in 81 seconds as a dozen other cops watched - demonstrated for white America what black America always has known: that police brutality is alive and well in the land.

And despite what the almost all-white Simi Valley jury decreed, the grainy black-and-white images of King on the ground getting his head handed to him will never fade away.

Black people have suffered from mistreatment at the hands of the police for as long as I can remember - with the perpetrators almost always white cops. Yet, all cops aren't brutal, and all of those who are brutal aren't white.

Some black cops also have been known to rough up people for no good reason. I know. My late uncle was a beat cop for years, and then a detective, and my sister was a police-

woman. And we're black.

So there.

As to the role of the media, millions watching live TV coverage and taped "highlights" of the looting of the City of Angels saw looters playing to the cameras. And what else is new?

The jugheads who got their kicks being on camera grabbing free goods in the guise of the Rodney King verdict were doing what camera hounds have done ever since television came on the scene in the late 1940s. You see it whenever a TV lens is out in public - from sports events to crime scenes to fires. People waving and mugging as a camera pans or a reporter reports or interviews.

But that doesn't mean the media ought to refrain from covering the news — especially civil disturbances. Hey, that's why they're in business. The notion that the presence of TV cameras or print reporters with tape recorders or notebooks encourage looters is hogwash. Bad actors are going to act bad, media or no media.

We've got to forget about killing the messenger and concentrate our efforts on changing the message.

✦   ✦   ✦

Just in case there still are some Americans out there who feel that what the nation saw over-and-over on videotape in Los Angeles was an aberration, let me say this:

African-American males who

weren't born yesterday know that being hassled and roughed up by white cops - and even severely beaten - goes with the territory. And our station in life doesn't change a thing.

We know because we've been stopped by cops as we walk along the street at night, questioned and searched for no apparent reason except being in a particular neighborhood - especially if it's not a black one.

We know because we've been pulled over while driving, asked where we're going, ordered out of our car and humiliatingly patted down while spread-eagled and grabbing the roof of a squad car.

We know that being black, we're subject to this treatment whether we're well-dressed or not. Whether we're alone or with friends, relatives or our wife. Or whether we live in town or are just visiting. We know that big city cops are big city cops no matter what the big city - from sea to shining sea.

How well I remember the teenage nights I spent wending my way home from a girlfriend's house in the Midwestern city where I grew up, only to be hit in the face with a powerful police spotlight, and unceremoniously told to lean on the hood of a squad car and "spread 'em." This happened with regularity.

Then there was the time I'd just finished my 6PM to 2AM shift at the Post Office, had my coffee at a nearby diner, and was waiting for a bus at the corner of a deserted downtown street. A black-and-white cop car came by once, twice, three times before its white, uniformed occupants stopped, rolled down a window and growled: "What the hell you doing here this time of night, boy?"

"What does it look like I'm doing," I calmly replied, gazing at the bus-stop sign.

The next thing I knew I was face-down on the ground, a knee in my back, my arms pinned at my side as one cop barked: "You keep up that smart mouth and you'll be riding an ambulance, not a bus." Needless to say I survived, but my psyche was scarred.

Then there was the incredible scene I witnessed from across a reasonably quiet inner-city street. One of three male members of a black family that owned a big, well-known car wash was berated by a white beat-cop for "talking back" when ordered to move a car the officer said was blocking traffic. The cop made the mistake of shoving the young man of 17, who was a

THE ULTIMATE
MEDIA
MANIPULATOR

CLICK
CLICK
CLICK

prize-winning amateur boxer.

In the next instant, the cop was on his back from a straight right. As he pulled out his billyclub, the young man kicked it from his hand. The cop, noting the presence of two more men, scrambled to his feet and ran to a corner call-box to summon help.

Within two minutes, three squad cars showed up and the young man, his brother and father found themselves face-to-face with seven big, billyclub-wielding officers. It developed, however, that each of the men in the car wash family was a boxer. The older brother, age 21, had won two Golden Gloves' lightheavyweight titles and the 43-year-old father was a middleweight Gloves' runnerup from days of yore who still looked able to hold his own with anyone.

The ensuing brawl was a doozy, with the outnumbered car wash clan knocking over the seven cops like 10-pins. Order finally was restored when four more squad cars arrived and the car wash contingent was overwhelmed, handcuffed and carted off to jail to tumultuous cheers of scores of black onlookers - including me.

Which brings me back to Rodney King and the thousands of others who aren't videotaped being beaten or publicly humiliated by cops.

What's really important is that all Americans regardless of race finally know the score on this stuff. They know it happens and that it must be stopped. But it won't be stopped by letting the guilty go free or blaming the news media for reporting the facts.

I think the media should be praised for getting the facts out.

And as far as I'm concerned, media-applied heat is responsible for Judge Stanley Weisberg's decision to hold the October retrial of Officer Laurence Powell in Los Angeles County. For him to rule otherwise would have been unthinkable. [Editor's note: As we went to press the media was reporting this charge against Powell might be dismissed, as all four officers were to be tried on Federal charges and the State charge would constitute double jeopardy.]

But remember now, this is the same judge who inexplicably chose to move the first trial of the bullboy LA cops' - ludicrous in itself - to Simi Valley, when there were more racially mixed sites available. And now he contradicts himself. Media pressure. Long may it live.

Finally, don't forget that some journalists got their asses kicked covering the post-King verdict riots. Think about that the next time you see some jerk on the street making faces into the TV camera. And be thankful that in America we have a free press, albeit an occasionally imperfect one.

Richard G. Carter, a freelance writer, is a former columnist for the New York Daily News

ABC's Ted Koppel begs to differ with Mr. Carter. As reported in the *Philadelphia Inquirer*, Koppel said about the medias role in reporting the riots in Los Angeles, "Live television was the carrier of the virus of violence that jumped from one part of the city to another." He indicated competition for ratings may have motivated local stations to cover the looting, arson and violence live, which may have inspired others to commit similar acts. Koppel feels, "Journalism is about editing. It is not just taking a live camera and putting it on an event. I always advocate serious journalism. That entails taking raw events and processing them ... That's the difference between journalism and technology."

The Art of Media Manipulation

Ed Cafasso

You've probably seen it by now in the newspaper or a lifestyle magazine or on one of those soft and fuzzy morning shows on television.

Ted Kennedy, the senior senator from Massachusetts, and his lovely new wife, Victoria "Vickie" Reggie, snuggling close — but not too close — as they happily discuss the joys of marriage and politics, Ted's love of painting and trick-or-treating with Vickie's kids, who, of course, worship Ted.

A "new" Ted Kennedy, the host or writer will explain, as numerous close family friends suddenly break their silence to describe how much he "changed" after he started seeing Vickie.

It is all true? Maybe. But consider how the story came to be.

Aides to the kinder, gentler and slimmer senator called news organizations and other media outlets this summer to pitch the idea and offer access to Ted and Vickie together.

No news reporters, they said. We want one of your feature people to do this, they said. No politics. No hard questions about Palm Beach or Chappaquidick or Clarence Thomas. Softballs only.

Editors who expressed reservations about the terms and conditions of the deal, some of whom had been trying for years to arrange a straight-forward news interview with the senator alone, were politely but firmly reminded of how many other media outlets had already climbed aboard.

The message was clear: If you don't want the story, fine. But your competitor will have it.

Manipulation has been part and parcel of the media game for centuries now, a great ethical tug of war driven by the eternal engines of politics, ignorance, love, hatred or greed that constantly challenges the idealism of the citizenry.

Only a handful of newspapermen traveled to Gettysburg to hear Abraham Lincoln's historic address. After all, the war was going badly and Lincoln, tremendously unpopular at the time, was not known as a riveting public speaker.

During last year's rape case against William Kennedy Smith, prosecutors publicly released affidavits from three women who claimed they too had been his victims, knowingly all the while how such explosive information would prejudice potential jurors and public opinion before a judge could rule on its relevance.

Smith had his manipulative moments too. By the time the trial was set to start, he had acquired a new puppy and a savvy media "liaison" and had posed for idyllic pictures along the ocean as friends and family rallied to his side.

Today, there are still some in the media who refer to the woman who brought the charge against Smith as his "victim."

Clarence Thomas was poised on the brink of fairly quick confirmation to the U.S. Supreme Court until an FBI interview with Anita Hill, which members of the Judiciary Committee had already discussed and disregarded privately, was leaked to two media outlets.

Boxer Mike Tyson was judged guilty of sexual assault within hours of the accusation being made public.

After all, Tyson, not exactly an expert in the field of human relations, was a hood as a kid wasn't he? Would have been in jail a long time ago if he hadn't been convinced he could get paid millions for beating the piss out of people, they said. And his "victim" was so petite and eloquent and convincing.

"I think before this case ever began, there was a real need to convict Mike Tyson," his attorney, Alan Dershowitz, told *Gauntlet*. "Smith had been acquitted, Thomas had been appointed and I've heard it said more than once: 'The women had to win one.'

"So, the defendant was stereotyped. He was black. He was large. He was athletic. He was sexual.

"And, unlike the Smith case and the Thomas hearing," Dershowitz said, "the Tyson case was not on TV where everybody could form their own opinion based on what they saw and heard.

"Instead the print media, specifically newspapers, could control the flow of information. It's hard to say whether racism was involved, although some stereotypes certainly came into play," he added. "But I'm convinced the fact that it wasn't on television played a very significant role in manipulating public opinion."

Most newspapers that bothered to cover the Tyson case with a member of their own staff sent sportswriters to do the job instead of reporters familiar with the subtleties of such proceedings.

Thus, unlike the Smith case, the Tyson saga was usually relegated to the sports pages.

Until of course he was convicted.

And when it was learned afterward that there was strong evidence that Tyson's victim had lied on the stand about discussing the possibility of cashing in on a civil suit against Tyson well before the trial began, the story was virtually ignored as some kind of desperate lawyer's trick instead of being seen as raising serious questions about her credibility.

How many times before and during the Persian Gulf War did you read or hear about the amphibious landing the Marines were expected to make on the shores of Kuwait to open up another front against Iraq's occupying forces?

That's exactly what Gen. Norman Schwartzkopf wanted you — and the Iraqis — to think.

"We continued our heavy operations out in the sea because we wanted the Iraqis to continue to believe that we were going to conduct a massive amphibious operation in this area," Stormin' Norman said during his famous post-war press conference.

"And I think many of you recall the number of amphibious rehearsals we had, to include 'Imminent Thunder,' that was written about quite extensively for many reasons."

No, Schwartzkopf said, he didn't want to characterize the amphibious landing ruse as "a deception," but, yes, he admitted he was "delighted" with the extensive press coverage at a time when the allies had insufficient ground forces in the gulf.

He neglected to thank the military press officers who made it so easy to cover those amphibious rehearsals — the same press flaks who later so strictly enforced the pool system of reporting the war; the same pool organized by the major media outlets to insure they got what battlefield access there was and their smaller competitors did not.

"When the Soviets did it, it was

called 'disinformation.' When we do it, its referred to as 'trial balloons,'" remarked Loren Thompson, deputy director of the National Security Studies Program at Georgetown University.

Thompson rattled off a list of such episodes: JFK's use of the so-called "missile gap" and "bomber gap;" JFK's successful efforts at persuading *The New York Times* not to break the story of the imminent Bay of Pigs invasion; the KGB's effort to turn the Third World against the West by starting a rumor about how the U.S. Army had secretly developed the AIDS virus in a lab in Maryland.

"Objective truth may exist, but finding out what it is is another matter," Thompson told *Gauntlet*. "The most important thing to remember is that, without the media, there can be virtually no communication between public officials and their public.

"Anything a politician wants to do to influence the public must be done through the media," Thompson added. "And, after all, how often are politicians politically objective?"

Virtually never and neither is the press most of the time, according to Gary Orren, a campaign veteran turned public policy professor at Harvard University's Kennedy School of Government.

In terms of manipulation of or by the media, "rarely is either side naively unaware of what's going," he said. "I suppose there are some instances where one is, in a sense, fooled by the other.

"But, more often than not, each side is aware of what's happening."

The relationship between the media and political leaders is "not unlike professional wrestling," he mused. "They know it's all an act and the audience, in many cases, is not naive either."

Orren believes that, with the increasing dominance of television as the preferred form of political communication, a "blurring of the lines" has intensified the nature of the inherently manipulative relationship between the press and the pols.

"Political leaders and the media have roamed into each other's traditional territories and have started performing some of the functions traditionally performed by the other side," he said. "Candidates and cam-

INVASION of PRIVY C

paign strategists have begun to act like news producers and reporters are acting like campaign strategists."

The "photo op" is a classic example of such media manipulation by campaigns, creating such scenic political tableaus as Bush's flag factory visits in 1988 or, in a larger sense, both party's national conventions.

Texas billionaire Ross Perot spearheaded a new mutation of media manipulation this year when he took his short-lived presidential run to the morning talk shows, where he could reach a larger share of the audience than on the nightly news and also exercise more effective control over the news he hoped to produce.

"If you want access to a politician these days, you have to take them in the form the campaign wants them to be in," Orren said. "In 1988, Mr. Bush hardly did any real press conferences during the course of the campaign. If you wanted to have the president, you had to go to the flag factory because he wouldn't be available otherwise."

Debates between presidential candidates are yet another example of how what appears to the public as an impromptu clash of political wills is actually a manipulation of message.

"Talk about professional wrestling matches," Orren said. "Debates today are scripted and designed by the candidates and brought to you courtesy of the networks.

"In 1988, Bush and Dukakis signed a very detailed agreement — a multi-page contract, in fact — stipulating everything: the size of the podiums, the camera angles, the topics, the subject of follow-up questions, the length of the questions, the length of the answers," he added.

In turn, most of the major television networks have manipulated the political process by requiring candidates to speak in soundbites suitable for the evening news.

Beyond the technical aspects of political manipulation today lies the age-old quandary of personal bias.

For example, a recent study by the Times Mirror Center for The People & The Press found that Democrat Bill Clinton "receives a significantly higher favorability rating from the press than does President Bush."

Among top level national editors, the survey pegged Bush's favorable-unfavorable rating at 43-48. He was even less popular among middle level news executives, who rated him at 35-53. Clinton's overall rating among the same groups came in at 55 percent favorable, 33 percent unfavorable.

As you might expect given the kind of press coverage he's had, Vice President Dan Quayle scored the worst among all members of the national media — a politically fatal 73 percent unfavorable rating.

The Times Mirror survey also found that the press and the public weren't reading from the same page.

While 56 percent of the press respondents felt they had "about the right amount" of influence over the selection of a presidential nominee, almost 60 percent of the general public thought the press had "too much" influence on the process.

Media bias may explain why the Center for Media and Public Affairs, an independent watchdog that tracks every story on the evening news, found that, between April 7 and June 2, Clinton received 53 percent favorable coverage from the networks; Bush got 22 percent.

In June and July, Clinton's favorable coverage mark reached 60 percent; the president's struggled to slightly more than half that — 33 percent.

Ask Arnold Zenker about media manipulation and he'll just chuckle a sly chuckle and deadpan: "Never heard of such a thing."

Of course, Zenker's job is manipulation and he's not afraid to use the word.

Based in Boston, he has been one of the nation's foremost imagemakers for the past 20 years, typically employed for anywhere from $3,500 to $10,000 a day by corporate clients seeking more than just a little damage control.

"My clients have a right to get their message across as best they can. I don't think of it as dishonest," he said. "If you are suddenly accused of hazardous waste violations or equal opportunity violations, you better believe you have a story to tell and you have the right to tell it as effectively as you can.

"When we work with a client, we leave absolutely nothing to chance. We anticipate all of the questions you might get asked at a press conference and we prepare all of the answers in advance," Zenker added. "We rehearse the demeanor that's going to accompany delivery of those answers, including what the client should wear and what the best camera angles are, and we determine the time of day that we want to release the story.

"Clearly, if you've got a story that's going to break negatively, you want it to break on a Friday after the six o'clock news," he said. "A good politician who wants publicity will issue his press release at two in the afternoon."

When a client is involved in a controversial issue, Zenker makes sure there is a tape recorder in plain view on his desk to send a subtle message about accuracy to the reporters gathered in the office.

Zenker has also prepared numerous clients for interviews on *60 Minutes* and each time he has made sure he had his own camera there to videotape the entire interview session.

"It has a slightly inhibiting effect on them," he said.

One of Zenker's recent clients was Dow-Corning, once the largest manufacturer of silicone breast implants.

"A no-winner," he recalled. "Once the media plays those emotional notes, there's no way you can win. Everything goes to gut and not to the head. Even if you have a story to tell, it gets lost in that visceral impact.

"The fact of the matter is that there was never any proven correlation between silicone implants and auto-immune disease or cancer," he added. "But when this thing picked up momentum and women were on TV saying their lives had been ruined by implants, it was all over."

A veteran of CBS News, Zenker sums up his philosophy succinctly: "If I can keep people in 18-second film clips, I can make Hitler look like Santa Claus."

Media manipulation became a growth industry for people like Zenker and for the media itself when advertising revenue changed television news from a public service into a money-maker.

Everyday across the country, small groups of editors sit in newsrooms and TV stations across the country deciding how much space to give a story, where it should appear and whether it should appear at all.

In a tough economy, those decisions get harder because there is not only less money to pay for the ads that support the space dedicated to news, but also less money for the consumer to spend to get that news.

Which is more appealing: The fact that most of the population of Somalia is dying of starvation or the latest news about Fergie, Diana, Woody and Mia, and Gennifer or Jennifer?

Which story would you read or watch first? If a row of magazines featured a cover story on these topics, would you buy the one about Somalia?

"The great tension in American media is between truth and entertainment," said Joseph Boskin, a professor of history at Boston University.

Boskin argues that that tension will continue to distort or overwhelm objective truth until the American public — the ultimate victim of media manipulation — enforces a new set of values on its masters.

"This is not a society that gives itself over to objectivity. American culture is not oriented toward thoughtfulness, or thorough discussion or thoughtful critique," he said.

"We love to think we're right, but that's icing on the cake. It's who wins that matters."

Have I manipulated you yet?

---

*Ed Cafasso is a reporter and city editor for **The Boston Herald**.*

TABLOID JOURNALISM AND MANIPULATION OF THE PRESS

Mark Di Ionno

Back in the good, old, jaundiced days of Yellow Journalism there was a legal epidemic so notorious, it became a standard part of law school curriculum.

It was called the Alienation of Affection suit and it was aimed at the industrial magnates and other high-powered brokers of commerce and government of the day. With money and fame, and reputations to protect, they became easy marks.

Alienation of Affection suits were legal extortion. The plaintiff threatened to make some unseemly matter involving the big shot very public. The big shot's choice was always easy. Even if he were innocent, he paid off the plaintiff, and kept it out of the papers. He knew what the papers could do to him.

There was fierce competition in the newspaper business in those days. Reputations of those involved and journalism ethics meant nothing to editors and publishers.

Today, competition has been replaced by survival for newspapers, and there is an intense competition for ratings among network, cable and independent television outlets. Perhaps that is why we are seeing a new rise in sleazoid journalism.

And it's just getting sleazier. We've heard Anita Hill testify that Clarence Thomas talked about his penis size, prowess and pornography, we've heard that William Smith (ah, almost forgot the media-bestowed Kennedy) had trouble maintaining an erection during sex (said he) or rape (said she) on the beach in Palm Beach, we've heard that Magic Johnson "tried to accommodate" all the girls on his way to contracting AIDS. The topper, of course, was Gennifer Flowers secret tapes bought and paid for by *The Star magazine*, who put on a New York press conference that was widely attended by the "legitimate" media. Here's a snippet that was recorded in all the papers and played over and over again on the air:

> In these days of dirty-laundry reporting, the media shows us all the unsightly human stains. No stone left unturned, no bedsheet left turned up.

CLINTON: If they keep asking, just say nothing went on.

FLOWERS: What am I gonna do, Bill. Tell them you ate my pussy.

Ah, freedom of press.

The media, unchecked by government and un-policed by itself, has us convinced we are a nation of voyeurs, driven by insatiable impulse to look through the bedroom curtains of our public figures, be they politicians, athletes or entertainers.

(Celebrity journalists, to date, are unsurprisingly exempt, except of course, the below-contemptible Geraldo Rivera who told the whole truth and something but truth in a tell-all autobiography, then shamelessly shilled himself not only on his own program, but those of similar ilk.)

In these days of dirty-laundry reporting, the media shows us all the unsightly human stains. No stone is left unturned, no bedsheet left turned up.

The only thing we never find out is how the media turns up the story. Well, here's a little trade secret. More often than not, it ain't from digging. It's from planting. Once the media shows a willingness to report anything, the rock is turned over and all the bugs come crawling out: political consultants and strategists, lobbyists, press agents, player agents, attorneys and a whole host of other unidentified sources who have a vested interest in seeing the story in print.

No one plants better than lawyers involved in civil suits. They litter court papers with outrageous allegations then tip off reporters that the suit has been filed, and, in many cases, furnish the press with a copy.

And the press is falling into the despicable habit of believing that just because information is "public" (in court papers or released police reports) it is fit to print. That is why we know names of high-profile suspects before they are arrested. Or even if they're never arrested. And that is why we get a laundry list of outlandish charges before they are ever proven.

And where is the media's responsibility in all this. Safe at home, hiding behind the First Amendment.

Lawyers exploit the media's irresponsibility by using sound-bite or headline language in court papers. Adjectives and invectives flow freely. You think the guy who called Mike Tyson a "Serial butt fondler" in a civil suit didn't know that sound-bite description would be all over the newspapers and TV news the next day.

"There are attorneys who use press agents and public relations firms to get publicity about their cases," said David S. Greenfield, who recently defended Howie Spira in a federal extortion case in which the complainant was George Steinbren-

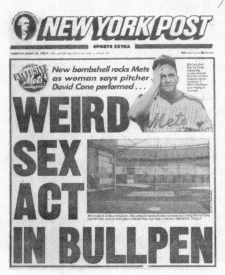

ner.

"They work the courthouses and drop little tidbits. They know certain reporters have certain likes or dislikes and know exactly where to steer the story."

Greenfield, who worked for the Bronx D.A.'s office on the famous Frank Serpico police corruption case, also said the use of reporters as press agents is getting worse.

"When I was in the D.A.'s office, if you leaked something to the press, you lost your job," he said. "And the other side (the defense) played by the same rules."

One of the most despicable examples of a pre-packaged journalism was a recent story about New York Mets pitcher David Cone. The Cone case may seem trivial. After all, he is not running for president or being nominated for the Supreme Court. But his case is the epitome of what's wrong with how today's media handles sleazy stories.

There was a day not too long ago when athletes private lives were off limits. (What, you think no one in the Cincinnati press knew Pete Rose was a degenerate gambler?) Sportswriters defended their lack of aggression into off-field stories by saying that what a guy did outside the lines was nobody's business, as long as it didn't effect his play.

But there was Cone, on the front page of *The New York Post* (and let's not pick on *The Post*. These days, it could have been The Times) accompanied by the headline, "WEIRD SEX ACT IN BULLPEN."

The paper got the story before anybody, even the court clerk. Cone and his lawyers did not have a chance to review the allegations that he masturbated in front of two of the three women who filed the suit, before he was splashed on Page One. Ouch!

The Cone story did not come from the cops. He was never charged or even investigated. It came from the lawyers of the three women, Phyllis DeLucia, Debra Hittleman and Joan Twohie. Want evidence? The picture *The Post* ran with their exclusive story were of the three women, conveniently posed and all made up and ready for the camera, in front of a book case in their lawyers' office.

To make matters worse, the women were seeking nothing but money. The Cone case was not criminal. It was civil. The alleged vic-

tims didn't want Cone locked up to make society safer. They wanted money. Big, SuperBucks Lotto Bonanza Money. Five million. Not a bad haul, even after you split it three ways.

The case has not been settled as of this writing. But if they win, they should vote a share for their friends in the press for its "shoot first, ask questions later" approach to this story.

The credibility of the three plaintiffs - Phyllis DeLucia, Debra Hittleman and Joan Twohie - was never questioned before *The Post* ran with the story.

So let's get some information and ask some questions that should have been asked before Dave Cone's reputation was irreparably damaged in a Page One non-story.

For instance, prior to becoming known to the public as the alleged victims of "Weird Sex Act in Bullpen," DeLucia, Hittleman and Twohie were well-known to the Met players as the Blow Sisters . . . and they didn't mean bubbles. Here's something else. DeLucia said in a radio interview (they all made the electronic talk show rounds the day the story broke) that her biggest complaint with Cone was not the "weird sex act." She was more offended that he referred to them as "groupies" in a newspaper item about an altercation he had with them while they were sitting in the player's family's section at Shea Stadium. The altercation was over the Blow Sisters allegedly harassing the wife of pitcher Sid Fernandez, who once dated one or another of the girls.

"How would you like to be called a groupie?" she asked the female radio show host after detailing a series of romantic encounters between a number of players and her friends. "We're not groupies."

Want more? Hittleman told the

press that just four months after Cone allegedly did the nasty in front of her in a back room of the Mets bullpen, she allowed him into the hotel room she was sharing with the Twohie at 3 a.m. and, wouldn't you know, he did it again.

"I was traumatized," she said. Twice!

(By the way, the hotel was in Montreal, where the Mets were playing the Expos . . . but they're not groupies.)

And here is a direct quote from Twohie about what happened when she tried to get him out of the room: "I grabbed him and broke one of my nails. These are my real nails and I almost had a fit. He's lucky I didn't kill him."

Why'd she let him in?

"He needed to borrow a towel."

At three o'clock in the morning!

Why didn't they tell him to call housekeeping?

And in a hotel with say, 600 rooms, how did Dave Cone know which one these women were in? Were they right next door? Or did a number of the other 599 guests, including teammates, turn down Dave Cone's request for a towel. Did any of this matter to the press? No. They were handed a copy of the suit and made arrangements to have "exclusive" interviews with the women. It was a tidy, packaged deal.

They never tested the credibility and motives of the people behind this frivolous lawsuit. Instead, they went with it full-speed ahead, lumping it in with a police rape investigation of Dwight Gooden, Vince Coleman and Darrell Boston (which was later dropped), and sent a female reporter to scout the bar scene at Port St. Lucie, where the Mets hold spring training to report on the night-life activities of the Mets.

As for Dave Cone, he may or may not be a pervert. At the very least, he's probably a bit of a jerk. Most athletes are, but it's almost impossible to be unaffected by the adulation the public bestows on them.

But whatever Cone did, it was obviously nothing but sex games with women who were, for a time, willing players. Regardless of the outcome of any court action, the damage has been done. Cone's name will always be accompanied by snickers of "WEIRD SEX ACT IN BULLPEN."

"It seems little or no concern is shown for the anguish of the person charged, who is really a defenseless target," Greenfield said. "Headline, byline and bottom line are apparently more important than the bright light of truth, justice and fair, balanced reporting."

Or like the say in the newspaper business: Don't let the facts get in the way of a good story.

Where is it all going? How much *A Current Affair* and *Geraldo* can we see before we are totally jaded? Newspaper readership and general consumer TV ratings are going down. More and more people are avoiding the news. They find is offensive to their senses and transparently manipulative.

Maybe it's time the media re-evaluates the newsworthiness of certain types of story. Maybe it's time to draw the line on certain subject matter and content. We always have to know everything. We don't always want to. Junk stories may sell today's paper, but over the long haul, they erode people's faith in the media as a credible source of information. And when that happens, the media serves no purpose.

---

*Mark Di Ionno is a former sports columnist for the **New York Post** whose work has also appeared in **The Sporting News**.*

Censorship and The Community Press

Caitlin Barry

[Editor's Note: "Caitlin Barry" is a pseudonym. The author does not wish to reveal her identify, nor that of the publications discussed in the following article, for fear of jeopardizing her current position with the paper and its parent-company — a very real concern in light of her situation both economically and professionally.

An award-winning, syndicated columnist, Barry has worked as a professional freelance writer for the past eight years.

The following article is the result of an interview she conducted with one of her editors, "Tim Stafford," who agreed to share his observations on the dynamics of censorship and "hidden agenda" at a community newspaper for which they both work, in return for a promise of anonymity — again for professional reasons.

The paper, which serves adjacent suburban communities outside a large Mid-Atlantic city, has been in publication for over fifty years; and was purchased some time ago by a company which also owns approximately 40 other community weekly and daily newspapers throughout the southern states. It is a typical "small town newspaper," covering county news and local events in much the same way it has done for over half a century.

Both Barry and Stafford live in the midst of the communities served by the paper. Barry moved to the area 14 years ago; Stafford was born and raised in this town, which prides itself on its over-200 year history and its middle-America-style family values.]

Tim Stafford is an award-winning journalist and assistant editor at a small town weekly newspaper for which I write. As an organization insider, he agreed to share his personal observations on the manifestation of censorship and "hidden agenda" at the publication.

I began our conversation by reminding Stafford of a story that appeared on the front page of our paper concerning the homelessness in the area. The piece was an up-beat account of local aid organizations that not only glossed over, but seemed to ignore, the actual situation; while the rival weekly, a tabloid format, commuter-oriented paper owned by a local corporation that produces some 20 look-alike community papers each week, had tackled the same topic with hard-edged prose and photos that graphically portrayed the plight of the homeless in the greater metropolitan area. Why the discrepancy, I wanted to know.

"It's not policy to cover up the facts, it's not stated policy," contended Stafford. "If it were (a cover-up), I would be the first one to be out, to bitch and moan, because I think I'm a highly principled person." But, "We always try to put the best possible light on our community . . . because it's a community paper and it's been (our experience that) the com-

CONGRESSIONAL DEFORESTATION

bore, and the fight was the most dramatic thing that happened."

Stafford, a graduate of a local high school, considers himself "extremely empathetic to (the school) and what goes on there." So, when he wrote a cutline for the photo and ran it with the story, "My intention wasn't to cause trouble," he insisted.

Even though the story never mentioned the fight, "We got more phone calls and complaints about the picture. You would have thought we had started at one end of the building and decided to tear the school apart, the community apart, by running one photograph. That's how much the community does not want to hear the truth."

It was a case, he said, "where all these sports parents — and they travel in packs — get together and they talk it over amongst themselves, and they blow the whole issue way out of proportion. We were hearing from a whole bunch of them within a couple of days of each other, and they were all pretty much spouting the same party line. It was pretty obvious that they had talked about it and decided they were going to put their little pressure routine on the (paper)."

Two letters to the editor were published, Stafford said, "Both of them erroneous. They saw in our coverage what they wanted to see — they never really did grasp the facts." It appeared, he said, that the writers had talked to other disgruntled parents and may not even have read the article at all, "and got all pissy about it."

The upshot of the "little pres-

munity wants it to be that way."

For instance, "Crime stories were always a big, touchy thing," Stafford explained, because one section of the community was "hypersensitive to the changes that were going on" as the black population there increased; and it was common, he said, for his supervising editor to question the efficacy of running "another 'bad' story" about the area.

Stafford cited other recent examples of the community setting the agenda for what it wants to read:

A photograph that ran in the sports pages managed to stir up a hornet's nest. When a fight had erupted among parents at a game between two area high schools, with students quickly entering the fray, "Our freelance photographer had turned in his roll of film and (the fight) was the best shot on the roll. The game, apparently, was a real sure routine?" "Since I was the one who (decided to run the photo), I would probably think longer about making a decision like that again," Stafford admitted. "I'm not sure I would change what I did, but I would think about it longer."

Local outcry over a lingerie shop selling sexual aids made front page news — and then the letters to the editor, noted Stafford. The report centered on a group of women who oppose the store, located in an area shopping center, as pornographic.

While there was never any question about running the piece, "We were all literally sweating it out, trying to figure out what was going to be 'too much' to handle," Stafford said. "Writing, working on the headline for the story, the question was, do we use the word 'dildo,' or is that too graphic for this community to handle?"

They decided in favor of 'dildo' — and other controversial nomenclature — and the negative comments started coming in almost immediately; proving that, if you offend certain segments of the community, "You'll hear about it unendingly," admitted Stafford, rolling his eyes. "That's not the worst thing that can happen," he hastened to add; "but you can't jeopardize the publication. It's a case where everybody knows everybody, and the advertisers are not removed from the scene, they're on the scene. You're getting pressured both ways, from up above and below too," he said.

Stafford doesn't believe that the practice of selective reporting — or advertising, since the paper is prohibited by home-office policy from running an ad for that same lingerie shop — is done maliciously. The bottom line is revenue; the paper is in *business* to serve the community, after all. "Kind of the tail wags the dog," he said; adding that while most newspa-pers keep advertising and editorial departments separate, "That's *never* been the case at (our newspaper)." In fact, experiments to create those types of boundaries over the past year "have been a total disaster," he reported; when ads and editorial work hand in hand, "We have a better product — the community is happier with the product."

Real estate pointed up the ad/ed bugaboo. "There was some documented racial steering going on by

> " . . . they probably want things censored. It's a self-imposed censorship."

realtors in (one) area (of the community). We lost advertising dollars from *all* the real estate companies there. They would not advertise (with us) because we had run some stories about the fact that this practice was going on," Stafford said. Later, when a similar problem arose, the supervising editor expressed concern whether they really wanted to "open another can of worms" by publishing the story, he recalled. "It was a concern on the part of management . . . so you have a kind of balance: Yeah, it's the wrong thing to do, if you're a dyed in the wool freedom of the press person; but if you're going to balance that against, well, suppose there's no mouthpiece at *all* for this community, there's nobody that's representing it or making a record of it — is that so much better?

"I think it was important to do the story, and we did it," Stafford went on. "And we got flak for it." But, at the same time, "I don't think it's something we should go out and look for (or ask) 'Is racial steering going on?' I don't think we should try to stir up racial pots all the time."

These types of situations lead Stafford to conclude that the paper is "controlled by the community. It's not so much the reporters or the management setting the agenda; the community sets the agenda." And, he said, while readers may not even realize that certain stories are being censored or white-washed, "I think, to be realistic, they probably *want* things censored. It's a self-imposed censorship," brought about by a "vocal minority."

That minority consists of what Stafford described as "a pretty small nucleus of people that we hear from week and week out"; either "the same people or the same *kinds* of people" who, by nature, rotate into various positions on community coordinating councils and the Chamber of Commerce; and "prominent community activists who have nothing better to do than call (the paper)," he said. These are the self-styled neighborhood leaders, what Stafford calls "the movers and shakers."

So, even though he views the weekly's purpose as "a chronicle of life in the community," one that he believes leaves a "generally accurate picture" of community life, "I think there are always people on the fringes that would pick up (the paper) and say, 'This is bullshit, this isn't what really goes on'; and there are probably mainstream people that do that too, on any given week. But I think generally it's a pretty good impression of what this place is all about.

"I may be deluding myself," Stafford mused; "it could be that the peo-

> "Obviously there's stuff we're not supposed to know, or they wouldn't be debriefing people."

ple even say to each other that's it's bullshit. But," he added with an ironic laugh, "to an outsider, they would promote it as the real McCoy." Because, while the paper's mission is to "mirror what's happening in . . . a mid-sized suburban town," he said, the responsibility is to do so in a "mainstream light."

With stories such as the lingerie shop, "I think we can hope that (the community) is mature enough to handle it. I don't know that that's very realistic . . . You can't force people. You can present things to people, but if you keep getting the same reaction, time and again, every time something like this happens — and it's been four years that I've been through it — I don't think it's going to change," Stafford observed. And even though a major portion of the community is currently considered a growth area, "It doesn't matter how cosmopolitan we get; they can build a thousand malls, a thousand housing developments, and invite the most free-thinking people in the world to live here — it seems like *they* conform, rather than act as a catalyst to change. The status quo kind of reigns here."

Stafford sees newspapers and other media being manipulated by the community they serve in other ways, too; including by "sources of authority that might be inclined to cover up." For instance, for the story concerning racial violence at a local public school, the reporter interviewed a school board representative; the principal; and a parent who called the paper, whose child was the target of an alleged racial attack. "The story he got is the story that the school system wanted to relay — that it was not a problem," Stafford said; and the piece never ran.

But what about the disgruntled parent? School officials, Stafford said, "gave (the reporter) their spin on where this parent was coming from" — an example of what he deems the "insurmountable relationship" between the press and certain sources. "We're not going to deal with (this school principal) one time and never have to deal with him again. (The reporter) has got to keep in mind that he's got to keep (the principal's) lips loose down the line." It's not a matter of taking the administrator's word as gospel, Stafford maintained; but, "You'll just have an unconscious tendency to go more with who you know, who you've dealt with, than you would some schmoe who calls on the phone one time and says, 'My kid got beat up.'"

This type of community-generated agenda is evident at all levels, contended Stafford; and is "an example of something that happens, to one degree or another, throughout the country"; though it may be more pronounced in his area, he allowed, given the conservative mind-set and self-imposed isolation of the community. "Obviously there's stuff we're not supposed to know, or they wouldn't 'debrief' people,": he added; "there wouldn't *be* such a

thing as 'top secret.'"

Stafford cited the metro area's daily, a nationally-acclaimed newspaper, as a "perfect example." "There's no doubt, when you pick up that paper, that the Democratic party has strong, strong inroads and pretty much calls the shots," he said. "And if that's happening here, you can draw some parallels, you can pretty much say that similar things are happening in other places too."

Then readership — and, it follows, advertising dollars — is the key to content, according to Stafford. Whether editorial or advertising, "There's a level between (our paper) and the (rival weekly). There's another level between our paper and the (city's alternative press newspaper) and the (metropolitan daily), in terms of what's appropriate. How far 'underground' do you have to go to get the whole truth?" he asked rhetorically.

Personally, "I don't think anything I've ever been involved with is something I can't live with, because (as an area native) I've always been able to see another side of it. If you always allow yourself to understand where they're coming from and what it is they're trying to accomplish — Are they trying to preserve something? The character of their community? I think very little of it is done maliciously," he concluded; "that's important to keep in mind."

Stafford views the "watering down" of reality to render it "inoffensive" to various groups as commonplace throughout society; "It's not just the news. You find this in organizations, schools, churches"; and, of course, "I've seen it at work. 'What will we tell them this week? How much truth can they handle.'"

HOW NOT TO BEGIN A CAREER IN RADIO

The strange case of the disc jockey, the journalist, Kiefer Sutherland, and the excrement heads

Duane Swierczynski

It took Karin Begin about three months to get herself into trouble in Philadelphia. That's not bad, considering it takes the city's politicians and lawyers years to do the same.

But even politicians can rarely get the media to fight itself.

When Begin arrived at University of Pennsylvania's public radio station WXPN early last December, she was a 24-year old unknown talent from Canada. Basically. Readers of such literary establishments as the *National Enquirer* and the *Globe* would recognize Karin Begin as the Canadian vixen who ruined Keifer Sutherland's fairy-tale marriage to Julia Roberts last summer.

Almost overnight, Begin became WXPN's late afternoon drive darling - but not because she was a Brat-Packer's "leukemia lover~." Begin the "Cool DJ" was talented - hip and funny - and gathered hundreds of fans, including local journalists. Her rise to Philly fame was so quick that by late December, *Philadelphia* magazine editor Lou Harry had caught wind of her success and thought she'd make a good profile.

Then Karin Begin's troubles began, or had already begun, depending on your perspective.

As he researched the piece, Lou Harry found out that Begin had lied on her resume about her movie and television credits. Not only that, but he couldn't find any verification for almost everything else she had claimed about herself - including the much talked-about Kiefer Sutherland affair. This became the center of the profile "Kiefer Madness" that appeared in the April issue of *Philadelphia*.

Begin's radio station and local journalists leapt to her defense, and it got ugly, even among grizzled journalists.

Professional writers called each other "excrement heads."

Columns were printed. Fact-checkers deployed.

Documents forged.

Finally, after those station managers and journalists found out that Karin Begin had lied to *them* as well, the "Cool DJ" was fired from her job.

Karin Begin is now in Annapolis, Maryland, a DJ at WHVY-FM.

In Philadelphia, they're still sorting it out.

Begin Unbound

Earlier this year, on the night before his first interview with Karin Begin, Lou Harry stopped into his local video store and rented *The Bay*

Boy, Kiefer Sutherland's early classic in which Begin was supposed to have had a bit part - as the "French Slut." It was always wise to be prepared for an interview. Harry didn't want to be caught not knowing his sluts.

But as he watched, he couldn't tell which character was Begin. She didn't appear in the credits, either. The clip that told him she was in *Bay Boy* only described her as the "French Slut." That could have been anybody.

"So which one were you?" he asked her the next day.

Begin quoted some dialogue, and soon Harry realized that she was a character who was the sister of a priest. "It was very clear she was telling me who she played. When you get something like that, there is no reason to doubt her." And Harry didn't. He listened to all of her acting credits (including parts in *Siege*, *DefCon4*, and *Happy Birthday to Me*), her illness that left her two hundred pounds heavier (aplastic anemia), and her childhood romance with Kiefer Sutherland.

According to Begin, "I felt bad from the beginning. I knew at the very end of the first lunch, when I mentioned something about *Bay Boy*. I told him I didn't want to talk about those things."

Harry recalls, "We had a lot fun at lunch. We were joking back and forth, and talked about everything from her birth till now. Nothing was hands-off." In fact, Harry's first doubts about Begin's story came much later, when he started doing some research before his second interview.

"When I met her in the studio, before her shift," Harry says, "I had my first moment of doubt." He'd read a clip in the *Atlantic City Press* that said Begin used to work with the famed Second City Troupe in Toronto. "I asked her if she had ever done comedy, and she said she never

had. I usually don't trust other journalists or other printed sources, because I can never guarantee that *they* got it right, but that was the first thing that alarmed me."

During the studio interview, Begin was the one who brought out all of her tabloid clips and tapes of the Canadian talks shows which dealt with the Keifer scandal. "She was not shy about anything," Harry insists. "The thing that really got me was when I started going through the clips and things from Canada, specifically, and none of them mentioned any other t.v. work she'd done. I thought, if all of this scandal is happening, if the tabloids were staking out her house, harassing her parents, and bugging her friends as she said, wouldn't they have found out that she had been a featured actress on one of the biggest hits in Canadian television?

"That's when I started tracking all of this stuff down, and tried to verify if she was in any of these things."

And started a fact-checking nightmare.

Begin Unfounded

More than anything, Harry was worried that his story was based on nothing more substantial than the airwaves Begin broadcast on every afternoon.

"My attitude was, I wanted to nail it down," Harry says. "If another person asked me about any job *I've* had, I could verify them."

Harry and magazine research editor Andrew Corsello, fresh from the research department of *The American Lawyer*, set out to verify anything they could.

They contacted the Canadian Broadcasting Company. The CBC never heard of her. They contacted the producers of *Hangin' In*. The producers of *DefCon4*, Salter Street films. The Canadian television actors' union, ACTRA. The Canadian Actors Equity.

That's not even to mention Kiefer Sutherland, whom Karin maintained was a good friend.

Nothing checked out. Most people Harry talked to hadn't even heard of a Karin Begin. Including Kiefer's agent, who swore that the actor had never met Begin in his life.

At this point, Harry still trusted Karin. "I went back to her and started saying, 'Look, I'm having trouble verifying some of this stuff, help me out,' because I thought I was missing something. That's when she started getting tense about things, and giving me names of people to call."

Names that eventually, would fail to check out.

There was a good reason: "Yes, I lied," Karin later told *Gauntlet*. "But the only thing I ever lied about was the television credits. I'm Canadian, and it's hard to get into this country. It wasn't like I was going to enter the country to go on welfare or something. So even though my television experience was minimal, my agent suggested I expand my acting credits, for instance, say I did two *seasons* of

Hangin' In (a popular Canadian show) instead of two *episodes*."

She laughs. "In Canada, being on *Hangin' In* is the equivalent of being on *Charles in Charge*. Besides, that resume changed once I got into the country. I never used it to get a radio job."

But why not admit that to *Philadelphia* from the beginning? "I felt trapped," Karin says. "Once you admit you've lied, you open yourself up to all kinds of things. But there is absolutely no reason for Lou Harry to delve into all of the things that he does, such as my illness. Some of my

Kiefer Madness

WXPN deejay Karin Begin's life story is straight out of the tabloids she stars in: too good to be true

By Lou Harry

"4 MONTHS WED—HE WAS BACK IN MY BED" screams the headline on top of Karin Begin's personal pile of tabloid articles. Maybe Elvis had more clips. Maybe the donor who wanted his kidney back sold more copies. But for a 24-year-old public radio deejay, it's a rather remarkable collection.

"I've never been known, when discussing sexual exploits, to break into verse," says Begin, offhandedly refuting the *News of the World* quote regarding her alleged relationship with actor Kiefer Sutherland while frantically looking for a three-minute song to plug in before the news. Begin may have had a brief moment of infamy, but now she has a job to do. Afternoon commuters in I-95 traffic are tuned in, and not only for Tom Waits, John Wesley Harding and Nancy Griffith tunes. They also want to hear WXPN's new 4-to-7 p.m. disc jockey, the one whose voice combines cool big sister, college girlfriend, and that strange high school buddy of yours who knew all the Monty Python skits by heart.

And the one who is reportedly the BRAT PACK STAR'S LEUKEMIA LOVER, who in 1988 had a LOVE-A-THON WITH MARRIED DAD KIEFER and last year was the REAL REASON KIEFER CALLED OFF WEDDING TO JULIA ROBERTS. The best story is probably the one about her cat fight with *Pretty Woman* star Roberts. No poetry in that report. But you can always count on the tabloids for evocative imagery.

"She hit me over the head with an Alpine wooden ship!" Begin quotes from memory, one eye on the console as she watches for a song to end. "She hit me with a schooner, and she said 'Get out of my house, you Canadian slut!'"

Begin smiles. "Yeah, Julie and I rolling around on the Persian rugs, breaking priceless artifacts over each other's heads. I'm

sorry," she suddenly bellows with equal parts bewilderment, merriment and indignation. "It didn't happen! There was no schooner! There wasn't even a ship in a bottle!" She slides an Elvis Costello CD into the player and prepares to switch to the news and a traffic update.

Okay, you know the tabloids are not to be believed. So we're not going to take their word for anything. But even if you ignore their colorful accounts of Begin's tumultuous quarter-century on this planet, the truth has a way of slipping through your fingers. And the line between the reality and the fantasy of this young woman's life starts to get a little murky.

"Every day of my life is like a bad movie," she says of that cool, warm, weird voice. "Every day is *The Adventures of Karin Begin*."

No, *Karin Begin was not involved with Dom DeLuise. That's her on the other Globe page.*

Adventure #1: Karin On-Camera

Karin Begin, born in New York City, raised in Halifax, Nova Scotia, was in ninth grade when she auditioned for a Canadian Broadcasting Company TV series called *Hangin' In*. Soon the overachiever was on her way to Toronto with her mother. "I had a good role," she says. "I played Jasmine, who was a counselor-in-training. I did that for two years, and it was great."

PHOTOGRAPH BY ERICA FREUDENSTEIN

APRIL 1992 PHILADELPHIA

acting credits were real. At least he could have included them. Instead, he focused on the others.

"Lou basically ousted me from Philadelphia."

Meanwhile, Harry and Corsello fought to find any kind of verification for Begin's story. With every dead end, Begin gave new contact numbers. When these failed, she gave more.

"It was like fighting a hydra," Corsello recalls. "You cut one head off, and two more appear. After a while, we just stopped."

Finally, with deadline looming, Harry turned in his story, and it appeared in the April issue. Harry presented to his readers both Begins's story and the results of his fact-checking. He felt confident that he'd given Karin Begin a fair shake.

The Columnists Vs. The Excrement Heads

Begin didn't think so. "I thought at the time, 'Why are they picking on me?'" says Begin. "Me, at the smallest radio station in town, a d.j. who's only been in the country for six months?"

So she called in reinforcements.

First, her station. WXPN administrators asked Begin if she had lied. "I said no," Begin told *Gauntlet*. "Later, after it came out that I had lied, Mark Fuerst (station manager at WXPN) asked me, 'Why didn't you tell me you lied?' I told him I was too incensed about everything else to worry about that." But at the time, WXPN believed their star d.j., and promised to back her up.

Then, Begin called the columnists in. Begin's primary defender was Philadelphia *Daily News* columnist Dan Geringer, who wrote a two-part column in early April. Geringer, who claims to have been "painfully misquoted" in the past by the maga-

There was never any secret love between the *Daily News* and *Philadelphia,* but this was turning into all-out war.

zine, wrote that Begin called him up and complained about "that excrement head from *Philadelphia* magazine."

To which Geringer replied, "Exactly which *Philadelphia* magazine excrement head are we talking about?"

Geringer later told *Gauntlet* why he'd sprung to her defense. "The magazine seemed to have - for motives I absolutely was not sure of - really gone after her. She's not an elected official. There are no public trusts involved. They took this small time show business personality, and basically called her a congenital liar. It angered me."

Geringer did some of his own homework, and assisted by some documents and numbers Karin supplied him, came to the conclusion that Karin's credits *did* check out, and that the only thing he couldn't confirm was the Kiefer affair. Regardless, called Harry's profile a bunch of "crock," having "reliable" agents and associates as well as "written proof" ready to back Begins's story.

Media writer Joe Logan from the *Philadelphia Inquirer* believed the same proof (also supplied by Begin), but reported the story as straight-news - minus Geringer's invective.

Harry and Corsello again set to work, not to fact-check the original story, but to save the reputation of the magazine. There was never any secret love between the *Daily News* and *Philadelphia*, but this was turning into all-out war.

Two of the major "proofs" were the existence of an agent, Ian Maynard, who verified Begin's credits, and Canadian television program listings.

As for Ian Maynard (whom Geringer based much of his proof), there was no such person listed at the CBC's Talent Resources Department, Employee Records, or the Jobbers department. *Hangin' In*'s creator, Joe Partington, never heard of Maynard. Andrew Corsello called Maynard himself, and noted that even though he sounded convincing, he failed to pass two small test questions, when he failed to recognize the names of the show's creator and producer.

The television listings Begin supplied were also blatantly faked. One listed a "Paul Schaeffer" as a guest. Not only was Letterman's sidekick Paul Shaffer's name blatantly misspelled, but Paul's agent, Eric Gardner, denied Paul's participation in the Canadian sitcom.

Finally, *Philadelphia* presented WXPN with this new evidence, not only resulting in Begin's suspension from the station, but an apology from Zachary Stalberg, editor-in-chief of the *Daily News*.

Stalberg wrote: "I should be clear about this: *Philadelphia* magazine was right. And our attack on its credibility was ill-timed and wrong . .

Our mistake was squabbling with the magazine over details instead of fully confronting the big issue: Did this stuff about Begin's past really matter to anyone outside the WXPN studio?"

Philadelphia's editor-in-chief, Eliot Kaplan, responded in a June "Letter from the Editor," calling Zack's apology a "class act," but noting "Curiously, we never did hear from Dan."

Dan Geringer, for his part, still feels the profile was completely unnecessarily mean-spirited, and feels no bitterness toward Begin. Whether he feels bitter about the magazine or not is a different story. "It's a weird publication," he told *Gauntlet*. "It's shallow to begin with."

As for Begin, the "Cool DJ" readily admits she forged the documents. "I did that so the reporters (Geringer and Logan) could focus on the other lies that Lou wrote. That was a big mistake. I'm not sorry about lying on my resume - it was the only way I could get into the country - but I felt bad about lying to Dan Geringer and Joe Logan. They were very supportive, even after they found out that I'd lied about the credits."

The same couldn't be said for WXPN. Begin was fired two weeks later. Mark Fuerst, WXPN's station manager, did not respond to repeated calls by *Gauntlet*, but the *Inquirer*'s Joe Logan reported that Begin had been fired because she failed to maintain a standard of integrity that all Penn employees are required to follow.

Begin herself speculates that her stunt embarrassed Penn's "higher-ups." "It's a lot different than commercial radio," she says.

Begin Again

Karin Begin is now working under the name Shannon Rock at a heavy metal station WHVY-FM in Annapolis (and part time at Philadelphia's WMMR, one of the market's top rated stations). Does she have a fear of reporters? "No, that would be like going out with one loser and then writing off men. I did get a lot of media attention out of it. I admit, a lot of it was me. I have to start refusing to talk about certain things. By expanding on things, it made them worse.

"It hurt me personally, and in terms of job security," Begin says. "But I don't feel it's done any irreparable harm to me."

Lou Harry, however, is still troubled by the whole affair. "I'm not pretending we took down a president, and our goal was never to take her down, but it's an interesting question: What do you do as a journalist when you're doing a profile of a celebrity and you find out that the person is bullshitting you, and you can verify it? This is a woman who claims that a Hollywood celebrity is a very good friend of hers, and he himself claims he never had anything to do with her. She sold a story to a tabloid about him. This makes her a public figure.

"If somebody had called me and said, 'I've got some dirt on Karin Begin, I think she lied on her resume,

check it out,' at best we would have run a paragraph item in the front of the magazine, if we found that out to be true. What happened is very different."

Dan Geringer continues to refer to *Philadelphia* as a souped-up furniture and restaurant guide.

Karin Begin may be gone, but some things never change in Philadelphia.

And Kiefer?

"It's all true," Begin still insists to *Gauntlet*. "Kiefer is denying it because he's trying to settle out of court with the tabloids. It's a money issue. That's why he's denying it."

As far as *Gauntlet*'s editor, Barry Hoffman is concerned it's a matter of privacy not worth pursuing.

It's better left to the tabloids.

*Duane Swierczynski is a freelance writer and regular **Gauntlet** contributor*

Florida State Attorney General John Turner in an attempt to drive video stores who rent X-rated videos out of business is attempting to get the names of individuals who rented such films, according to the National Coalition Against Censorship.

A Tale in "Twin" CITIES

by Kate Worley
art by Reed Waller

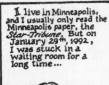

I live in Minneapolis, and I usually only read the Minneapolis paper, the *Star-Tribune*. But on January 29th, 1992, I was stuck in a waiting room for a long time...

...so I read both the "Strib" and the *St. Paul Pioneer Press*. There was a story in both about a crime that had happened the night before.

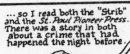

A woman who was employed at the Relax-a-Lounge sauna in Minneapolis was forcibly kidnapped and raped. A terrible thing... but there was something odd about the two stories...

In Minneapolis, the incident happened at a "sauna," which had been the site of "alleged prostitution activities."

The St. Paul paper referred to the location as a "bordello" and a "whorehouse."

(Classy, huh? Shows great concern for the victim)

Rebecca Rand, the sauna owner, was, in the *Strib*, the "Owner."

She was a "madam" in the *Press*.

Welcome to the **TWIN** Cities. Home of *balanced* reporting.

Quotes from Wayne Wangstad, staff writer - St. Paul Pioneer Press ✻ Jill Hodges, staff writer - Minneapolis Star Tribune.

CANDIDATES WITH NO BALLS

Greg Hotchkiss

With 1992 being a Presidential election year, it's to be expected that throughout the summer Americans would get plenty of exposure of the candidates through that magical electronic window: the television set.

But what's different this summer is when and on what programs we are seeing the candidates. No more are the early evening news programs the place the find Presidential wannabes.

Sorry Tom Brokaw.

Sorry Dan Rather.

Sorry Peter Jennings.

This summer you either had to get up early or stay up late to see your favorite candidate.

Hello Bryant Gumbel.

Hello Larry King.

Hello Arsenio Hall.

Yes, during the summer of 1992, the morning news shows and evening/late-night talk programs were the shows of choice.

A quick check of where the Presidential candidates spent some of their summer is like a tour through the morning and evening sections of the TV GUIDE.

Ross Perot *twice* stopped by *Today*, answering questions from both Bryant Gumbel and Katie Couric and also taking phone calls from viewers across the country. Perot was also on CNN's *Larry King Live* twice.

Bill Clinton chatted with Phil Donahue on *Donahue* and Arsenio Hall on *The Arsenio Hall Show*. He also fielded questions on both *Today* and *CBS This Morning*.

Finally, the President himself, was interviewed by Barbara Walters on *20/20*. An interesting non-appearance for Bush was when he officially told *The Arsenio Hall Show* that he wouldn't by making an appearance on their program. What makes this interesting is not that he didn't go on, but that he even considered it.

So what does this all boil down to? Well, it seems that George, Bill, and Ross are avoiding Tom, Dan, and Peter. And why are they avoiding them? It's simple, because they're afraid.

Follow me here; Presidential candidates want to be on TV. TV equals exposure, and exposure equals votes. Simple, right? Except for when the candidate's TV expo-

> . . . it seems that George, Bill, and Ross are avoiding Tom, Dan, and Peter. And why are they avoiding them? It's simple, because they're afraid.

sure is bad. This takes away votes.

So the candidates this summer are staying away from television situations which could be disastrous; namely a traditional stop along the campaign trail: the network evening news shows.

These news anchors are trained journalists who ask the tough questions (i.e. Where do you stand on this issue? What are you going to do about this situation?) and don't give up until the questions have been fully answered. You can be sure that an interview with Mr. Rather, Mr. Jennings, or Mr. Brokaw won't be a walk in the park, and the chance of the candidate looking bad in such an interview is quite high. The candidates know this.

So where do they go to get their TV exposure? They go to more entertainment-driven programs where they believe they will have an easier time. And they do, because of two reasons: the nature of the program and the people who are going to be conducting the interview.

Let's digress for a moment.

I can remember a few years back when Andrew Dice Clay was on *The Arsenio Hall Show*. The controversial comedian had just finished a short monologue and Arsenio began questioning the Dice Man about his combustible personality, about whether or not it was just an act to stir up controversy.

Well, Dice said no, but Arsenio kept badgering him to come clean. The comedian kept denying it was an act and Arsenio remained relentless.

Then something amazing happened. The studio audience began to turn on the host. A few even booed the

A-Man. That right, the fist-circling, woof-yelling crowd of Arsenio did not like what he was doing to his guest. The slightly taken-aback Arsenio quickly gave up his current line of questioning.

The reason I mention this was to emphasize how talk shows want to avoid conflict and just be a laugh-a-minute program. Arsenio tried to deviate from this, he tried to ask some tough questions, and it didn't work.

Clinton was recently on *The Arsenio Hall Show* and he started off by playing the saxophone. During the subsequent chat between Clinton and Hall, it seemed that Arsenio was more concerned with telling jokes than asking any real questions.

Arsenio had learned his lesson with Andrew Dice Clay, and he wasn't going to make the same mistake twice.

That appearance was exactly what Clinton wanted. It got his face in America's living room with little or no risk of an image-killing interview.

This is true for all the shows that I've mentioned above. It certainly is much easier to be interviewed by Katie Couric than Peter Jennnings. Do you think Larry King is going to push a candidate until they answer the important questions?

A problem now arises because these questions aren't getting answered. We are learning all sorts of superficial stuff about the candidates, but is any of that information important? Not really. Bill Clinton being able to play the saxophone isn't going to make him a better President, but that's about all we learned from his appearance.

We, as Americans, have to be aware that the Presidential candidates have censored themselves and their views by avoiding the evening news shows and their tough questions and are gravitating to more entertainment-driven programs.

The candidates are so afraid that one bad appearance will kill their drive to the White House that they avoid putting themselves in such situations.

So now, come November, when we Americans go into that small booth to cast our ballot, we can't count TV as a helpful influence on our vote.

Greg Hotchkiss is a freelance writer.

A 65-year old woman, attacked in Miami and left with a fractured back, was awarded $50,000 in full disability because she panics at the sight of black man. The case, being appealed, the *USA Today* reports could open the floodgates to similar claims. "The possibilities are endless," says Robyn Blumner of the ACLU in Miami.

HATE AND THE ART OF QUEER MEDIA SPINS

Andy Mangels

Four years ago, I was involved in a protest against *The Oregonian*, the largest newspaper in the state of (where else?) Oregon. Sponsored by Queers United Against Closets (QUAC), Portland's early version of ACT-UP, we were distressed with the gay-bashing editorials by editor David Reinhart. He blamed the AIDS crisis on the gay community, and refused to cover anything positive relating to the gay community. We staged a "die-in" on sheets of butcher paper, tracing outlines of our bodies and writing in the names of deceased Oregonians who had died of AIDS.

The butcher-paper roll was delivered to Reinhart's office door, and our demonstration ended. One TV station hurriedly covered the event, and even *The Oregonian* had a small piece on it. Staffers later told people that Reinhart had cried when he saw the butcher paper roll, representing the lives lost.

That was an election year, and the gay community in Oregon already faced a bitter battle. The governor had passed a bill which protected state employees from job discrimination due to sexual orientation. A small conservative group called Oregon Citizen's Alliance began a petition drive to overturn the bill, succeeding in getting a confusingly-worded measure on the ballot.

The OCA misdirected the public with a commercial showing a fearful child about to be adopted by two male lovers, obvious "child molester" caricatures. They claimed that the governor's bill allowed such evil to corrupt the children. While TV stations pulled the ad, little play was given in the media as a whole, to the struggle into which the gay community was entering.

Despite last-minute newspaper non-endorsements of the OCA's Measure 8, the outlying country areas of Oregon pushed the ballot box to the brink of bigotry. The measure no one thought would win became a cold reality.

Last year, the OCA sniffed the winds again and felt that the time was right to make their grand play. They introduced to the public a petition that declared "perverse and unnatural" homosexuality, sadism, masochism, pedophilia, and necrophilia (these last three already illegal). The wording of the measure would ban government promotion or protection of any of these, and require schools to teach that such lifestyles were wrong.

This time, not only did Oregonians themselves wake up to the threat of the bigoted fringe, but so did *The Oregonian* itself, along with the rest of the media. As OCA cronies went signature-gathering in the malls, positive news pieces about the gay community began popping weekly, then several times a week. When several store chains and shopping malls had to go to court to keep the OCA from petitioning on their doorsteps, the reporters crowded in to flaunt the hoped-for failures of the right-wing bigots. When a poster appeared around the state declaring "Free Jeffrey Dahmer, All He Did Was Kill Homosexuals," and listing the OCA's address, the cause became a national phenomenon.

The TV magazine, *20/20*, shot an unflattering portrait of the OCA and its leaders, comparing them to the Ku Klux Klan and labelling them a "Hate Group." The segment helped strengthen both sides, however; while it gave the gay community new supporters, it also gave the OCA a new infusion of interest and money from bigots around the country.

Meanwhile, the OCA's video of San Francisco Gay Pride antics meant to shock the public, didn't find the venues it had hoped for. *The Oregonian* and other state newspapers became targets of the OCA-sponsored boycotts due to their editorial policies; these were called off after meetings with the OCA, yet, if anything, the gay coverage became stronger and more visible than ever before.

The OCA attempted city-wide measures of the same sort as their statewide initiative, in Portland, Corvallis and Springfield. When the Portland signatures were turned in, a large percentage were disqualified, and the measure did not qualify for the ballot. Corvallis, a college town, handsomely defeated the measure. Springfield didn't. Immediately upon passage, the OCA was calling for the removal of "pro-gay" books from the town library.

July 3rd, the day before Independence Day, the OCA turned in their statewide signatures. Far in excess of the required amount, many civil rights activists spent a non-celebratory weekend. The signatures were counted and recounted, but the devils had done their deeds. The "No Special Rights Initiative" soon became Measure 9.

What will Measure 9 accomplish, if it passes in November? All books, encyclopedias, and recordings which do not label homosexuality "perverse and unnatural" will be removed from public and school libraries. All school teachers and any state workers who deal with children will be grilled about their sexuality; if found to be - or *suspected* of being - homosexual, they will be removed from any access to children. The State of Oregon will be forced to abolish any kind of anti-discrimination laws regarding housing, employment, medical aid, etc.

Not chilling enough? All Hate-Crimes laws will be removed from books as well, removing gay-bashing as a crime. Business and liquor licenses, all state-controlled, will be pulled and/or denied to any business thought to cater to gay clientele. Public television and radio, if it received any government money, will be forced to air anti-gay propaganda. All state-funded AIDS agencies will also be forced to espouse anti-gay rhetoric, or be shut down.

Constitution be damned, the OCA is fighting *faggots* here!

Into this vicious climate of hate, the civil rights activists have finally seen the media stepping in to represent them. *The Oregonian* now has daily articles on gay themes, and every movement of the pro-OCA or anti-OCA forces are carefully tracked. Electronic media is not far behind. Marchers in this year's Gay Pride Parade noted humorously that, for perhaps the first time in national history, the media estimated the same number of marchers and participants as the Pride committee itself!

The media is having an easy time presenting a case against the OCA. The hate-group has recently split from the Republican Party, who denounced them, the Oregon Medical Association gave the OCA's message a bad diagnosis, and coalitions of churches are preaching anti-hate and anti-OCA messages from the pulpit. Even the Oregon Council of Architects recently changed their name to Council of Oregon Architects due to the embarrassment over their monogram.

With stormclouds rending the horizon, some gay leaders are thanking the OCA for bringing civil rights solidarity to the state, yet such thanks are premature. Still, a victory has been won in the media. Four years ago, a roll of butcher paper with traced bodies of death gained only tears. Today, a measure which threatens to split a state and destroy civil rights has gained much more attention to the plight of the beleaguered gay community.

Ironically, the politics of hate have impassioned the media far more than the politics of loss.

Andy Mangels is a mainstream comic book writer whose work includes Nightmare on Elm Street and upcoming issues of Quantum Leap and the Batman Adventures. He is the editor of Gay Comics.

New York's WABC-TV was the *only* affiliate, out of more than 200, who decided against airing a recent *Sally Jessy Raphael Show*, the *New York Post* reported. Raphael was to interview former-Miss Arkansas Sally Perdue, who claimed she had an affair with Bill Clinton. Sources at the station told the *Post*'s Jill Brooke they were concerned with the veracity of Perdue's story. It's a shame the other 199 stations are more interested in ratings than in integrity.

With stormclouds rending the ...
the OCA for bringing civil rights solidarity to the state. ...
premature. Still, a victory has been won in the media. Four years ago, a roll
of butcher paper with the dead bodies of death gained only tears. Today, a
measure which threatens to split a state and destroy civil rights has gained
much more attention to the plight of the beleagured gay community.
Ironically, the politics of hate have empassioned the media far more
than the ...

I'M ALSO AN ACTIVIST IN THE WORLD OF COMIC BOOKS. MY CHOSEN PROFESSION. INSPIRED BY THE EARLIER UNDERGROUND COMIX WRITERS AND ARTISTS, LIKE **HOWARD CRUSE**, I BECAME THE FIRST OPENLY GAY **MAIN-STREAM** COMIC PROFESSIONAL BACK IN '88

THE MEDIA WAS ALL AFIRE WITH NEWS ABOUT THE *TRUE CRIME TRADING CARDS* FROM ECLIPSE. IT WAS AN IDEA THAT COULD BE UTILIZED. I STARTED LAYING THE GROUNDWORK FOR A SET OF CARDS CALLED THE *TRUE BIGOT TRADING CARDS.*!

IT MEANS I **DON'T** GET A LOT OF WORK, AS THERE ARE SOME HOMO-PHOBIC EDITORS IN THE COMIC INDUSTRY, BUT THAT'S A STORY FOR ANOTHER TIME. AFTER PRODUCING A SET OF LOCAL FUNDRAISERS TO FIGHT THE **O.C.A.**, I THOUGHT I'D USE MY TALENTS IN THE COMIC INDUSTRY TO DO THE SAME.

I APPROACHED A NUMBER OF COMIC ARTISTS FROM THE NORTH-WEST, AND **LOTS** OF THEM AGREED TO DO A CARD. WITH DIFFENT ARTISTS ON EACH CARD, THEY'D BE COLLECTABLE IN THE **COMIC** MARKET, AS WELL AS IN THE **POLITICAL** ARENA.

THEN I HIT ON A **SECOND** IDEA. REMEMBER THE "CARTOONISTS AGAINST HUNGER" A FEW YEARS AGO?
MOST OF THE NEWSPAPER COMIC STRIP ARTISTS DEDICATED A WEEK'S WORTH OF STRIPS TO THE TOPIC OF ENDING **WORLD HUNGER.** I BELIEVE IT WAS THANKSGIVING WEEK.

OUT CAME THE "**CARTOONISTS AGAINST HATE**" PROJECT. MY IDEA WAS TO ASK ALL THE CARTOONISTS TO DO A WEEK'S WORTH OF STRIPS ON THE SUBJECT OF **BIGOTRY** AND **HATRED** -AGAINST **ANYONE,** NOT JUST GAYS AND LESBIANS. THEN ON ONE DAY THEY'D ALL DO A **SPECIAL** STRIP AGAINST HATRED.

THE **O.C.A.** WAS GIVING THE OREGON GAY COMMUNITY A CHANCE TO RAISE A LOT OF **CONSCIOUSNESSES, BUT HERE** I THOUGHT IT COULD BE DONE ON A **NATIONAL** LEVEL.

WHO, I THOUGHT, WOULD REFUSE TO DO A STRIP AGAINST HATRED?

MEANWHILE...

EVEN CALLING THESE PEOPLE "TRUE BIGOTS" SEEMED TO BE A CONCERN. OKAY. SO I CAN CHANGE THE NAME TO "TRUE HATE TRADING CARDS." TASTES GREAT, LESS LIBEL.

STILL, NO ONE WOULD GO FOR IT. THE PUBLISHERS WANTED EITHER A COMPLETED CARD SET TO SOLICIT FOR DISTRIBUTORS NOW, OR THEY WANTED TO BRING IT OUT AFTER THE ELECTION.

TRUE HATE

Tast as GREAT Less LIBEL

I WAS GETTING NOWHERE WITH THE TRUE BIGOT TRADING CARDS. SOME PUBLISHERS WERE INTERESTED, BUT NERVOUS ABOUT THE LEGAL IMPLICATIONS. JESSE HELMS AND DAVID DUKE WERE PUBLIC FIGURES, AND ONE COULD SAY ALMOST ANYTHING ABOUT THEM WITHOUT FEAR OF LIBELING OR SLANDER. BUT WHEN IT GOT DOWN TO LON MABON AND SCOTT LIVELY, HEAD O.C.A. HATE MONGERS, THEIR "PUBLIC FIGURE" STATUS BECAME QUESTIONABLE.

BUT WAIT! THAT RUINS THE PURPOSE! IT DOESN'T RAISE MONEY OR CONSCIOUSNESSES IN TIME!

WHICH LEFT "CARTOONISTS AGAINST HATE." THE ADVOCATE THOUGHT IT WAS A GREAT IDEA AND PROMISED TO DO A FEATURE. COMICS BUYER'S GUIDE THOUGHT IT WAS A GREAT IDEA AND PROMISED TO HELP PROMOTE IT.

ON A ROLL, IT WAS TIME TO CALL THE SYNDICATE

COMICS BUYER'S

WHEN THE ANTI-O.C.A. GROUPS IN OREGON SEEMED LESS-THAN-ENTHUSED WITH MY IDEA (THEY STOPPED RETURNING PHONE CALLS) I GAVE IT UP. DESPITE THE FACT THAT IT COULD HAVE RAISED A LOT OF MONEY, IT WAS GOING TO BE TOO HARD TO DO THE WORK. AS A VOLUNTEER I DIDN'T HAVE THE TIME OR THE ENERGY. THE "TRUE BIGOTS/TRUE HATE TRADING CARDS COMMITTED SUICIDE.

SO, THAT SEEMS TO BE THE END OF "CARTOONISTS AGAINST HATE."

TO REVIEW:

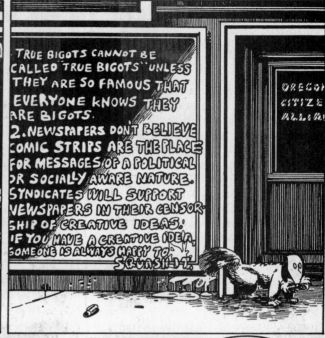

1. TRUE BIGOTS CANNOT BE CALLED TRUE BIGOTS" UNLESS THEY ARE SO FAMOUS THAT EVERYONE KNOWS THEY ARE BIGOTS.

2. NEWSPAPERS DON'T BELIEVE COMIC STRIPS ARE THE PLACE FOR MESSAGES OF A POLITICAL OR SOCIALLY AWARE NATURE.

3. SYNDICATES WILL SUPPORT NEWSPAPERS IN THEIR CENSORSHIP OF CREATIVE IDEAS.

4. IF YOU HAVE A CREATIVE IDEA, SOMEONE IS ALWAYS HAPPY TO SQUASH IT.

OREGON CITIZE ALLIAN

WELL, SO THERE YOU HAVE IT.

I'M GOING BACK TO PROMOTING OTHER FUNDRAISERS AND GETTING INFORMATION OUT TO THE PUBLIC ABOUT HATE GROUPS LIKE THE O.C.A.

OF COURSE, FAR BE IT FOR ME TO STOP ANY CARTOONIST WHO VOLUNTARILY CHOOSES TO INCLUDE A MESSAGE ABOUT HATE AND BIGOTRY IN HIS OR HER COMIC STRIP

OCTOBER   11-17

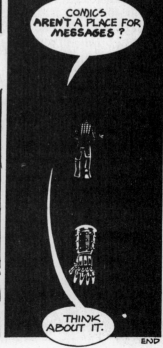

COMICS AREN'T A PLACE FOR MESSAGES?

THINK ABOUT IT.

END

STILL LURKING IN THE SHADOWS, AFTER ALL THESE YEARS

Michael C. Botkin

National Geographic, that stalwart bastion of mainstream blandness, recently published an article about West Hollywood. I was curious as to how they would deal with the fact that the township is a majority Queer community, and indeed, this was a major factor in its secession from the city of Los Angeles. What would the mainstreamers make of the colorful natives on their little safari to this urban jungle?

They did what most of the press does with the Queer issue: ignored it as much as possible, and wildly distorted the little they could perceive.

There was one mention of the gay community in the several thousand words of text, and this was a brief reference to the Gay and Lesbian community center. However, the mention came only in the context of a more prolonged discussion of a heterosexual woman with AIDS who received services from the center. The 98+ percent of the center's clients who are gay and lesbian remained invisible.

On a graphic level, there were two photos of gay men. The first was a teen-age junkie hustler working the streets, the second a horribly emaciated Person With AIDS clearly on his death-bed.

This pretty much sums up the conservative stereotype of gays: outlandish degenerates and/or Dead Meat Specials. *NG* was striking a "compassionate" pose, along the lines of "isn't it a shame that homosexuals are doomed to brief and miserable lives of quiet desperation cut short by an early and painful death." The more hard-core right-wingers take a harsher tack, cruising Gay Pride festivals and selectively targeting the most outlandish leather queens and motorcycle dykes they can find for portrayal in videos designed to support crusades against gay rights.

The liberal wing of the media offers a far less pejorative view of the queer community, but ultimately it is almost as skewed and distorted. The *New York Times,* which for years refused to use the word "gay", insisting upon the clinical term "homosexual", recently began providing extensive coverage of gay and lesbian issues. Currently, scarcely a week goes by without them publishing a major article on Queers, whether it's the latest purge of gays from the military, our presence at the Democratic convention, or a lawsuit against the Boy Scouts of America for homophobic discrimination.

But this awareness extends only to the most yuppified aspects of the Queer community. It's as though they can only recognize those of us who most closely resemble their own image of the Ideal Citizen; exemplary soldiers, delegates to presidential conventions, perfect Eagle Scouts.

This is particularly noticeable in the *Times* almost obsessive attention to "the Gay Market." Announcing that major mainstream advertisers have finally decided that the gay market is "too big to ignore", they've printed several articles on the prospects of "the Gay Slicks", glossy magazines targeted at moderate, upscale "gaystream" audiences. In today's tight advertising markets, the prospect of wealthy, high-living GUPpies (from "Gay Urban Professionals") just waiting to buy name-brand Vodka, expensive household toys, and costly vacations is simply too alluring to resist.

This is not to say that the Queer community doesn't have its fair share of junkie hustlers, terminal PWAs, leather queens, bike-dykes, and well-heeled gaystreamers with high discretionary incomes. It's just that these easily recognizable sub-groups are clearly, to anyone at all familiar with the community, just the tip of the iceberg. And as far as I can tell, the mainstream media is totally unaware of this.

In all fairness, I don't think most editors have a fixed, homophobic policy. But they see what they expect to see, and anything that goes counter to their expectations so confuses them that they simply ignore it.

This confusion was apparent in the local papers' recent, bewildered attempts to cover the rise of the Queer National movement. Like ACT-UP, its role model, Queer Nation began in New York City (in 1989) and quickly spread to the other Gay Urban Meccas, like San Francisco and LA. Queer Nationals favor in-your-face demonstrations, civil disobedience, bizarre acronyms (my personal favorite: DORIS SQUASH for "Defending Our Rights in the Streets, Super Queers United Against Savage Heterocentrism", an anti-queer-bashing group) and an ultra-democratic openness based on consensus process. Finding the AIDS focus of ACT-UP too restrictive, local QN chapters sponsored a multitude of aggressive consciousness raising events, like Queer "outings" to suburban malls, demonstrations at fundamentalist churches and protests of homophobic movies like *Basic Instinct*.

The media just didn't know what to make of us. They weren't sure if the obscure acronyms were serious or not (mostly not), they couldn't see if or how we were different from ACT-UP. A writer for one of the local dailies followed a crowd of Queer Nationals around during the rather spirited protests during the invasion of Iraq; in his column he called them "ACT-UP types" (which actually wasn't a bad description). But he was dinged for mis-attribution and had to admit that he didn't really know who they were or what group they actually "represented".

The absurdly decentralized structure of Queer Nation/San Francisco drove local journalists up the wall. They would attribute a demonstration to QN, only to be huffily informed that it had been sponsored by this or that "focus group", imprecisely affiliated with QN but NOT endorsed by the parent organization. After about eighteen months of frenzied and troubled existence, QN/SF folded last year, but only after having sparked a plethora of now free-standing committees and activist grouplets. To me, its obvious that all these fragments are distinctively Queer National in their goals, membership, and heritage, but to the mainstreamers they're just a swamp of random acronyms.

Back in 1989 it had been so easy! There was just one, single Queer activist group. If any Queer militants in black leather jackets showed up disruptively someplace, you could simply call them "ACT-UP" and you knew you'd be right. But ACT-UP/Golden Gate split from the parent ACT-UP/SF, in 1990, and QN was formed soon there-after (no need to go into the details of the split, as it

> ... the overall effect of Queer Invisibiltiy is to keep more gays and lesbians in the closet and disempower the Queer community as a whole.

was totally arcane to the mainstreamers). Then, to top it all off, QN implodes and splinters into a dozen fragments, which scatter across the political horizon like cue balls.

To them this new movement was an impenetrable maze, and their instinctive response was, therefore, to ignore it as much as possible. When Queer Nationals trashed San Francisco Chief of Police Frank Jordan during a riot, ripping one of his shoes off, many attributed this anarchistic militance to (of all people!) the Revolutionary Communist Party, a group that scarcely exists anymore and has not, for some time now, dared to show its red flags in the Queer Castro district, where the Jordan melee took place.

(Since Jordan became mayor of San Francisco shortly afterwards our community deemed it advisable to play down the whole incident as much as possible, and didn't particularly challenge the mis-attribution. The shoe itself was ritually immolated, mounted upon a donut box.)

Likewise, the above mentioned protests of the Iraqi war, and, more recently, demonstrations against the Rodney King verdict were heavily Queer events in San Francisco, a de-tail the media largely ignored (or, to be fair, perhaps just didn't notice). Of course, there's a certain advantage to this, for this lack of basic knowledge impedes mainstream intervention and counter-action. As Mark Pritchard, editor of *Frighten the Horses*, puts it: "For now I take comfort in the momentary inattention of the law enforcement/intelligence community: 90s groups like Queer Nation can bloom overnight, scandalize the squares for a year, then blow apart like dandelions before the Feds even notice."

Tactical considerations aside, it is clear that the overall effect of Queer Invisibility is to keep more gays and lesbians in the closet and disempower the Queer community as a whole.

Few groups in the U.S. have as little control over how they are portrayed in the mainstream media as we do. While racist and sexist commentary is discouraged, or at least allowed rebuttal (on the rather frequent occasions when it happens anyway), talk-show hosts can openly fag-bash away for hours, and Hollywood can grind out endless empty thrillers based on psycho-killer Queers without fear of any serious reprimand. If we suggest that these attacks entitle us to equal time to respond, their jaws drop in amazement. If we protest so effectively that we can't be ignored - as we did around "Basic Instinct" - they declare us "terrorists".

I see two factors on the horizon that are likely to alter Queers currently shadowy status. The first is the growing militance of the Queer community, which is already hyper-sensitive to our portrayal in the media. A major national gay group is GLAAD, Gay and Lesbian Advocates Against Defamation, with numerous local chapters and a policy of aggressively monitoring media coverage of Queer issues. Combined with Queer National zaps against the worst of the homophobes, and the contrasting lure of the lucrative Guppy market, this influence is likely to tilt the balance of power in media representation debates in favor of the Queers and against the reactionaries and fundamentalists, who until now have succeeded in cowing advertisers with (probably empty) boycott threats.

The second is the emergence of openly gay and lesbian journalists in the mainstream media (e.g. the National Association of Gay and Lesbian Journalists). These closeted workers have been there for decades, of course, but only recently have they begun to feel entitled to representation and input into editorial policy. Ironically, although they have clearly benefitted from the new Queer militant wave they are, as a group, fairly hostile to it. Now they have begun to organize, to "come out" on the job, and to agitate for better mainstream coverage of Queer Issues. It was the influence of just such a group at the *New York Times* which inspired their newly awakened interest in such things as the Gay Market. When the militant wing develops enough clout to require mainstream change, the newly out mainstream journalism Queers will be ready to step in and provide it. It will doubtless still be skewed, but Goddess, it's got to be better than what we've got now.

Michael C. Botkin is a San Francisco Queer activist, regular columnist for The City's queer Bar Area Reporter, and "Sleazy Editrix" of Diseased Pariah News, THE HIVer humor 'Zine.

UNHEALTHY MORALITY

David Gilden

Last summer's Eighth International Conference on AIDS was buffeted by contradictory impulses from the very beginning. The conference opened with its widely respected chairman, Jonathan Mann of Harvard and formerly of the World Health Organization AIDS program, warning that the epidemic was careening without hindrance about the world. Mann called for a "blue" political party to promote health care to the top of the world agenda. But when asked about specific reforms (beyond catch-phrases such as "world solidarity" or "social equality"), Mann demurred, claiming that it was not his place to come up with the details. And thus he rendered his eloquent pleas meaningless, but safe. He will continue jetting about the world to conferences of the rich and mighty.

"Play it safe" has been the watchword for coping with the epidemic all along. A disease that should call into question everyone's long-held views of sin's place in the universe instead has summoned up the usual reflexes, and the very conditions that spawned the epidemic continue unchallenged.

One of the greatest failures in this whole affair has been the media's handling of AIDS. America's sources of news have distinguished themselves by shallow writing that plays on the fears of modern society: a fascination with death, an obsession with death's connections to sex, and an overall hesitancy about interpersonal intimacy. As the eighties progressed, other human beings appeared more and more untrustworthy. It seemed safer to rely on material consumption to fulfill human needs.

As the AIDS conference unfolded, the three major US newsweeklies all gave vent to major AIDS stories, exemplifying how far the media has come and how little they have seen in a dozen years of AIDS coverage.

The magazines' theme, like Mann's, was that AIDS is out of control, but they had even less to say than the professor about what to do. First out of the gate was *US News & World Report* with "The Hidden Cost of AIDS." In the year 2000, the magazine estimates that AIDS will be costing the world as much as $514 billion dollars, or 1.4% of all countries' gross domestic product put together. Although it is indisputable that AIDS is going to cost a lot, especially as the epidemic moves into Asia, the magazine does not explain how it reached that particular figure.

Had *USN&WR* bothered to do that, it would have had to go beyond its off-the-cuff assignment of blame for the epidemic, which it concluded is the fault of a world hooked on prostitution and psychoactive chemicals plus short-sighted leadership. The magazine might find that the epidemic is linked more deeply to the social dislocations resulting from world-wide poverty. Mann at least is quite clear about this in a general sort of way.

The AIDS epidemic around the world has fed on the mass migration to urban areas, the spread of intravenous drug use and the curtailment of public health systems. These took place within the context of the eighties' international financial crisis — an economic dimension *USN&WR* alluded only in mentioning Brazil's need of $600 million for AIDS care, truly a paltry sum compared to the country's $100 billion foreign debt.

A few days after *US News & World Report*, *Newsweek* chimed in with its cover story "Teens and AIDS: Love, Sex and Shattered Dreams" to fill us in about how "white-bread" adolescents are catching AIDS from their first sexual adventures. This is just untrue. Most AIDS educators are now up in arms about such generalized scare mongering because its scattershot message misses the youth populations desperately in need of targeted education, namely IV drug users and young gay men. The two groups combined represent at least 70 percent of all 13 to 25 year-olds diagnosed with AIDS in the last year. (The number of AIDS diagnoses in this age segment amounted to less than four percent of all AIDS diagnoses last year.)

Funny thing about *Newsweek*: It did find one gay man in his twenties to profile. But Wally Hansen of San Francisco, unlike the other people in the article infected by the AIDS-triggering virus HIV is still "reckless," he admits to using speed and practicing unsafe sex! All the other profiled cases are just innocent girls who trusted the wrong man and now spend their lives preaching to their peers about condoms. Yet Hansen better represents the reality of AIDS, and his inconsistent use of condoms represents real, underlying contradictions in safe sex. Those contradiction cry out for a sympathetic examination that the mass media are incapable of giving.

Time's post-Amsterdam AIDS coverage at least tried to appear sensitive to gay issues. In an article appended to the longer description of the conference's scientific achievements, *Time* surveyed the "gay community," which *Time* said, was created by the epidemic: "The crisis turned an often hedonistic male subculture of bar hopping, promiscuity and abundant 'recreational' drugs... into a true community, rich in social services and political lobbies, in volunteerism and civic spirit . . . "

Excuse me, but I think I met the gay community long before AIDS. Its defining moments in the modern era were the Stonewall riots and Gay Liberation, not AIDS and Gay Men's Health Crisis. The community arose out of a shared sexuality (in all its varied expressions, of which the bathhouse style obsessing *Time* is but one example) and the need to defend that sexuality. And from the cohesion founded on sexual community arose the response to AIDS, not the other way around.

The rest of *Time's* AIDS coverage, labeled on the cover "Losing the War against AIDS," summarized the AIDS Conference proceedings in a sensational way that transformed the somewhat hopeful conference proceedings into an unpromising session. Nothing can check AIDS' escalating dangers according to *Time's* reportage, which in fact was filled with unchecked mistakes. The biggest blooper concerned the new Thai strain of human immunodeficiency virus that supposedly is specially adapted to heterosexual transmission. Actually, the researcher reporting on the Thai virus strains specifically stated that he had no evidence to substantiate this possibility.

Time, like *US News & World Report*, concluded that myopic governments, including the Bush administration, were short-funding the effort against AIDS. Unfortunately, the obstacles go beyond negligence to downright *malevolence*. My sources among Washington AIDS circles have long complained about the right-wing ideologues planted in key positions at the Health and Human Services and Justice departments. This invisible network's purpose is to ensure official purity on the abortion issue. At the same time, it promulgates the whole "traditional family values" social agenda.

The Bush and Reagan administrations as a result have consistently refused to mount any sort of effective AIDS education effort, leaving local community groups to carry the load without adequate funding. Last spring, the Center for Disease Control's latest AIDS prevention campaign drew this response from Rene Durazzo, Director of Public Policy for the San Francisco AIDS Foundation:

"Once again, the CDC has produced a pathetic and woefully inadequate public education campaign about AIDS that fails to target people who are most at risk of HIV infection, gay and bisexual men of all colors and injection drug users and their partners. The CDC's campaign disgrace-

fully ignores direct messages about condom use."

One four-city study found that a 20 year-old gay man had a 50 percent chance of contracting HIV by the time he was 55. Young, nonwhite, and non-self-identified gay men have largely escaped contact with AIDS prevention programs in the past. But they are not the only ones to display the insufficiencies of safe sex education. A report this winter by San Francisco's AIDS Office estimated that each year, 1.5 percent of gay San Franciscans older than 25 contract HIV. This is a group that not only has had extensive exposure to safe sex education, but also vast first-hand experience with the AIDS epidemic.

Even as the AIDS Conference was occurring, the government was at it again. Posters erected at San Francisco bus stops by the National Institute of Drug Abuse displayed to what lengths AIDS would be used to attack teenagers' attempts to construct their own relationships outside family domination.

The posters were divided into

three horizontal panels. The top one showed a smashed-up car with the caption, "THIS FATAL ACCIDENT WAS CAUSED BY TEENAGERS GETTING STONED AND GOING TOO FAST." The bottom panel showed a similar, but intact car with an adolescent, heterosexual couple kissing. The bottom caption amazingly read, "SO WAS THIS ONE."

In between was a white panel with the following explanation: "Every year thousands of young people die in car accidents caused by drugs and alcohol. But now you can wreck your life without hitting the gas pedal. The number of expected AIDS cases has increased by 96% in the last two years. If you get high and forget even for a moment how risky sex can be, you're putting your life on the line."

The tragedy is that simple, forthright approaches avoiding this absurd confounding of sin with death could easily block the AIDS epidemic around the world. But you'll never know it from the mainstream media.

Largely unreported in the gloomy AIDS stories mentioned above were reports at the AIDS Conference of the synergistic effect between HIV infections and other, more conventional sexually transmitted diseases. Gonorrhea and illnesses causing genital ulcers, in particular, seem to increase the transmission of HIV. Immune deficiency, meanwhile, makes all the standard STDs more severe and long-lasting. They are then more contagious.

All the usual STDs are *treatable*. Eliminating STDs could prevent as much as 40% of all heterosexual HIV transmission in Africa, according to one estimate.

Circumcision also was reported to have a high protective effect. Studies found that circumcised men, gay and straight, had half or less the rate of HIV than similar uncircumcised men had.

Under present political conditions, you're not likely to see the US promote sexual hygiene, whether to reduce the enormous STD caseloads in Third World countries or reverse the soaring syphilis rate at home. Nor are you likely to see another obvious, simple measure to reduce HIV transmission: increase the availability of new syringes for heroin and other IV drug users.

At the Amsterdam conference, a Yale University report showed that New Haven's needle exchange program had reduced HIV transmission among participants by one-third. That was in a limited, cumbersome program with no other components to directly improve the conditions under which addicts live. In Amsterdam, syringe distribution is part of a general health and outreach program for addicts that includes massive methadone distribution.

The Dutch are quick to point out, though, that their efforts have at best slowed the spread of AIDS, not eliminated it. Educated white gay men in the urban centers of America and Europe are the only group to effectively block the epidemic. They were able to accomplish this feat because their sex-positive community generated credible organizations that could provide clear, frank information about the risks of contracting AIDS. Members of the gay community also came up with the condom solution because it was obvious that forbidding high-risk practices was untenable. Safe sex saved the community while demanding only a minimum of change. Its introduction refuted homophobic interpretations of the epidemic.

Drug users remain completely stigmatized in American society. With their lives defined by their illegal status, they have no community organizations to formulate a self-affirming responses to the epidemic. Closeted gay and bisexual men living underground in straight cultures, Hispanics and African Americans in particular, are in a similar situation. Little has been done to communicate with these hard-to-reach populations in a culturally sensitive way, and the AIDS epidemic continues is spread among them. Obviously, the first step to halting AIDS here is a little acceptance of their lifestyles by the mainstream. Would that be so hard?

As noted above, some AIDS transmission continues even in the most organized gay centers. One could just moralize about safe sex, attempting to shame the so-called relapsers into using condoms. One could also supply support groups to overcome supposed psychological barriers, such as self-esteem and grief issues. But the first thing should be to recognize and alleviate the physical limitations of condoms in real life use —among other things, their awkwardness and their interference with sensual pleasure. This will require some simple research. Merely developing a condom that will fit on a flaccid penis would make safe sex considerably more accessible.

Jonathan Mann was right when he said that we know how to prevent AIDS, we just don't do it. That's true, although he should have said *"won't do it,"* not *"don't do it:"* We *won't* do it because really preventing AIDS entails acknowledging the forbidden pleasures as important in themselves for human survival. The religious fanatics influencing the government refuse to accept the necessity of sin. They want everyone to be part of one community composed of traditional families that look to them for moral guidance.

It's enough to drive you to drugs . . .

The human spirit rebels against moral straightjackets because it craves the intimacy of shared enjoyments, sex in particular. Behavioral experimentation is a basis for alternative communities that attempt to fulfill human needs better than the mainstream. Trying to suppress those communities is what brings about epidemics like AIDS. Accepting deviance, allowing alternative communities to come out in the open, provides the preconditions for effective anti-AIDS work.

In contrast to the ideologues, the mass media seem liberal. They talk bluntly about AIDS and safe sex. Homosexuality comes up without being totally condemned. Yet doesn't it all boil down to the same thing? The right says sin equals death while the liberals say sex, at least, is OK, only there is this and that unfortunate problem (for instance, pregnancy and degenerate habits that ruin your life), and besides which, now you could die. By the time they get through, you're so worried, you don't want to have sex anymore. Covering AIDS from this perspective reflects the structural biases of the media, whose sponsors — the corporate advertisers — are busy taking advantage of sexual frustration to sell their products.

*David Gilden is a San Francisco free-lance writer specializing in the impact of technology on society. For the past two years, he has been AIDS and health correspondent for the **Bay Area Reporter**, a gay newsweekly.*

BASIC INSTINCT:

THE MYTH OF THE PLAYING FIELD . . .

AND THE QUEERS WHO RAN WITH IT ANYWAY

Angela Bocage

[Editor's Note: This is a rebuttal to an article written by Rebecka Wright in issue #3 of Gauntlet]

What they witnessed and what eyewitnessed

Contemporary mainstream journalism, its controls concentrated in increasingly fewer hands (in this country, those of 17 megacorporations) often reminds me of Hannah Arendt's commentary on propaganda-by-"Big Lie" in *Eichmann in Jerusalem*, or "newspeak" in Orwell's *1984*. Reading mainstream accounts of the *Basic Instinct* protests I witnessed, reinforced my respect for those works' prophetic insights.

What *I* saw in the latter half of April, 1991 was a ragtag, creative little group of dykes and fags and PWAs and mom-and-pop magazine publishers and diminutive but courageous journalists getting infiltrated, intimidated, wrongly arrested, whacked, threatened, even anonymous-death-threatened, by some very, very rich and powerful interests—*and the media made it look like it was the activists who posed the threat to free speech!* I guess

when you're a very, very rich and powerful corporate interest you can pay people to write press releases that rival Orwell's fiction . . . and you can expect the newspapers and TV stations owned by your golf buddies to pick up your line.

What Really Happened?

A chronological look at the campaign that's become a footnote to most mainstream coverage of gay activist group Queer Nation could well begin with the visit to their April 10 general membership meeting by the Gay and Lesbian Alliance Against Defamation (GLAAD). While QN concentrated on direct actions, GLAAD tends toward researching societal sources of anti-queer prejudices, and they're ace media-watchers. They heard about *Basic Instinct* — and, upon reading the script, brought it to the attention of Queer Nation.

The script to the film was circulated. (Contrary to the ignorant-philistine-activist myth, most everybody had read the screenplay before the protests. It was passed around at meetings of other groups, even handed about at parties I attended. Hilarious readings were attempted at barbecues. The thing *stunk to high heaven!*)

Discussion of cinematic homophobia ensued. Hollywood, the assembled queers acknowledged, certainly seemed to hate them. What could be done about it? How could this industry be made to see that hatchet jobs on a whole subculture promoted hatred, served nobody? Hadn't these movie guys ever *met* any lesbians or bi-women? And just how much money was Ray Chalker, the owner of the Rawhide II gay country-western bar where some scenes were filmed, *making* off Hollywood homophobia? Estimates ranged from ten to twenty thousand dollars.

This last topic was bitterly fascinating to some, because Chalker delighted in using the weekly paper he also owned, the *Sentinel*, as a forum for lengthy diatribes against feminism, AIDS activism, progressive politics in general—and Queer Nation in particular. Always rumored to be moribund, with old, slightly-rewritten press releases from "alternative" drug companies printed as AIDS news, letters to the editor printed as hard news, and a stratospheric staff turnover—especially, according to one ex-*Sentinel* journalist, *female* staff unwilling to tolerate open contempt—the *Sentinel's* no pinnacle of journalistic quality, and Chalker is not, especially to younger, more radical elements of the gay and lesbian community, a very well-liked man. The next day, a small group of women from QNSF's focus group LABIA, Lesbians And Bi-women In Action demonstrated in front of the Rawhide II.

Please note—the women brought signs expressing their opinions, and held a peaceful demonstration in front of a commercial establishment. As Cris Gutierrez writes, in part two of the valuable dialogue on this subject presented in *Frighten the Horses,* the activists "[never] sought, or made any statement supporting, the censorship of this movie or any form of speech. In the grassroots response to Basic Instinct, there has been no drafting of laws or lobbying of government officials to pass new laws; ... no formulation of legal arguments that would make the producers . . . liable." Gutierrez' essay further asserts that even such official impositions as ratings or labeling for homophobic content were never discussed; as free speech advocates, the demonstrators sought more public access to more information—broadening, not curtailment, of free expression. Unfortunately, they didn't have the bucks the other side did to buy clout with the San Francisco bureaucracy, credibility with the media, or attention from the cops, even when they were the victims of crimes ranging from harassment to assault to murder threats.

This first small demonstration was photographed and written up in the *Bay Area Reporter,* San Francisco's other gay weekly. *BAR* boasted Daniel Mangin, an erudite and insightful film scholar, as arts editor, and he wasn't about to let homophobic trash be filmed in his backyard without comment. Between photographs, stories, and Mangin's unanswerable question—why can't Hollywood ever portray all the lesbians and gay men who *aren't* "Twisted Sisters and Psycho Killers"(the title of his presentation on queers in cinema)?—the April 11 *BAR* brought a lot of people to the April 17 QN meeting.

The film company, meanwhile, was in Marin County north of San Francisco to shoot car scenes, so activists had time to brainstorm. The group on the 17th was so big it subdivided—one committee would talk to the *Sentinel's* advertisers, asking for a symbolic one-month boycott to protest Chalker's collusion with the film company. The other was the action committee, people willing to demonstrate at filming sites. Also at the meeting were representatives from GLAAD and San Francisco's Board of Supervisors, some of the latter on record as condemning the film's defamation of San Francisco and its gay and lesbian citizens.

Rick Ruvolo, of Supervisor Harry Britt's office, worked with GLAAD to urge the SF Film Office, the bureau assisting moviemakers with permits and locations, to release (*Basic Instinct* production company) Carolco's shooting schedule. Even though such documents are legally on public record, the community group and the elected representative were stonewalled for several days, denied the information. Mark Pritchard, heading the aforementioned action committee, had gotten angry when he read the script. Now he was angrier.

The script had convinced him that the *Basic Instinct* filmmakers didn't care about making a *good* movie— "It was the same trashy, violence-packed, Hollywood stuff that always makes me mad, full of stupid ideas about sexuality and about how people actually live their lives, and extremely insulting portrayals of queers and women in general—not to mention insulting presumptions about the audience. It has no emotional insight, no real people." And the stonewalling convinced him they didn't care about their public relations, either, at least not in San Francisco. "That's another thing we resented, people coming from out of town to portray San Francisco to the rest of the country in this terribly negative light, as though we're so mindlessly obsessed with sex that we just go out and murder people if anything impedes our sexual obsessions." Pritchard, a writer, performance artist and editor/publisher of the aforementioned *Frighten the Horses: A document of the sexual revolution,* sought out writer friends who'd had Hollywood dealings to research how he and his friends could make their voices heard.

"The only thing they really did care about was coming in on budget," Pritchard continues. "So our strategy was to disrupt and delay their shooting schedule as much as possible." His sources told him about the disastrous effects of reflected light on filming. Glitter, aluminum foil, and mirrors became props for the show the protesters planned to stage, and the first large demonstration was officially announced for April 24 on the publicly accessible "Queer Line" telephone bulletin board.

Telephone tag gets deadly? The papers get it dead wrong...

The less accessible phone messages in this story are another matter the media, and unfortunately the previous *Basic Instinct* piece in *Gauntlet,* got all wrong. It was widely reported that "lesbians" threatened to kill Ray Chalker. This was never substantiated. However, calls threatening "the fucking lesbians" with violence and death were kept on tape long enough for three other local journalists to listen, and identify—Ray Chalker!

"Chalker never offered to produce his tape. But *his* story dovetailed so well with national prejudices it was easily believed," asserts Michael Botkin, writer of the popular Queer Watch column in *BAR.* (One of the first victims of police overreaction in the demonstrations, Botkin, a person with AIDS who often bicycles rather than walks in part to avoid fatigue, found himself chased away from the crowd—and up a one-way street— by an entire squad of motorcycle officers, who dispersed when faced with five lanes of oncoming traffic. Witnesses compared their performance to the Keystone Kops. "A bicycle is easier to maneuver in a situation like that," adds Botkin modestly.) "This is our *objective media*," laughs Botkin; "On the one hand, Ray Chalker, business owner, rich male Republican newspaper publisher; on the other, lawless, faceless, scary lesbians. It's the *Basic Instinct* stereotype at work! It's doubly ironic that in a debate that's supposed to be about challenging stereotypes the media was so willfully suckered."

"College journalism should've been able to deal with this. To my knowledge, the media, and the police, ignored completely the alleged death threats against the Queer Nationals by Chalker. Who cared? What's in operation here is the myth of the level playing field!"

Excuse me but my side of the playing field is quicksand

Attorneys for Carolco reached Pritchard at work April 23 to inform him officially that they had gotten a superior court hearing to bar protest in the vicinity of the production. He was told they were specifically targeting Queer Nation, the focus group, and any citizen who chose to join in: "Does 1-500," as in John, Jane, or anybody opposing Carolco. That night, the focus group meeting at a private home in the Mission district was infiltrated by at least one agent.

The man, admitted early in the meeting, stood up after about an hour, passed around photocopied notices of the hearing the next day in superior court, then left. "It really wasn't that big a deal," Pritchard insists. "But people really were freaked out about it. All it was was a notice of a hearing, after all, not a subpoena or lawsuit." As intimidation, however, and a none-too-subtle notice of the power of their enemies, it was effec-

tive. Still, planning for the next day had to go on.

First would come a meeting, at the ritzy downtown Hyatt Regency, that as Michael Botkin points out, "*They* demanded. They were here to spend millions to make millions and we were in their way. They could send lawyers into our meetings to spy on and intimidate us, set up meetings in plush hotels with the media eating out of their hands, and then *they* asked *us* if we wanted script changes!"

The meeting featured director Paul Verhoeven and screenwriter Joe Eszterhas confronting representatives of GLAAD, QN, and the Board of Supervisors. Oh, sure, said the activists— here's some script changes: run a public service announcement before the film opposing homophobia and queerbashing. And make the Michael Douglas character a woman. ". . . And we might as well have said, 'Make sure everybody's accessories are tasteful,'" laughs Frida Malo of AQUANET (Anarchist Queers Advancing Necessary Educational Terrorism). "I see the script change demands as just more evidence of the exquisite queer sense of humor and irony," continued Malo, "because it seemed obvious they were just setting us up."

Sure enough, Carolco snagged a lot of mainstream press sympathy from that meeting. Perhaps it was the hors d'oeuvres, but their masterful sound bite decrying "censorship by street action" made more papers than any criticisms of the movie's hatemongering. As Gutierrez wrote, "The hatred, beating, maiming, and killing of queers seemed to be the least important aspect of the *Basic Instinct* issue to those who criticized our position." On the positive side, the judge who heard Carolco's lawyers argue for suppressing protest refused to grant their whole wish list:

while a restraining order was issued, it only obliged demonstrators to stay 100 feet from the shooting site.

The April 24 general meeting of QNSF attended the filming en masse! There was yelling and screaming and singing and chanting, glitter tossed and mirrors flashed! There was one arrest—when "Wrongway" Botkin, realizing he couldn't elude motorized pursuers forever, at least managed to get nicked in front of witnesses; it seemed wise, since the police were noticeably unimpressed by the high spirits.

For similar reasons, tactics changed the following night. Besides the police, Carolco had hired lots of big guys who not only *looked* as if they'd like to hurt you—they'd say so. Botkin encountered them: "The people on the crew, as well as the hired goons, took our protest as an intolerable attack on their privilege. They could have said, this is just a job, but they were more than willing to inflict any pain they could." Two other journalists, a female photographer and a male news reporter, both from gay media, neither over 5"6', were battered.

But weren't the protesters citizens with the right to assemble and express their points of view? "It's our *right* to exercise free speech—to get out in the streets and scream in pain at being used as scenery in the propaganda against us," Botkin acknowledges; but the playing field *isn't* level—it's mined. "It's only in theory that this huge company and a couple of dozen activists are equal before the law, or before the media. They were enraged that anyone could even question them, that people could say or do anything. The producer pointed his finger, and the cops made arrests. It was obvious whose side the 'vast machinery of the law' was on!"

That old "exquisite sense of irony" had served the activists well on the second day of protests, April 25, when they held a "49er pep rally" squarely within earshot of the shooting. Displaying emblems of San Francisco's popular football team, their signs successfully encouraged passing traffic to "Honk if you love the Niners!" and "Honk if you Support the Troops!" That week—because someone had discovered how easily accessible the filmmakers' elaborate Clementina Street sets were from the freeway offramp and redecorated them with paint-filled eggs—filming in San Francisco was delayed until Monday, even though, according to Pritchard's informants, "The city made a huge effort to clean up the sets, sending a firetruck *immediately* to hose them down."

The night of Monday, April 29, the producer himself, in what was termed a citizen's arrest, indeed pointed out to the police some thirty marching, singing film critics, who may or may not have been within 100 feet of the filming. They continued to sing Broadway show tunes in the paddy wagons all the way to the Hall of Justice, and in its garage until they were cited and released. (All charges were dropped by the May 30 court date.)

Pritchard, coming down with a cold, was out of action for the next few days. This included more picketing; an ingenious scheme whereby protesters got inside the film company's police barricades by printing up bogus birthday party invitations; and further unauthorized set decoration.

Was it worth it? Was it "censorship?"

Pritchard believes he and his friends were successful on several levels. First, their example sent a message that queers don't have to sit quietly while hateful propaganda against us is perpetrated in our neighborhoods. Second, even if reports were pretty skewed, people all over the country heard about the protests. Third, the group had some success in making the filmmakers "feel it in the pocketbook—" "We didn't have a tremendous effect on the filming, but it was delayed, and we kept hearing about 'nerves' among the crew—a lot of messups, a lot of things having to be redone, reshot, overrunning schedule."

What about the "censorship by street action" accusation? "A common political tactic in use by privileged groups . . . is to turn definitions inside out—to accuse [minority] groups of being oppressive themselves," writes Gutierrez. This "implies that a disenfranchised group who protests, at significant physical and financial risk to themselves, a dangerous and insulting commercial exploitation of their identity, is in the same position as the government and the owners of the media." Or as Pritchard says, that a little rubber raft from Greenpeace is the same as an oil company's supertanker.

Pritchard agrees that Carolco's accusation is doubletalk. "Censorship is either some kind of official, governmental effort, or, stretching the definition, the silencing by the powers-that-be, the media, of marginalized groups, minority viewpoints. The viewpoints of queers, ethnic minorities, and women, it could be argued, are censored out of American public discourse by the media itself. *Basic Instinct* to me was a really good example of this phenomenon—it represented only one very narrow viewpoint about a subject, namely lesbian and bisexual women, that the filmmakers obviously knew very little about." The focus group's use of their own free speech rights to protest the film, Pritchard argues, was no more censorship than other community groups who organize to exert pressure on private commercial interests whose actions affect them; "like when neighbors protest a shopping center going in across the street, or when the state wants to put a freeway through a neighborhood and people in the community lie down in front of the bulldozers. *Basic Instinct* was purely a commercial product, and while the makers had the right to express their views, I had the right as an audience member to give them my reaction."

"People protest in a way that interferes with business as usual because they can't be heard any other way," writes Gutierrez. "*Basic Instinct*, in spite of its lack of artistic truth, may have to be considered art (as compared to, say, the production of rubber truck tires) in a discussion of legal speech rights, but we can treat it like very bad art, the sort of art that gets booed off the stage."

Finally, of course, the movie was neither amended nor prevented. "The movie company had millions and millions of dollars, lots of lawyers, the support of the San Francisco government and r well-armed force...and we had a couple of hundred angry people with a bunch of whistles and glitter. It certainly didn't amount to censorship!" But Pritchard concluded with a defiantly mischievous "what if:" "Even if we'd had ten thousand people, and overrun the set—I'd call it a community response to some really bad art! I'd call it art criticism!"

Washington D.C.'s all news station WTOP-AM, according to *The Sporting News*, banned its announcers from using the word "Redskins" on the air, as derogatory to Indians. Advertisers on the station, however, won't be under such constraints. The moral? Money talks.

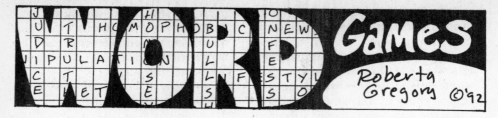

WORD Games

Roberta Gregory ©'92

The panel on the right is from my 1976 comic book, Dynamite Damsels ... In this story, a lesbian woman is upset by a newspaper item describing her as an "admitted" homosexual.

16 years later, as Gay service personnel, for instance, come out of the closet, there are more "admissions" in the news these days...

EVERYBODY READS THAT DAMNED GOSSIP COLUMN, TOO---

"ADMITTED"... WHY DIDN'T THEY JUST SAY "CONFESSED"...

THEY MAKE IT SOUND LIKE MURDER!

Initiative 489 would prevent practicing homosexuals from teaching in public schools.

That makes sense. We SURE don't want those people practicing on our KIDS...

SHEEP DIP

COW CHIPS

... there are also (less often) "acknowledged" and "avowed" gays (among reporters a bit more conscientious about their choice of words.) Look at the other uses of these words: we "admit" guilt, but we do "acknowledge" the truth. Subtly, this affects the manner in which these infobits are interpreted by the public.

And look how often we hear about the "gay lifestyle" from preachers to politicians, as if one's sexual identity were a frivolous choice rather than a matter of one's psychological (and often physical) survival! AND, that word "homosexual" is NEVER going out of style as long as that attention-grabbing 3-letter-word is the center syllable!

Hmm.... How should I accessorize my homosexual ensemble today?

Black Plastic and White Sheets:
The Censorship of the Art of Dayton Claudio

Mike Baker

Dayton Claudio is a professional artist who supplements his income by teaching art at Butte Community College in Chico, California. A painter, Claudio typically works in a style he refers to as "mixed media with realism woven into it"; an eye-catching melding of painted and photographic images.

For the past ten years, Claudio has made extensive use of the Cooperative Use Act—a public service-related law which opens the lobbies of government buildings for the display of artwork—to show his work. In addition, his paintings have hung in art galleries, corporations, and museums throughout the country, and he's never had any problems or complaints about his work, until recently, that is.

It all started in November of 1991 when eight of Claudio's paintings were hung in the lobby of the Sacramento Federal Building. Soon after the exhibit began, *Madonna*, a nude, was covered with a sheet of black plastic. This was the first time

Madonna

Claudio had experience censorship of this sort, and he was both confused, and dismayed, by it; he'd shown nudes before with no problem and he didn't consider *Madonna* to be in any way obscene. Neither did the local media; during the extensive coverage which resulted from the censorship of the painting, *Madonna* was shown, without any alterations or touching-up whatsoever, in both newspapers and television newscasts.

A week after the media blitz began, the plastic was removed from *Madonna*. It came off, Claudio believes, not because the censors had a change of heart, but because they had been made to look bad by the media and were trying to get out from under public scrutiny with a modicum of grace.

Three months later, in March of 1992, it happened again, this time in San Francisco. Less than a day after a two-painting exhibit (*Madonna* and *JFK*, one of Claudio's few politically-themed works) was set up in the lobby of the Federal Building, it was ordered taken down. When he discovered what had happened, Claudio contacted the California Lawyers for the Arts (a non-profit organization) as well as the local branch of the American Civil Liberties Union. Working together, the two groups contacted the Building Manager's office (the people who, technically, are in charge of the exhibition) and asked them to reconsider hanging the paintings. The powers that be initially declined, then changed their minds two weeks later when the threat of a lawsuit was raised.

The most recent incident occurred in May of 1992 in Raleigh, North Carolina. The painting under dispute this time was *Sex, Lies and Coathangers*, which, according to Claudio, "makes a pro-choice comment" with its depiction of a nude, a fetus, and a coathanger (no action is shown in the painting, the three images are separate and the viewer is left to draw their own conclusion). *Sex, Lies and Coathangers* hung in the Raleigh Federal Building lobby for mere minutes before being covered with, ironically enough, a white sheet. Less than an hour later it was removed from the lobby and taken to the Building Manager's office. The ACLU once again got involved, stepping in to ask the proper authorities if they'd be willing to negotiate. The answer was no. They then asked the regional GSA advisor for an appeal, but the response was the same. Having had no luck at arbitration, the ACLU took the next logical step and filed lawsuits against both the Building Manager and the local Federal Branch. At the time this piece was written (mid-August), the case was

JFK

still pending.

According to Claudio, the lawsuit wasn't filed for monetary reasons; there is a monetary restitution named in the suit, but it is minimal and was included solely for legal purposes. No, all Claudio asks is that his contract be honored and his artwork displayed for the month it is supposed to be.

Claudio believes that there are two reasons why all of a sudden he's having trouble. First, he feels that the countries' political climate is becoming obsessive when it comes to political correctness; if anything shows even the slightest sign of being controversial, it's deemed bad and steps are taken to remove it from the public eye. (In other words, freedom of speech and expression still exist, but only so long as you do and say what you're supposed to and you don't offend anyone).

The second reason is that since it's an election year, government officials are trying to make examples of society's so-called bad (i.e. controversial) elements in order to curry political brownie points and increase public opinion in their favor. Artwork which would have been ignored a year earlier is suddenly attacked with a manic fury which far outweighs the potential harm, if any, the piece would cause if it were shown to the public.

Claudio believes that this second reason is why the Raleigh officials are being so stubborn. According to the ACLU, the local Federal Branch has an extremely weak case, yet they refuse to back down; they're dead-set on legally sticking it out and settling in court even though they have little, if any, chance of actually winning. Rational, intelligent people (even politicians) don't tend to behave in such a manner, unless ordered to by higher-ups, that is. It's his opinion that there is a high-level elected official (or officials) manipulating the proceedings in order to benefit their image as a defender of all things morally right and good, a self-serving knight in shining armor who'll keep on fighting the good fight for the glory of God and country as long as it makes them look good in the public eye.

Though his recent bouts with censorship have troubled Dayton Claudio quite a bit, he's not going to let it stop the creation, and exhibition, of his work. Artistic freedom is something he believes quite strongly in; to him, it's the backbone of civil rights in our country.

To end things on a more positive note, a exhibition of Dayton Claudio's work, including *Madonna and JFK*, recently opened at the Federal Building in Los Angeles. It's been running for over a week now and the Building Manager's office, which was, understandably, a bit wary of the show at first (they even asked that photos of the paintings to be shown be sent to them prior to the exhibition) is proud to announce that, so far, they've received nary a complaint. We can only hope that future showings of Claudio's work have the same kind of luck (and understanding audiences).

[Editor's Note: There is currently no photo available of Sex, Lies and Coathangers as it is being held as evidence in North Carolina for a court challenge. We plan on running a photo of the picture in our next issue] Mike Baker is GAUNTLET's West Coast Correspondent

Born to Raise HELL:
The Lowbrow Labors of
Robert Williams Continue

S. C. Ringgenberg

Certain individuals, no matter what they do, sometimes become lightning rods for controversy just because society's values change around them and they suddenly realize they're behind the curve. Lately, painter Robert Williams can't be blamed for feeling zapped. He's probably lost track of all the groups he's offended with the bizarre, shoot-from-the-id imagery his canvases can barely contain. If you've never seen his work, Williams's visual style is a feverish amalgam of E.C. horror comics, blended with the twisted iconography of the hotrod culture of the '40s, '50s, and '60's, tattoos, commercial art, movie posters, carnival art,

and old under-the-counter porno. It is not designed to be reassuring or comfortable art.

Williams, a personable, friendly sort, is hurt that anyone would think him a racist, sexist, gay-bashing bigot. But underneath his easy-going manner, you sense that he's damned if he'll change what he paints to suit anyone, no matter how vocally they attack him.

In the first issue of **Gauntlet**, Doug Martin interviewed Williams to learn why women's groups had picketed record stores carrying the Guns 'n Roses album that used his "Appetite for Destruction" painting as its cover. "It was a hell of a contro-

Oscar Wilde in Leadville, April 13, 1882

Two Bull Dykes Fighting For the Privilege of Buying a Prostitute a Banana Daquiri

versy," Williams recalled. "There were six or seven women's groups picketing up north over that thing weekend after weekend."

Guns 'n Roses' record label, Geffen Records, eventually bowed to the intense pressure and moved the offending painting, which feminists allege had a 'rape' motif, from the record's cover to its inner sleeve.

What most appalled Williams, a self-described "liberal young artist", is that his work earned him the scorn of people he felt should be his natural allies. "I've always fancied myself something of a liberal. And what's happened is that I've pretty much followed the same road of ethics and ideals all along my life, but the world has changed around me to a certain extent. And the people that are liberal now look at me like I am some

archaic stick in the mud that's an adversary of theirs." What many of his detractors undoubtedly forget is that Williams had paid his artistic dues many times over as one of the original *Zap Comics* artists. In the '60s and '70s *Zap* frequently aroused the official wrath of both the postal service and local law enforcement authorities. Yet, Williams, like the rest of his underground peers, refused to bow to community pressure and produced some of the most shockingly bizarre and visually striking comics in the underground canon.

However, Williams notes ruefully that in the politically correct '90s, "I'm no longer feeling any pressure from the right, but I'm getting it from my comrades on the left." Like many of his contemporaries, Williams sees the artist's natural role as an adversary of society's repressive, right-wing elements, "I think the best thing that ever fuckin' happened in this goddamned country was old Jesse Helms blowin' it like he did. Look at all the stimulation he created, you know? I mean that guy did so much to get the American artist in an aggressive stance like they should be."

Complaining that he "would rather fight Jesse Helms and Meese and people like that, people I really don't fuckin' like, Williams finds he's made enemies he never wanted. "I am obviously a target of the feminists. I am an out-and-out adversary in neon to these people, when, in reality I'm very sympathetic to their movement. Now I've discovered that there's some elements of the gay movement that I've offended. And this is a whole new thing to me." The "Helter Skelter" show, presented at Los Angeles's Museum of Contemporary Art from February through May, 1992, was picketed by a women's group Williams identified as, "P.I.G.S.: Politically Involved Girlfriends, a large women's group down here. And then the gay group Queer Nation said they were going to picket but then they backed out. I guess they realized that maybe I wasn't fair game, maybe I wasn't a legitimate problem or not, I don't know. But I've gotten a lot of criticism from them."

Queer Nation's members were outraged by the titles Williams wrote for a painting in the "Helter Skelter" show depicting a true incident from the life of Oscar Wilde. The painting's full title is: "Oscar Wilde in Leadville April 13th 1882". Williams, however, insists that his painting is, "in reality, pro-Oscar Wilde, but there were some subtleties in it that were misconstrued." The painting, far from condemning Oscar Wilde,

was motivated by Williams's desire to celebrate Wilde's life.

"I've always been a fan of Oscar Wilde, and one thing that really stuck out in my mind was when he visited the United States in 1882 and he gave a lecture in Leadville, Colorado (which) at this time, was one of the meanest towns in the world, period. This was the most incredible thing, to visualize him on a stage dressed in these Edwardian tights lecturing about beauty to these people." Claiming he'd "researched the hell out of" the painting, Williams also notes that "when I wrote the titles, I wrote it in kind of an air of negativity toward Oscar Wilde so you'd get the sense of tension of him standing there on the stage confronting all these roughnecks and cowboys and prostitutes and miners and gunslingers. I did a painting that I'm very proud of on this subject. But in the titles, I used the language that was used against Oscar Wilde when he faced trial in England for sodomy. So when these sensitive gay people came in and they heard about this, they immediately flipped out as me being a gay basher."

To his credit, Williams *has* tried to make peace with the gays, noting that he has been "written up in a couple of papers defending this

"I'm sure I do these things in very bad taste."

thing so I've got the (situation) kind of calmed back. I've always had a pretty big gay following and I don't know how much this has hurt me or not. But I'm finding myself more intention(ally) worrying about my political correctness these days."

Ironically enough, three years earlier Williams found himself at odds with Los Angeles's lesbian community when his work was shown at LACE, a small, publicly funded gallery that would later find itself at the center of the censorship controversy. "I was in a group show there and I had a bunch of my Zombie Mystery Paintings there that had nekkid women with big tits. And one painting depicted two lesbians fighting each other over a prostitute." Unfortunately, the gallery's staff of gay women was highly offended, and in Williams's words, "I caught hell. They

wouldn't take my books in their bookstore, and they just really came down hard on me."

Then, in the wake of the assault on the arts in the 1990's, spearheaded by Jesse Helms, LACE became one of the battlegrounds in the conservatives' war on artists' rights of free expression. "Three years later," Williams notes with slight bitterness, "they're the head core of the fight against censorship. And I remember they wouldn't even let me put my fuckin' books in their bookstore."

Women's groups, Williams realizes, are often offended by his objectified portraits of women, which, he says, "they relate to me rendering blacks as Uncle Toms and Steppin Fetchits". Williams frequently depicts women's bodies nude or deconstructed as a pair of breasts, buttocks, or a lascivious mouth. Yet,

A Tribute to the Management of Still Sewage — Women's Group P.I.G.S. Picketed Helter Skelter Show Due to Williams Work

despite the abuse feminists have heaped on Robert Williams, he remains sympathetic to their perceptions, " . . . to a certain degree, I have to agree with them, but I don't agree with them fully." However, he freely admits that as an artist, "I like nekkid ladies, and. I've just got a fuckin' dirty compulsion about rendering nekkid ladies. I'm not that big on big breasts, but for some reason to express a breast, they always seem to come out a little bigger than they should be. I really like women with small tits." But in fairness to Williams, he is perceptive enough to acknowledge, "I'm sure I do these things in very bad taste."

Standing in stark contrast to his attitudes as an artist, Williams's stated attitude about the opposite sex borders on the reverential. "I am a big, big admirer of women. I worship women. I'm not a religious person, but the closest thing for me, that I would come to worshiping, is females. I mean, in my twisted mind a woman can do no fuckin' wrong, even when she attacks me. Even ugly fuckin' lesbians that come up and drive me nuts and hate my guts. I see fuckin' virtue in them."

Women and gays aren't the only people offended by Williams's paintings. When his work is reviewed, he often finds that the fine art world's most prominent critics have their knives sharpened for him. "When it come to reviewing (the MOCA show), a couple of papers came out with it and then the rest of the papers watched how it was slowly being written up, and then jumped in and followed suit, and cut it to pieces. And Robert Hughes was the last one to cut it to pieces in Time magazine. And he really butchered it."

Fortunately, to balance out the chorus of criticism from art snobs and humorless zealots there is Williams's immense popular appeal.

The three books of his artwork have remained in print continuously since their publication, and will soon be joined by a fourth collection published by Last Gasp. In addition to his success in publishing, Williams has a list of over two hundred people who've put down deposits on one of his canvases, and will undoubtedly find a ready audience for his new series of prints.

Williams produces twenty to twenty-five canvases a year and routinely sells out every gallery show he puts on. In an era of tight budgets and hard times for the art world, Williams is acutely conscious of the envy his success provokes, "here I am coming into town with this fuckin' sold-out show, you know, and tryin' to feign humility. I've been told that they're going to be waitin' for me. You know, that the head critic in the *New York Times* is a feminist that belongs to the Guerilla Girls, and I'm just going to catch hell."

You get the feeling that Williams's paintings wouldn't be so misunderstood if his critics would simply talk to him. He's obviously an intelligent, culturally literate man whose speech is equally peppered with profane expletives and knowing references to Benvenuto Cellini, Cro-Magnon spearpoints, Thomas Hart Benton, and the prehistoric cave paintings of Lascaux, France. He is certainly not blind to the mind-irritating effects of his paintings' dense imagery. Rather, what he paints is inherent in his approach to his work. "First you've got to have a lot of notions of what you'd be interested in seeing; what kind of anxieties do you have. Then you start taking notes of all the little things that interest you, whether you want them in the picture or not. Then you sit down with a thesaurus and as much research material you can get. And then you start finding offshoots of the things that interest you; what reaction does one thing have to another thing."

Williams's frequent pairing of nude women and food, for instance a naked Indian woman embracing a titanic, phallic, mustard-slathered corn dog, is part of his overall strategy for getting under his viewers' skin, "...the food makes your mouth water and the female irritates your prostate. You've got those two wants working against each other. The painting was designed to work on human beings' anxieties, to hold them there long enough to have a few ingredients happen. Then, when they walk off from the fuckin' painting, these ingredients are still gnawin' on their fuckin' cerebellum. They'll say, 'I hate that fuckin' painting.' and they'll look for more paintings like that to hate while their appetite's developing for them."

All Robert Williams really desires is what any artist craves, a chance to pursue his own peculiar artistic vision in peace, "What I want is to live with the damn art world. I'm not tryin' to deny these people their right, but I want my fuckin league. You know? I want to be able to circulate in the world of art too."

But as much as Robert Williams may hope for peaceful coexistence with his artistic peers and his gay and feminist comrades, as long as his work remains as searingly weird and perverse as it is now, Robert Williams will keep right on painting in the eye of a critical shitstorm.

_____

[Editor's Note: Robert Williams paintings will be featured in a show at the Bess Cutler gallery in New York City, from October 3-November 21, 1992. The gallery is located at 379 W. Broadway in New York City. For further information call (212) 219-1577]

ABORTION WARS:

THE CANNING OF POPEYE COMIC STRIP WRITER BOBBY LONDON

Steve Ringgenberg

Though on the surface, they may seem like unrelated events, Bobby London's recent firing from the *Popeye* comic strip is another chapter in America's war over abortion. Even the mere mention of abortion is too controversial for the conservative editors and management of King Features Syndicate. Bobby London was fired by King features because he attempted to do a storyline that contained a thinly-veiled allegory about abortion. To get the entire story we interviewed Bobby London:

G: What was the *Popeye* brouhaha with King Features?

BOBBY LONDON: Well, on October 25, 1991, I did a gag where the Sea Hag uttered the words: 'Drat! There goes Roe v. Wade.' and didn't hear a peep out of the syndicate and since I always heard from them whenever they objected to any kinds of punchlines or other nonsense that I might have injected in the strip, which was seldom, but it did happen occasionally. I automatically assumed that Roe v. Wade was considered fair game by them and I proceeded to prepare a full-length story about the

subject.

G: That's the storyline that they recently found objectionable with Olive Oyl wanting to send back the baby she'd gotten?

LONDON; She didn't get a baby, she got a *baby robot* that she did not remember ordering from the Home Shopping Network. It was an allegory designed specifically to keep Olive Oyl's innocence intact, and it was designed primarily to lampoon all the misguided good intentions of all the characters concerned.

G: So it was intentionally a veiled reference to the whole abortion issue?

LONDON: Well, of course, but I knew that, I respect Olive too much to sully her reputation or her good nature, or anything else about her and I would never directly be that blatant where she's concerned. I've known her for many years and she's a fine woman, and a good Joe.

G: You're a long-time *Popeye* fan, aren't you?

LONDON: A long-time *Popeye* fan, from way back when I was a kid.

G: Would you consider E. C. Segar one of your seminal influences?

LONDON: As far as making a deci-

sion to be a professional cartoonist, Segar was *the* seminal influence in my career. I've been drawing cartoons since I was four years old. I grew up as fascinated with the Max Fleischer Popeye because I used to get beat up by big, fat kids all the time, so naturally I sort of gravitated to *Popeye* because he kind of took care of all the fictitious bullies in my head. But as I got a little older, as I reached junior high school age, I stumbled upon the legendary E.C. Segar version, which I had heard about from my dad, when he would talk to me about it. He regaled great stories of Olive Oyl's mysterious little brother, Castor Oyl, and the Sea Hag and a lot of other characters, so when I actually saw these old strips, I was mesmerized, and it joined the ranks of some of my other favorite old-time strips that I admired at the time, like *Mutt and Jeff*, and *Barney Google*. But I would chance to say that it really took front and center in my imagination.

G: How long have you been drawing the *Popeye* strip?

LONDON: Since 1986.

G: How did the syndicate notify you that your work was unacceptable and that you were being terminated?

LONDON: Very briefly and very abruptly. The editor, Jay Kennedy, just called me up and told me that they were unhappy with the storyline and I was fired. It was simple as that.

G: And was Kennedy a friend of yours, in addition to being a colleague?

LONDON: Kennedy was an acquaintance from his tenure at *Esquire*, and when I was still drawing for slick New York magazines in the late Seventies. He came to my attention when he published an underground comic buyer's guidebook that contained an article with some derogatory references to me by George Shenkman, a fellow underground cartoonist from my early days.

G: Did you have a cordial relationship?

LONDON: Well, we ironed out that difference. It was mainly a matter of when I told him that I was sort of offended by the things that Shenkman wrote, he said, 'Well, you believe in freedom of speech, don't you, Bobby?' You know, that made me

laugh, but it was also kind of a poke in my eye at the time. But I forgot about it. I let it ride. I'm not the kind of person who holds grudges, you know? I tend to let things go, and I certainly did let this go. We became friends.

G: And how long had Kennedy been your editor?

LONDON: I can't be specific about that. I think it was about a year and a half to two years. It's all a blur.

G: So, how many strips do you still owe them?

LONDON: I owe them three weeks, which I'm working on as we speak. Ha! Ha! Excuse me.

G: the syndicate just notified you the strips in question were unacceptable? Had they had any complaints from their client papers?

LONDON: Not that I know of, no. I

never got anything but positive fan mail.

G: So this was just the execs at King Features deciding they didn't like it?

LONDON: Well, yes. There was a rumor that I heard from somebody there that they'd been considering dismissing me for quite some time because they other plans for *Popeye*, but I just sort of, I just kind of ignored that. I was continually ignoring rumors like that because they're just rumors. I tried to concentrate on my work, and see that it improved.

G: Prior to this whole thing with the Olive Oyl storyline was *Popeye* doing all right in syndication? Had your work attracted more papers?

LONDON: I'll tell you the truth, it was beginning to attract new clients when this dismissal happened. However, it was due more to word-of-mouth than any effort that the syndicate would make to promote it. It's a strip that's slowly been losing papers since the creator died. That's pretty much the natural chain of

events. You can look at *Pogo* or any other old strip where the creator passes away and that's bound to happen. And even when Bud Sagendorf left the daily because he had been with it so many years, people were used to seeing him. So I expected some amount of readership loss, but I also expected new readers to be gained if enough people heard that I was doing it. And I think that was beginning to happen. I think that I didn't underestimate my draw, my drawing power. No pun intended. There've been a number of the papers that have already dropped it because I've left.

G: About how many papers is it running in, you think?

LONDON: They never told me and I can only guess that it's about twenty-four, which is what they're telling the press, but I don't really know. This whole thing started when a client newspaper in Chicago insisted on running the cartoons in question, and a reporter called me and asked me what the story was and I had just been freshly fired at the time, so I just told him, and then all off a sudden I found, I found seven networks at my doorstep.

G: What's your opinion of King Features right now?

LONDON: No comment. (Laughter) You can just say, I'll be eating neither spinach nor fried chicken for some time to come, you know.

G: Has all the media attention brought you any offers of new work?

LONDON: Well, I've been getting illustration offers. I'm not especially worried about what I'm going to do next. In fact, I probably need a vacation. I've been working for six years on this strip without a any time off, plus two years at Disney before that. It adds up to a whopping eight years without a rest, so I want to take a breather and get all my ducks in a row as it were, and see where to go from there. I have to clean my room, too.

G: Were you pleased with the way you were treated by the media, by how they handled the story?

LONDON: Yes, they were all great. That was amazing. I had dozens of television reporters in here and nobody stole anything from my studio. It was really terrific.

G: And what about *Playboy*? Are they planning on running anything on you, because I know you're a long-time contributor with *Dirty Duck*.

LONDON: I haven't heard from them. I haven't heard from *Playboy* in a long time, I might add. (Laughter) But there's always that outside chance, you know. There are people who've been calling me that I haven't heard from in years, so I assume I might hear from Michele Urry eventually...

G: Are you planning any legal action against King Features, or are you just going to drop it?

LONDON: Not at this time. So far there's been no reason for me to. You know, my reputation doesn't seem to have been hurt terribly, and so far I don't think my reputation has been hurt at other major newspaper syndicates, but time will tell.

G: Would you ever consider doing a syndicated strip again?

LONDON: Yes, I would consider it. It would depend on the syndicate. It would depend on the editor. A whole lot of things would be, would have to be considered before I would do that. I've certainly learned a lot.

The Bobby London saga continues in the next issue of **Gauntlet**, *in which Bobby discusses his role in the infamous Air Pirates controversy of twenty years ago and reveals the secret origin of Dirty Duck. Stay tuned!*

TYSON DIDN'T GET A FAIR SHAKE

Pete Hamill

At night now, before sleeping, I often think about poor Mike Tyson. Out in Indiana, he is trying to sleep, too, and I see him there in a cell, tossing and moving and trying to find stillness. No image is sadder.

That's not the only image of Tyson that comes to me late at night. Sometimes I see him walking across Sheridan Square with my brother, Brian, on a summer afternoon. I see him laughing at the big front table in Columbus or sparring in the Teikin Gym in Tokyo or signing autographs for kids on 57th Street. He is sweet and soft-spoken and intelligent, asking a hundred questions to discover how he should live his life. He is not Jack the Ripper.

Sometimes, again and again, I see him in triumph after taking out Michael Spinks and he's smiling that gap-toothed smile and shouting to the cameras of the world: "Brownsville *awright!* Brownsville, *awright!*" That night, it was if he'd knocked out the whole lousy past, that Brownsville childhood of cruelties and abandonment; up ahead lay the limitless, golden future. But in victory he was affirming that past, too, saying to Brownsville that he would never forget. That night, it seemed certain that Tyson could never go back.

He's back now, part of the Brownsville Archipelago, just another black man in a jail cell. And I think that's an outrage. I don't think Tyson should be in jail. I don't think

he's a rapist (although I can't prove it). Above all, I don't think he received a fair trial.

In all the years that I've been visiting courtrooms, I've never seen a more inept defense on a major trial than the one prepared for Tyson by Vincent Fuller. The Washington-based lawyer was chosen by Don King, who had been successfully defended by Fuller a few years earlier on a tax rap. Fuller's basic theory of the case was my-guy's-a-pig-and-she-should-have-known-it. This was nuts.

The truth was that Fuller did not really know Tyson; at the sentencing, with Camille Ewald sitting in the audience, Fuller tried to blame Cus D'Amato for failing to teach young Tyson about character. I knew Cus for 30 years; character was at the core of his system. His sermons on moral character drove some of us into deep sleep. But Fuller slandered Cus, parroting some Don King routine, while Camille had to listen. She lived with Cus for decades and was as much a loving, nurturing mother as Tyson ever had. Fuller seemed to know nothing of this.

But the inept ignorant defense was compounded by a dreadful performance in Marion County Superior Court by Judge Patricia Gifford. During the trial itself her worst decision was to bar the testimony of three defense witnesses who might have supported the case for consensual sex. One was Carla Martin who said that on July 19 last year, at about 2AM, she saw two people in the back of a limousine outside the Canterbury Hotel. They were "all over" each other, hugging and kissing, and then got out of the car and went into the hotel. Martin says that the two were Tyson and Miss Washington.

The other witnesses were Pamela Lawrence, who remembered Martin telling her about the behavior of the couple in the back of the limo, and Renee Neal, who remembered seeing Tyson and Washington holding hands as they went into the hotel.

These witnesses were produced near the end of the trial. Fuller explained (plausibly) that the delay was caused by several factors. Martin's aunt was a lawyer and she told the young woman that the case was so weak it would probably never go to trial; it wasn't worth the effort. Then, when the women did call Fuller's office, the lawyers needed to check out the truth of their stories, separating them from the many hundreds of nut calls his firm had received about Tyson. That took time.

But the prosecutor, a vaguely smarmy "hired gun" named Greg Garrison, was furious at the production of these three witnesses. To bring them in now made his work "awkward." Hey, man: he would have to bring back some witnesses who had already testified. "It destroys what rhythm we've been able to build up."

A good judge would have reminded the prosecutor that she was not charged with maintaining "the rhythm" of the prosecution case. Her job was to ensure a fair trial, during which the jury would try to determine the elusive truth. Awkward? A man's *freedom* was at stake.

A good judge would have slapped down the prosecution on this motion, but Gifford is not a very good judge. She ruled in favor of the

> A good judge would have slapped down the prosecution on this motion, but Gifford is not a very good judge.

prosecution, the witnesses never testified, and the inexorable rhythm of the prosecution case led to a conviction. Maybe the last-minute witnesses were phonies. But maybe they were *the real thing*. Either way, Tyson, as an American citizen, had the right to present them in a court of law. That right was denied.

Worse, when the trial was finished, Gifford botched the charge to the jury. It was not enough for the prosecution to prove that Miss Washington did not consent to have sexual intercourse with Tyson. Under the law, they must also prove that "the defendant did not reasonably believe that she had consented."

This comes from the theory of criminal intent. Many feminists and some prosecutors hate that part of rape law. In the view of some legal theorists, it gives the rapist the right to determine whether a rape had taken place. Still, it is the law. If Tyson had a "reasonable belief" that Miss Washington had consented to sex, he would have been acquitted. From his point of view, such reasonable belief surely existed. He'd called the young woman at 1:30AM, she'd met him outside her hotel, traveled to his hotel, went to his room, necked with him. From his own testimony (corroborated in some ways by hers), it's clear that Tyson must have believed that she wanted sex with him, no matter what words of protest she uttered. But Gifford did not explain this aspect of the law to the jury. She didn't explain that this is fundamental to our system; criminal intent must be proven *beyond reasonable doubt* to convict a person of a felony. That insistence on proof is not waived when the serious crime is rape. Gifford explained none of that to the jury. In our appeals process such an omission is usually an automatic reason for the overthrow of a verdict.

For a while, Tyson should be all right in jail. He knows the codes of the can; he learned them the hard way as a boy on Amboy Street. But if the appeals system is fair, he shouldn't stay long in the N-Dorm of the Indiana Youth Center. I just hope that late at night, as he struggles for sleep, he starts making sense of his life.

*Reprinted with permission from Pete Hamill. Pete Hamill is a columnist for the **New York Post**.*

DEATH OF A MAD-MAN

William M. Gaines (1922-1992)

Steve Ringgenberg

"What, Me Dead?" gibed the *New York Daily News* headline for Bill Gaines's obituary. If it had been anyone else, such an irreverent death notice would have been the height of bad taste, but for *Mad* magazine publisher William M. Gaines, it seemed just right. For over four decades the comics and magazines Gaines published had offended the sensibilities of adult bluenoses the world over while giving the world's adolescents (and some subversive adults) a chortle as said sensibilities were parodied, satirized, mocked, and on one memorable occasion, given the finger.

Bill Gaines was a true American original, an eccentric, maverick publisher whose gross, sophomoric humor magazine made him a multi-millionaire. Gaines was never part of the publishing establishment of prep-school old boys and old-time editors who'd worked their way up through the ranks. Instead, Bill Gaines acquired his publishing empire the old-fashioned way, by inheriting it from his father, M.C. Gaines. In publishing comics, Bill was simply carrying on a family tradition, because M.C. Gaines was one of the men most responsible for the creation of the American comic book. Bill went his father one better, by publishing what is perhaps the best line of

comics in American history, E.C. Comics, comics of such quality that they are still being reprinted today in a variety of formats, and which have inspired two horror films, *Tales From The Crypt, Vault Of Horror*, and the ongoing HBO series, *Tales From The Crypt*.

Upon his father's death in a boating accident in 1949, young Bill Gaines inherited a million dollars and his father's failing comics company, Educational Comics, which published comics with titles like *Picture Stories From The Bible* and *Tiny Tot Tales*. A bright young man with a voracious capacity for reading short stories, Gaines set to work with editor Al Feldstein to change Educational Comics to Entertaining Comics and find some formula for success. And find it he did, Gaines and Feldstein came up with some of the most shocking, tasteless and grotesque horror stories ever written for the comics. At the same time, they were presiding over the two of the most imaginative, well-written science fiction comics ever published. It should also be noted that E.C. published the finest war comics of all time, *Two-Fisted Tales* and *Frontline Combat*, written and edited by Harvey Kurtzman, who refused to have anything to do with the horror comics because they were simply too gross.

Gaines is remembered here, not just for the excellence of his publishing output, but also because he was no stranger to censorship battles. In 1954, at the height of the anti-comics hysteria largely generated by a book entitled *Seduction of the Innocent*, which blamed comics for a whole raft of offenses, ranging from juvenile delinquency to the younger generation's bad grammar, Gaines voluntarily testified before the Senate subcommittee on Juvenile Delinquency. E.C. Comic titles such as *The Vault Of Horror, Tales From The Crypt, The Haunt Of Fear, Crime Suspenstories, Shock Suspenstories, Weird Science* and *Weird Fantasy* printed stores about werewolves, vampires, axe-murderers, zombies, cannibals, and man-devouring alien plants. *Crime* and *Shock*, while they ran some science fiction and terror stories, mainly concentrated on searing tales of rape, murder, racial prejudice, drug addiction and other modern horrors. Make no mistake, E.C. Comics were strong stuff for the conservative 1950's. Gaines's trio of horror comics, his most popular titles, were the best-selling horror comics of the '50's. Because E.C. was so successful and because E.C. Comics were so graphic, William Gaines wound up taking a lot of heat. Parents' groups, headline-seeking politicians, and of course, the retailers and wholesalers who controlled the comics business, singled E.C. out as among the most flagrant offenders of the public taste.

Gaines freely admitted that the comics E.C. published *were* gruesome and often explicit in their gleeful depictions of torture, dismemberment, cannibalism and murder. But, unlike most of its competitors, E.C.'s horror comics were done with style and intelligence, and with tongue planted

"I REMEMBER THE HORROR I'D FELT DURING OPEN SCHOOL WEEK WHEN MOM WOULD COME INTO CLASS. I DREADED THOSE DAYS. I CRINGED AT HER BROKEN ENGLISH...HER FRANKNESS ...HER SENTIMENTALITY ... HER NAIVE IGNORANCE ..."

SUCH A DIAMOND LIKE MY MARK YOU WON'T FIND IN A MILLION YEARS! YOU ARE LUCKY TO HAVING HIM IN YOUR CLASS, MISTER OTIS! SUCH A GOOD SON HE IS! AND IN THE STORE, HOW HE HELPS HIS PAPA...

L-LET'S *GO*, MA! LOTS OF *OTHER* PEOPLE WANT TO TALK TO MR. OTIS ...

"BUT MA WAS OBLIVIOUS TO EVERYBODY. IT KILLED

"I REMEMBER A VACATION TRIP THAT LEFT ME LIMP. MA ALWAYS SPOKE AT THE TOP OF HER VOICE, NOT THINKING HOW SHE LOOKED AND SOUNDED TO OTHERS..."

PLEASE! ASK THE CONDUCTOR—MAN! IS THIS THE *RIGHT* TRAIN? MAYBE WE GOT ON THE *WRONG* TRAIN, HEAVEN FORBID? I'M SO WORRIED...SO AGGRAVATED! VACATION TRIPS WE NEEDED!? A HOLE IN THE HEAD I NEEDED!

MA! PLEASE! QUIET! IT'S THE *RIGHT* TRAIN! SIT DOWN! THE CONDUCTOR IS GIVING US DIRTY LOOKS!

I WAS *MISERABLE* AND YOU WERE *ASHAMED!?*

In this story from Psychoanalysis, Mark Stone felt buried resentment at his parents because they were Jewish. The Comics Code, however, refused to allow E.C. to mention Stone's religion, thereby rendering the character's conflict meaningless.

This story from Impact #4 revolved around the conflict between "Miller," a Jewish
G.I. and his anti-Semitic tormentor. The Comics Code prevented E.C. from
mentioning "Miller's" religion or giving him a Jewish surname. Copyright © 1992
William M. Gaines estate.

firmly in cheek. Gaines and his
writer/editor Al Feldstein also
dished up their horror with large
helpings of black humor, which is one
of the reasons why E.C. Comics are
still being read and reprinted today.

But because E.C. and some
other comics companies were seen as
a threat to the morals of America's
youth, the Comics Code Authority
was inaugurated in October of 1954.
The Comics Code Authority was an
organization designed to assure
America's parents that the comics
bearing its seal were clean, wholesome entertainment. Every comics
publisher that subscribed to the Code
was expected to submit its comics to
a review board for approval before
publication. The Code specifically
forbade the use of the words "Horror" and "Terror" in comic titles, and
the word "Crime" could only be used
if it was used with "restraint". The
code also forbade "All scenes of horror, excessive bloodshed, gory or
gruesome crimes, depravity, lust, sadism, masochism . . . " as well as the
"walking dead, torture, vampires . . .

ghouls, cannibalism and werewol-
fism."

Gaines knew his days as a horror
publisher were numbered when he
couldn't get distribution for his non-
Code-approved comics, so he killed
them off and created a new line of
titles, his "New Direction Line".
These comics, with titles like *M.D.*,
Psychoanalysis, Valor, Impact, and *Pi-
racy*, while more restrained than the
original E.C. line, were still intelli-
gently-written, beautifully drawn
comic books. Unfortunately, they
weren't as successful as the more
shocking stuff, so after a year of trying, Gaines killed off the "New Direction Line" and turned *Mad* the comic
book, which had been created by
Harvey Kurtzman, into *Mad* Magazine. Even after Kurtzman's departure from *Mad* Magazine, Gaines
maintained the anarchic E.C. spirit in
Mad, which, under the editorship of
Al Feldstein, went on to become one
of the two most successful humor
publications of the 20th Century.

Despite being out of reach of the
Comics Code Authority, *Mad* did not

escape controversy. In the nearly forty years since its inception as a magazine, *Mad* was accused of everything from being a bad influence on the minds of America's children to being unpatriotic to simply being in bad taste. *Mad* also had the distinction of being sued by one of America's most eminent composers, Irving Berlin. Back in the '60's, Mr. Berlin took exception to several parodies of his songs in *Mad*, feeling that if his work was being parodied, he was owed royalties. He was wrong and the ensuing court case set a precedent about how much parodists can take from the source material they are lampooning.

As a man, Gaines will be remember as a kindly, paternal boss, who was a good friend to his staff. He had a taste for fine wine, gourmet food, *King Kong*, zeppelins, and outrageous practical jokes. Gaines also liked to travel, and for decades, took the *Mad* contributors on yearly trips all over the world. But, when all is said and done, and the echoes of his eulogy have faded away, it will be remembered that Bill Gaines made his mark on

An implied reference to "Miller's" Jewishness that you'd have to read very carefully to notice. Copyright © 1992 William M. Gaines

Twentieth Century Pop Culture. The publishing industry will henceforth be a poorer, less interesting place for his passing. He will be missed.

Bill Gaines on censorship: "Oh, I've never believed in any kind of censorship against anything in any way for anybody nohow."

Bill Gaines on the Mappelthorpe controversy: "I'm glad I don't have to be a judge on that kind of thing because I tend to think that there's a difference between things that are done with public money and things that are done with private money. If part of the public was offended by this, and they were paying for it, I can see their point. If it had been a private museum, they don't have a leg to stand on."

Bill Gaines on the Lyle Stuart's Anarchist Cookbook, a book for bombmakers: "I thought it was horrible. Lyle and I don't see eye in many ways. And he's one of my dearest, probably my dearest, closest friend. But, over the years we have had many differences of opinion. I think it's a disgrace that he publishes the Anarchist Cookbook. On the other hand, I'm delighted that he can get away with it because that shows that this is a free country after all."

Bill Gaines on child pornography: "I personally have no objection to it. They might arrest the guys for what they did to the kids, but I don't have any objection to the pictures they took."

WE'LL CARRY ON WITH THE LAUGHTER, THE IRREVERENCE, THE MISCHIEF AND, OH YEAH, THE MAGAZINE, TOO. WE'LL MISS YOU, BILL

LOVE,

"THE USUAL GANG OF IDIOTS"

OH, THE HANDWRINGING OVER "P.C.!" JUST ANOTHER FABRICATION OF THE CONSERVATIVES, I THOUGHT; ANOTHER EFFORT OF THE CREEPS IN POWER & THE SHEEP WITH PRIVILEGE TO TURN WORDS INSIDE OUT IN THE ATTEMPT TO CLING TO WHAT THEY HAD. IT WAS JUST LIKE THE GUYS WHO LOVE TO RANT AGAINST "P.C. in ACADEMIA--" THEY OFTEN DON'T SEEM TO HAVE EXPERIENCED "ACADEMIA" FIRSTHAND, BUT THEY SURE ARE INCENSED WHEN OTHERS INSIST OUR VOICES ARE AS IMPORTANT AS STRAIGHT, WHITE MALES'! BUT SUDDENLY--THANKS TO DR. DON FRANCIS' COURAGEOUS FAREWELL ADDRESS AFTER 20 YEARS AT CENTERS FOR DISEASE CONTROL--I REALIZED THERE WAS A SPECIES OF "P.C." THAT WAS ALL TOO REAL A DANGER! I UNDERSTOOD HOW--

WHEN A VIRAL EPIDEMIC OF UNPRECEDENTED FATALITY IS AGGRESSIVELY IGNORED OVER YEARS, DESPITE PUBLIC HEALTH OFFICIALS' PLEAS--BECAUSE TO TALK ABOUT IT, TO TEACH ABOUT IT, WE MIGHT HAVE TO USE NAUGHTY WORDS OR ACKNOWLEDGE THE VARIETY OF HUMAN SEXUALITY--THAT'S P.C.!

WHEN 10% OF OUR CHILDREN FACE A TEN TIMES GREATER RISK OF SUICIDE, SUB-STANCE ABUSE, AND STD'S, INCLUDING AIDS, BECAUSE CONSERVATIVES FIGHT TOOTH AND NAIL AGAINST ANY SEX EDUCATION FOR YOUTH, MUCH LESS GAY-POSITIVE EDUCATION OR SUPPORTIVE COUNSELING--THAT'S P.C.!

WHEN EVERY 2½ MINUTES A WOMAN DIES OF A BOTCHED ABORTION BECAUSE THE POLITICAL PRESSURE FROM RIGHTWING EXTREMISTS HAS DENIED HER CHOICES, HEALTH CARE, SAFE CONTRACEPTION, &, ULTIMATELY, HER OWN LIFE--THAT'S P.C.!

THOUSANDS MORE PEOPLE WERE INFECTED WITH H.I.V. IN THE TIME IT TOOK CITY TO DECIDE FOR SIMPLE HEALTH MEASURES TO BE OFFERED THEM--BECAUSE THEY WERE ONLY DRUG USERS, AND GIVING THEM CLEAN NEEDLES JUST WASN'T P.C.!

THE TRUE FACE OF P.C.--JUST LIKE THE APOCRYPHAL--IS A PURE PRODUCT OF RIGHTWING NARROWNESS, IGNORANCE, & HATE. AND HOWEVER THEIR SPIN DOCTORS TRY TO PRETTY IT UP, TRY TO MARKET IT...... IT STILL LOOKS LIKE DEATH.

© 1992 BY ANGELA BOCAGE

CHERRY, ME & CENSORSHIP; OR NO FLIES ON ME.

Larry Welz

The specter of Censorship hangs over my head all the time, but it never shows its face; not directly to me, anyway; I'm baiting it, trying to get it to come out in the open where we can get a little better look at it. Of course, it doesn't really want to do that. For ten years now, I've been doing this little black and white comic book that started out being called *Cherry Poptart* but was later shortened to simply *Cherry*, for reasons I will explain shortly. They were what used to be called "Underground" Comix. Now they don't know what to call them.

Cherry Poptart was conceived as a one-off parody of Cute Teenager Comics in general, and a certain more popular line in particular. I made Cherry generic to make her more . . . uhhh . . . universal, as well as to cover myself in case I managed to piss somebody off enough to try and sue me: "any resemblance is purely coincidental, etc. . . . " *Cherry* comics feature lots of hard core sex. That's part of the setup, which was something like "What if there were a Cute Teenager Comic that showed something more like what teenagers really do? . . . taking lots of drugs, fucking, and doing stupid things." And what if it was done in the same cutesy, wide-eyed "everything is beautiful" style as the ones you find at 7-11? Cute Girl Who

Likes To Fuck.

Another part of the setup: "Underground" or "Alternative" comics at the time (mid '70s) seemed to me to be getting blander and/or more disgusting, and when sex came up, it was usually accompanied by dismemberment and/or disembowelment or something even worse. Some of this I'm sure has its place and all that, but I wanted to see something positive about sex, so I wondered how "disgusting" I could make a comic with explicit sex, without it being really disgusting: that is, no violence (well, as little as possible), and not too graphic. Only cute violence (like Dis-

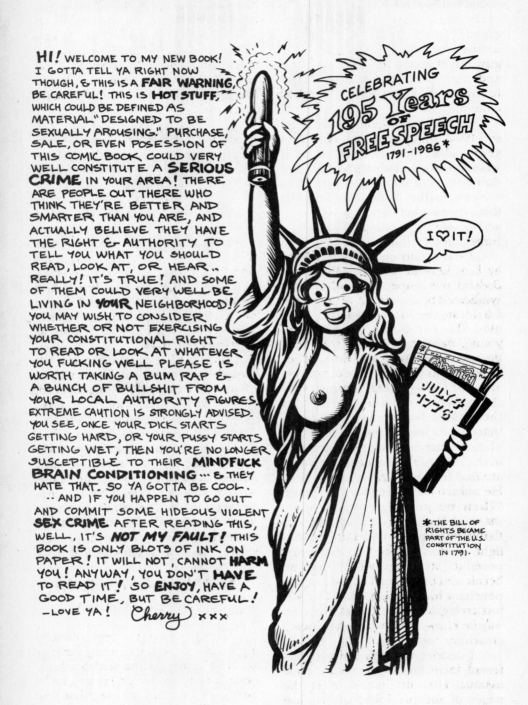

HI! WELCOME TO MY NEW BOOK! I GOTTA TELL YA RIGHT NOW THOUGH, & THIS IS A **FAIR WARNING,** BE CAREFUL! THIS IS **HOT STUFF,** WHICH COULD BE DEFINED AS MATERIAL "DESIGNED TO BE SEXUALLY AROUSING." PURCHASE, SALE, OR EVEN POSESSION OF THIS COMIC BOOK COULD VERY WELL CONSTITUTE A **SERIOUS CRIME** IN YOUR AREA! THERE ARE PEOPLE OUT THERE WHO THINK THEY'RE BETTER AND SMARTER THAN YOU ARE, AND ACTUALLY BELIEVE THEY HAVE THE RIGHT & AUTHORITY TO TELL YOU WHAT YOU SHOULD READ, LOOK AT, OR HEAR .. REALLY! IT'S TRUE! AND SOME OF THEM COULD VERY WELL BE LIVING IN **YOUR** NEIGHBORHOOD! YOU MAY WISH TO CONSIDER WHETHER OR NOT EXERCISING YOUR CONSTITUTIONAL RIGHT TO READ OR LOOK AT WHATEVER YOU FUCKING WELL PLEASE IS WORTH TAKING A BUM RAP & A BUNCH OF BULLSHIT FROM YOUR LOCAL AUTHORITY FIGURES. EXTREME CAUTION IS STRONGLY ADVISED. YOU SEE, ONCE YOUR DICK STARTS GETTING HARD, OR YOUR PUSSY STARTS GETTING WET, THEN YOU'RE NO LONGER SUSCEPTIBLE TO THEIR **MINDFUCK BRAIN CONDITIONING** ... & THEY HATE THAT. SO YA GOTTA BE COOL.
.. AND IF YOU HAPPEN TO GO OUT AND COMMIT SOME HIDEOUS VIOLENT **SEX CRIME** AFTER READING THIS, WELL, IT'S **NOT MY FAULT!** THIS BOOK IS ONLY BLOTS OF INK ON PAPER! IT WILL NOT, CANNOT **HARM** YOU! ANYWAY, YOU DON'T **HAVE** TO READ IT! SO **ENJOY,** HAVE A GOOD TIME, BUT BE CAREFUL!
—LOVE YA! Cherry xxx

CELEBRATING
195 Years OF FREE SPEECH
1791-1986 *

I ♡ IT!

* THE BILL OF RIGHTS BECAME PART OF THE U.S. CONSTITUTION IN 1791.

ney), no gore, no rape . . .

"What? No rape? How am I supposed to have this chick get fucked in every single story if she never gets raped?" Don't get me wrong, I'm as aroused by rape scenes as the next guy, but at least I feel guilty about it and rape is not funny. I wanted a funny book. I mean they're called comics, right?

I didn't feel up to the challenge, so I tried to ignore it for a couple of years. But after a few years, it wouldn't let go, and nobody else was doing it, even though it seemed so obvious to me that something like this was needed. So I hashed it together as best I could and tried to forget about it.

I was greatly inspired at the time by Dan O'Neill, creator of the *Odd Bodkins* newspaper strip which was syndicated by the *San Francisco Chronicle* during the Sixties. Dan had assembled the Air Pirates, a group of young, naive cartoonists from Seattle, and was gunning for Disney. They took the old *Mickey Mouse* characters and did "disgusting" things with them, O'Neill's premise being that these characters aren't even drawn that way anymore, they're now part of American Folklore and therefore in the Public Domain. It was a frontal attack. He wanted Disney to sue him. He wanted the raging bull to charge. When he got his subpoena, he thanked the server effusively. The flames he went down in didn't exactly light up the sky like they were supposed to, but nevertheless, it was an heroic and ballsy act. O'Neill has that penchant for lost causes, and he was just trying to make it work the only way he knows how, which is by being creatively obnoxious.

I decided to apply a slightly different tactic. Rather than a frontal assault, I would dance along the edges of the precipice, staying just inside the line of what was, supposedly, legally acceptable, and just outside the line of what was "socially acceptable," hanging BAs and waving my penis at anybody who might be offended or amused as I go. If anybody reaches out and smacks me down, the sham of "Free Speech" will be exposed for all to see. I'm playing the game of "Nyaah nyaah! Can't catch me!"

Nobody wants to play. But the Phantom Blot of Censorship is out there, and if I can't get them to bite, I want to at least raise his blood pressure a little.

S. Clay Wilson, when he burst onto the scene in the Sixties, didn't really open the door like people are fond of saying; he merely showed us that the door was already open. If it's only "line on paper" we can do whatever we want, who gets hurt? And how far can we go? I'm not a Pioneer or anything, but I am out here checking for the "edge of the envelope" as they say these days.

Maybe it's something about offense being the best defense, maybe it's just because I want to be censored, and as we all should know by now, "You can't always get what you want." Not the way you want it, anyway. The Phantom Blot is a sneaky guy. He would rather dribble in around your ankles than bite you on the nose while somebody might be looking. Self-censorship is very subtle, like termites. You don't even know they're there until you try to sell your house so you can move somewhere else.

Self-Censorship in *Cherry* Comics

The guy who has been publishing *Cherry* for lo these many years is an old Hippie, but he is also a businessman and a survivor. He gets nervous. If I dance too far over that line and the Phantom Blot decides that it has to kill *Cherry*, said publisher will be in the line of fire. At least that's what he thinks. I don't want to see him go down; if there's going to be any flames, I want them around me. So I dance along, defiling any sacred taboos I can find within arm's reach.

There are certain things that I don't mess with. The biggest one is Cherry's age. The idea is that she's a teenager, right? But if I depict her as being under eighteen, then she's a child, and it can or could be classified as child pornography, a "bustable offense" in my publisher's words. He wants me to have her be in junior college instead of high school. I take my original line of defense which is to be generic. It's just a school. Might

be a trade school, might be a fucking Vassar. But it makes me wonder . . . is the act of putting blots of ink on paper that is not even all that white and that vaguely suggests the image of an underage girl having sex equivalent to the act of actually abducting an 11 year old girl, tying her up in the basement and forcing her to have sex while you torture here and shoot videos of it? That's a hideous crime, and anyone who does that should be shot in the head immediately. But what about allowing grown men and women to even think about the idea of an underage girl having sex? When nobody gets hurt in the process? Is that legal? We're talking mind control here.

So what I do is just make a big joke of it. I make a big deal about how she's just turned 18, she has always just turned 18, she will always have just turned 18, as fresh as you can get, legally. Its okay with me for now; there are plenty of sacred cows to tip. The other thing is directly assaulting current public figures in too blatant a manner, as I was about to do on the front cover of the book during the Meese Commission hearings. I wasn't really pressured or anything, I was just led to think about it a little. So I changed the one-liner into something really tepid and yes, generic. I'm glad I did. The gag would have been dated and obscure and not funny by now, and that issue is still in print, as are all 13 (so far), so I need to be dealing with classical, timeless, immortal themes and larger pieces of history. High flown talk coming from a Smutmonger. A Phantom Blot dribbles and oozes in around my ankles.

Okay, so what about the shortening of the title? No, I didn't receive any shit from Kellogg's of Battle Creek, Michigan about the use of the word "Poptart." After I finally did the second issue and it became apparent that we had a seller on our hands, a friend of ours wound up acting as my temporary manager. She was, and probably still is, a hot young bleached blonde megababe who managed head-banger Heavy Metal rock bands. She had so much style she managed to make the spikey black leather torn-up punky-look look cute and sexy. She suggested that we drop the Poptart to avoid the possibility of any such conflict with the Poptart People. I said well, I doubt if they're going to be a serious threat as long as I don't go into the snack food business. Then they'll be all over my ass.

But I now begin to notice that the core concept of the thing is going over well enough that the gag of her full name really isn't necessary. "Cherry" by itself actually says it quite nicely and it's a shorter title that can be blown up larger and be more easily read from a longer distance when it's sitting on the rack in the adult section of a comic book store. That's it. It wasn't a chickenshit move, it was a design decision, okay? I'm glad I did it and I think it works.

Part of O'Neill's plan with the *Air Pirates* comics was to have the covers, even though they did indeed have some kind of Anarchistic Bad Stuff right there in plain sight look, at superficial glance, just like a perfectly normal Comics Code Authority-approved wholesome everyday comic book, so that it could be surreptitiously placed on any comic book rack in any 7-11 or Circle K or whatever, and no one would know the difference. So when some harried housewife with a cranky kid comes into the store and the kid wants a comic book and he's really loud and obnoxious about it so she says "Okay, but I'm gonna pick it out for you, 'cause what do you know? Oh here's one that looks wholesome, isn't that the Comics Code thingy in the corner there? Sure. Here ya go kid, take it and shut up!" So the kid's brain ends up getting permanently twisted and he never trusts authority again. Sort of a psychological letter bomb.

So far, after a full decade, I have received precious little response from the groups, movements, organizations or Powers that I have been trying to annoy. I did get, through my publisher (in the line of fire, right?) a couple of cranky letters from a staid New England Law Firm representing Archie Comics demanding that we cease and desist and destroy all copies etc. . . . That was after the first issue, which contained a story by Larry Todd that directly lampooned the Archie Comics characters in an extremely rude fashion. Copyright Infringement blah blah blah . . . So we took the story out, and stuck something else in there in subsequent reprints, of which there have been many. So now the first ten thousand printed are all collectors items.

Then after #2, they wrote again noting that we had left out that particular Bad Stuff, but Cherry looks an awful like . . . and her best friend is a dead ringer for . . . and the cover layout is too similar to our unique design and color scheme so cut it out. Bull's Eye! Tee-Hee!

I've gotten no shit at all from feminists of any kind. Actually, it turns out that a whole lot of my fans are women, a goal that I used to dream about but gave up as too hard to do. But Cherry is usually in control of her own destiny, even if she's being silly about it, which was at the time considered an especially Revolutionary Idea. Just a fantasy of mine; what if there was this gorgeous young woman who really loved sex, and didn't have a bunch of hangups about it; she just liked to do it? Naaaahh . . . couldn't be. Not where I come from. To my most extreme delight, I have been proven

wrong on that one. There are lots of them, and some of them are even cute!

I'm looking for censure, I'm coming on with this chip on my shoulder (although I do wrap it up in a semi-sarcastic cuteness), and what I get is warm fuzzies from all different kinds of people. I got one letter, well, it wasn't really a letter, it was a small cluster of tiny notes, from a Black guy (I assume he was black, I could be wrong), taking exception to the way I portrayed Black People in my books. The way I portrayed Black People was a parody of the way White People (a lot of them anyway) still view them. Anyway, this guy cursed me and wanted my dick to shrivel up and fall off into the toilet "like a piece of shit that it is . . . " He didn't even want to cut if off himself. That's as close as I've gotten to a Death Threat.

I don't get it. Am I that smart, or just lucky? Am I living in a Fool's Paradise, and any minute now they're going to erase my whole existence? Does my warm jovial nature shine through that clearly? Am I that good a dancer? Am I so low and vile in the eyes of Those Whom I Wish to Offend that I am beneath their contempt and not worthy of the merest response or acknowledgement? Hmmm . . . born an' raised in a briar patch!

At this point I'm just a mouse fart, beneath notice, not anywhere near big enough to be considered dangerous, not worth the trouble it would take to wipe me out. I'm just hangin' out here in the briar patch where nobody wants to go. But it's been ten years now and *Cherry*'s still alive and kickin'. In fact, she's growing every day, even though she remains "just 18." So we'll see. If they find my body on a bathroom floor with a needle in my arm, then you'll know that I was right, they were out to get me. And you're next.

"God, did you hear that? He just compared himself to Lenny Bruce! The nerve of that motherfucker!"

"Really! He doesn't even *do* heroin!"

I remember thinking, as I was dreaming *Cherry* up, that for a comic book to call itself "Underground" it should be dangerous in one way or another. If they even think it's dangerous, then it is. Showing explicit sex as if it was a fun, positive, wholesome, healthy thing could be considered dangerous by some people. I certainly hope so. I wanna be an outlaw. I just don't wanna get outta my chair.

"I wasn't no backslidin', knee-crawlin', commode-huggin' drunk, I was God's Own Drunk! . . . And a fearless man!"

Jimmy Buffet
"God's Own Drunk"
from a Lord Buckley routine

Cherry can be purchased from your local comic store. If your store doesn't carry it, it probably doesn't carry Gauntlet either. In any case, write to the editor and we'll steer you to where you can obtain copies.

SPORTS ILLUSTRATED SWIMSUIT ISSUE REVISITED

Trisha Sherrick

In response to Jeannette M. Hopper's article, "Yes Celebrate the Beauty of the Female Form" written in response to my article on the *Sports Illustrated* swimsuit issue (issue #1 of **Gauntlet**) there seems to be some confusion as to the reasoning behind NOW's protest of the swimsuit issue. There are two main reasons for our protest:

(1) *Sports Illustrated* is a sports magazine. (I don't think anyone would argue this point). The women featured in the swimsuit issue are professional models, not sports figures, not athletes.

(2) Professional women athletes receive little coverage from *Sports Illustrated*.

We would like people to question the logic behind the publication of the swimsuit issue. Somehow I doubt that the powers that be at Time-Warner, Inc. got together one fine day in the boardroom and said to one another: "Yes, let's celebrate the beauty of the female form," and behold of birth of the swimsuit issue. In keeping with their claim to fame as a sports magazine they could publish an issue dedicated to professional women bodybuilders. This is an issue I would *love* to see. This issue would have it all; lots of beautiful women, beautiful bodies, skimpy bathingsuits *and* a tie-in to sports.

Being photographed in a swimsuit is not demeaning to women. This is clearly ridiculous. However, the fact that women athletes receive such a small amount of coverage from *Sports Illustrated* while a special issue is devoted to models *is* demeaning to women. It is the *concept* of the swimsuit issue which is offensive. An annual swimsuit issue published by a sports magazine simply makes no sense unless one buys into the concept of **women as sport**. This is the message being sent by *Sports Illustrated*.

Ms. Hopper argues that men's bodies, as well as women's bodies, are being used to make money for *Sports Illustrated*. I believe that the men are being paid for their athletic skill, not solely for the shape and proportion of their bodies, although these qualities certainly add to the development and degree of skill. "For some reason feminists have decided that it's wrong for a women to be proud of her body." How does she come to this conclusion? How does one make the decidedly radical leap from protesting the swimsuit issue and raising awareness about its underlying absurdity, to the charge of being ashamed of our bodies. I protest the swimsuit issue and I'm not ashamed of my body. I rather like it, thank-you-very-much.

Celebrate the beauty of the female form - certainly, we should celebrate the beauty of the *human* form, both male *and* female. However, any random photo of a female body is not necessarily a celebration of that body. There is celebrating the female form and there is cheapening it. A nude photo by Robert Mapplethorpe is a celebration of the beauty of the human form. A photo of a model in a skimpy swimsuit with the words *Sports Illustrated* above her head cheapens and dehumanizes it by portraying this body, this human being, this *woman*, as *sport*.

TEMPEST IN A TEAPOT

John Rosenman

AWRIGHT, YOU!! **HOLD IT** RIGHT THERE.!! BEFORE YOU GO ANY FURTHER— LET'S SEE SOME I.D.!

If Ms. Sherrick wants to protest something that demeans and exploits women, she should focus on what is significant, not trivial. Our society is filled with serious and offensive abuses of women that Ms. Sherrick and NOW should address instead, such as porn magazines which she only briefly mentions. From brassiere/panty/girdle/garter/black-lace-stocking/sanitary napkin/feminine deodorant/douche ads and commercials, to magazines like *Cosmopolitan*, where women often exploit themselves by appearing small-minded, man-hungry and conniving, we find countless examples where women are reduced and dehumanized.

As one example of the *truly* serious abuses I'm talking about, see the "found poem" below, which I took from Sears and J.C. Penney catalogs. Notice that it exploits and demeans women as *Sports Illustrated* does not, and treats them, to use Ms. Sherrick's phrase, **"as sport."** (The photos of seductively clad models are more prurient and salacious too, and lack even a peep show's honesty. Sometimes, in fact, the faces aren't even seen, and we are shown objects, depersonalized fragments of bodies.) In addition, some of the language in these catalogs exploits *pubescent girls*, treats them as sexy little Lolitas. Mothers take this disguised kiddy porn home and pass on these stereotypes to their daughters, whose own daughters, in turn, will pose in similar catalogs.

Moreover, the language and accompanying photos are sex-coded and discriminatory; there is *no* comparable sexy and suggestive selling of males in these catalogs. Finally, the last three words ("buy, Buy, BUY!") are mine, but they reflect the blatantly materialistic purpose which the females - some of them children - serve.

FROM SEARS AND J.C. PENNEY . . . WITH LUST

Natural looking
figure-flattering
                bra in solids
     and lace-patterned
                power net panties
softly-appealing seamless-cup bras
     a wardrobe of bras for Today's Teen
                Her first bra
     styles for the young girl just beginning to develop
                Softbody Plunge Bra
                Long-leg Panty Girdle
          FOR A MORE PROVOCATIVE *YOU*
with removable extra-full pads
     GLISTENING BRIEF   LEISURE BRAS
     INTIMATE THOUGHTS   MY SATIN FANTASY
This glamorour underwire bra
          romances you with the enticing touch
                of stretch satin
     Bust enhancers
     Deep Plunge, Contour Demi-Bra
Fuller-Figure Sports Bra provides maximum support
                and minimum bounce
     Our Pretty Lace Crossover Bra
          features three-section cups that
     lift and separate
     enhance figure with foam rubber padding

     It's no secret . . .
          WHAT'S NEW IS WHAT'S UNDER THINGS!
     NICE TOUCH
          CLING-ALON
     Our Curve Conscious Bustier
Ventilated nylon crotch
                Nylon tricot split crotch
1 layer gently holds and shapes derriere
          HARD-TO-FIND SPECIAL OCCASION BRAS
Lustrous, lightweight nylon
     and Spandex fabric hugs your body like a
                second skin
Wear with removable, fiberfill pads for push-up
                silhouette
     fiberfill pads that push-up and contour
          for a soft, sensuous shape
     Comfy cotton-lined crotch
Sheer inserts at Neckline highlight our Ah-h Bra
     Teddy in Two-Tone Silk
          The softest, most irresistible layer
                of coverage
          PANTIES WITH PIZZAZZ

     buy

          Buy

               BUY!

Enoch

Robert Bloch

(Editor's Note: "Enoch", a short story by Robert Bloch, became the center of controversy on the teaching of values in the Conestoga Valley School District in late-1991. The story, which appeared in Scholastic Scope magazine, was part of the 8th grade English curriculum to teach short story craft. According to the Philadelphia Inquirer, many of the stories posed moral dilemmas and left endings unresolved and these became a springboard for discussions about values - choosing between right and wrong. Nikki Arnold, parent of one of the students in the English class was outraged and brought three stories, including "Enoch" to the attention of the School Board, demanding their ouster. "Stories for young teens," Nikki Arnold told the Inquirer, "should have an ending that says you get punished if you lie or cheat or steal." The Board voted to get rid of "Enoch", while allowing the other two stories to remain part of the curriculum.

Robert Bloch, in an exclusive introduction for GAUNTLET, discusses the exclusion of his story from the schools curriculum. The full text of "Enoch" follows, so the reader can decide whether its ban was warranted.)

Introduction

"Enoch" is, as eighth-grade student Meagan Arnold accurately described it to her parents, "really weird."

That's exactly what I intended it to be - an obvious fantasy/horror story, when it first appeared way back in 1946 - long before Meagan was even a twinkle in her father's eye. For that matter, her father wasn't yet a twinkle in *his* father's eye. So obviously this bit of fiction was not written with the express purpose of corrupting the morals of little Meagan.

Over the past forty-six years "Enoch" has been reprinted two dozen times or more, including a half-dozen appearances in other countries: it was even the basis for one of the episodes in an anthology film. And it has been part of the curriculum of any number of schools, along with some of my other stories. It's hard to tell just how many youngsters have been exposed to its influence by now, after almost half a century of its existence in print.

If it is any reassurance to Meagan's parents, I've yet to have other reports of "Enoch's" capacity to harm readers. Whenever it's been published, the story has been clearly labelled as a work of fantasy.

I strongly doubt that anyone old enough to peruse it would think otherwise. I don't feel that anyone would believe that an unseen familiar ever dwelt on the head of an obviously mentally-disturbed youngster, or that it had been obtained by supernatural means.

To address the present situation, I don't for a moment accept that little Meagan would read the story and confuse its fantasy with reality - be inspired to identify with its narrator, feel it worthwhile to emulate him, or imagine her own mother could be a witch. There are no role-models here, and no incentives to indulge in anti-social behavior.

As for Meagan's parents, I fail to see why they are so lacking in faith.

From what I've learned about Fundamentalist Christian beliefs, a basic tenet is that God possesses awesome power. In which case, I'd expect devout believers to put their trust in Almighty God's ability to prevail against any evil which might be lurking in the pages of my fairy-tale.

I sometimes wonder why the people who most strongly and loudly proclaim their faith in divine power are so frightened at even the mere hint of anything they imagine could possibly be interpreted as disputing it. My feeling is that the nits they pick may be their own. Which, of course, is their privilege. As long as the apprehensive citizens of Conestoga Valley School District wish to impose their own variety of "moral absolutes" on their children, so be it. Imposing their variety of "moral absolutes" on everybody else's children is just the logical next step. And since history offers precedents, the step after that is to burn the book in which my story appears - preferably, in a fire that also burns me.

If so, may smoke get in their eyes. And in the eyes of the Conestoga Valley School Board members whose actions so eloquently attest to their motivations.

ENOCH

It always starts out the same way. First, there is the *feeling*.

Have you ever felt little feet walking back and forth across the top of your skull? It feels like that.

You can't see who does the walking. If you suddenly brush your hand through your hair, you won't catch him. Even if you clamp both hands to your head, he gets away.

When he stops walking, he goes down the back of your neck. You can feel his body, cold and tiny, pressed against the base of your brain. You can hear him whispering in your ear.

You try not to listen. If you listen, you have to obey him.

I used to try to fight against him. But he knows how to threaten and frighten me. Now, as long as I listen, things don't seem so bad. Besides, he gives me wonderful rewards.

Folks think I'm poor because I live in and old shack on the edge of the swamp. They laugh at me. The girls in town call me "scarecrow." But after I do what he wants, he gives me riches.

He takes me away - out of myself - for days. There are other places in this world, you know - places where I am king.

Just dreams? I don't think so. It's the other life that's a dream - the life in the shack by the swamp. That life doesn't seem real any more. Not even when I kill people.

I kill because Enoch tells me to. Enoch is the thing that lives on my head.

Sometimes he leaves me alone for days. Then, suddenly, I'll feel him there. I'll hear him whisper. He'll tell me about someone who is coming through the swamp.

I don't know how me knows about them. But he describes them perfectly.

"There's a tramp walking this way," he'll say. "He's short, fat and has a bald head. He's wearing blue overalls. He'll come to the swamp in about 10 minutes. Get the hatchet. Then hide behind that tree. Sometimes I ask Enoch what he will give me. Usually, I just trust him. I know I have to obey him anyway. Enoch is never wrong about things - until this last time.

That time he told me about this young woman. "She will come to your door and ask you to help fix her car. She had taken a shortcut into town. The car is in the swamp right now. One of the tires needs changing.

"You will go out to help her when she asks you. Don't take anything. She has a wrench in the car. Use that."

This time, I said, "I won't do it."

He said, "If you don't, you know what I'll do to you."

"NO!" I said. "I'll do it."

"After all," Enoch whispered, "I can't help it. It keeps me alive. It keeps me strong enough to give you rewards."

"I'll do it," I said. And I did.

She knocked on my door a few minutes later. She was pretty. I was glad I didn't have to harm her blonde hair. I hit her behind the neck with the wrench.

Enoch told me what to do, step by step. After I used the hatched, I put the body in the quicksand. It sank out of sight. Enoch told me how to use the end of a log to turn the car over. I didn't think it would sink, but it did.

Then Enoch told me to go home, and I did. I felt the dreamy feeling coming over me now.

Enoch had promised me a reward. He went off into the swamp for *his* reward.

I don't know how long I slept. When I finally started to wake up, Enoch was back with me again. Then I woke up all the way, because I heard the banging on my door.

I waited for Enoch to tell me what to do. But he

was asleep. He always sleeps afterwards. Nothing wakes him for days. But now I needed his help.

I got up and answered the door. Sheriff Shelby came inside.

"Come on, Seth," he said. "I'm taking you to jail." His mean eyes were looking everywhere inside my shack. He couldn't see Enoch, of course. Nobody can.

Then he said, "Emily Robbins' folks say she was going to cut through the swamp. We followed the tire tracks up to the quicksand."

Enoch had forgotten about the tracks. I didn't say anything.

"Anything you say can be used against you," the Sheriff said. "Come on, Seth."

I went with him into town. There was nothing else for me to do. A crowd was waiting foe me outside the jail. They wanted to kill me. But Sheriff Shelby held them off.

I was tucked away safe and sound in the jail. I was locked up in the middle cell. The cells on each side of me were empty. I was all alone - except for Enoch. He was still asleep on top of my head.

Sheriff Shelby went out, leaving Charley Potter in charge of the jail. Charley kept asking me questions.

I knew better than to talk to a fool like him. He thought I was crazy. Most people in town thought I was crazy. Because of my mother, I suppose, and because I live all alone out in the swamp.

Charley told me about the search for Emily Robbins, and how the Sheriff began wondering about some other people who disappeared. He said there would be a big trial. The District Attorney was coming to town. They were sending a doctor to see me.

Sure enough, the doctor came. He sat down outside the cell and talked to me. His name was Dr. Silver-smith.

Until now, I wasn't really *feeling* anything. It all happened so fast, I didn't get a chance to think. But the sight of this Dr. Silversmith changed things.

He was real, all right. You could tell he was a doctor by the quiet way he talked. He sounded like the doctor who wanted to send me to the institution, after they found my mother.

That was one of the first things Dr. Silversmith asked me - what happened to my mother? I found myself telling him how my mother and I lived in a shack. How she made potions and sold them. About the big pot and the way we gathered herbs. About the nights when she went off, and I heard strange noises far away.

I didn't want to say much more. But he knew that they called her a witch. He knew the way she died. Santo Dinorelli came to our door and stabbed her, because she made the potion for his daughter who ran away with that trapper.

He didn't know about Enoch. But somehow I began telling him about Enoch. I wanted to explain that it wasn't really I who killed Emily. So I had to mention Enoch and how my mother had made a bargain in the woods. She hadn't let me come with her. I was only 12. But she took some of my blood, sticking a needle into me and dropping it into a little bottle.

When she came back in the morning, Enoch was with her. I couldn't see him. But she said he would look after me when she was gone. And I could feel him when he jumped onto my head.

I told Dr. Silversmith why I had to obey Enoch. Enoch protected me, just as my mother had planned.

I thought Dr. Silversmith would understand. I was wrong. He said, "Yes, yes," over and over again. He had the same kind of eyes as Sheriff Shelby. Mean eyes. Eyes that don't trust you.

He asked me if I heard any *other* voices. He wondered if I saw things that weren't there. Why, he talked to me as if I was some kind of - crazy person!

I wouldn't talk to him after that. Finally, he went away, and I went to sleep.

When I woke up, a new man was outside my cell. He had a fat, smiling face and nice eyes.

"Hello, Seth," he said very friendly. "My name's Cassidy. I'm the District Attorney. Can I come in and sit down?"

"I'm locked in," I said.

"The Sheriff gave me the keys." Mr. Cassidy opened my cell. He sat down next to me.

"Aren't you afraid?" I asked. "I'm supposed to be a murderer."

Mr. Cassidy laughed. "Seth, I know you didn't mean to kill anybody. How's Enoch?"

I jumped.

"Yes, that fool doctor told me," Mr. Cassidy said. "He doesn't understand about Enoch, does he? But you and I do."

"That doctor thinks I'm crazy," I said.

"Well, just between us, Seth, it was a little hard to believe. But I've just come from the swamp. Sheriff Shelby and his men are still there. They found Emily Robbins' body and saw other bodies."

I watched his eyes. They were still smiling. I knew I could trust this man.

> "One more thing," he said. "The heads are missing from the bodies we found in the swamp. Where are the heads?"

He said, "They'll find other bodies, too, won't they?"

I nodded.

"Enoch made you do it, didn't he?"

I nodded again.

"You see," Mr. Cassidy said, "we do understand each other. So I won't blame you for anything you tell me."

"What do you want to know?"

"How many people did Enoch ask you to kill?"

"Nine," I said.

"Are they all buried in the quicksand?"

"Yes."

"Seth," he said, "I'm going to be at your trial. Now, you don't want to have to get up in front of all those people and tell them what happened. Right?"

"Right. Those mean people in town hate me."

"Then you tell me about it, and I'll talk for you. Okay?"

I wished Enoch could help me, but he was asleep. I made up my own mind.

"Yes," I said. "I can tell you."

So I told him everything I knew.

"One more thing," he said. "The heads are missing from the bodies we found in the swamp. Where are the heads?"

"I don't know," I said. "I give them to Enoch. That's why I kill people for him. He wants their heads."

"Why do you let Enoch do such things?"

"I must. Or else he'll do it to me."

Mr. Cassidy suddenly seemed nervous. When I came close to him, he leaned away.

"You'll explain all that in the trial?" I asked. "About Enoch and everything?"

"I'm not going to tell about Enoch at the trial," Mr. Cassidy said. "If I did, people would say you're crazy!"

"How can you help me?" I asked.

Mr. Cassidy smiled. "You're afraid of Enoch, aren't you? Well, I was just thinking - suppose you gave Enoch to me?"

I gulped.

"Let me take care of him for you during the trial," he went on. "Then he wouldn't be yours. You wouldn't have to say anything about him. He probably doesn't want people to know what he does anyway."

"That's right," I said. "Enoch is a secret. But I hate to give him to you without asking him. And he's asleep now."

"Asleep?"

"Yes. On top of my head. You can't see him, of course."

"Well, I can explain everything when he wakes up," he said laughing. "I'm sure he'll realize that it's all for the best."

"You'll give him what he wants?"

"Of course."

"You know what will happen if you don't," I warned. "He will take it - from you - by force."

"Don't worry, Seth."

All at once, I felt something move. Enoch was waking up.

"He's awake," I whispered. "Now I can tell him."

I could feel him crawling towards my ear. "Enoch," I whispered. Then I explained to him why I thought I should give him to Mr. Cassidy.

Enoch didn't say a word. Mr. Cassidy didn't say a word. He just smiled.

"Go to Mr. Cassidy, Enoch," I said.

And Enoch went. I felt the weight lift from my head.

"Can you feel him, Mr. Cassidy?" I asked.

"What? Oh, sure," he said and stood up.

"Take good care of Enoch," I told him.

"The best."

"Don't put your hat on. Enoch doesn't like hats."

"Sorry, I forgot. Well, Seth, you've been a great help to me. That Dr. Silversmith is going to try to tell folks that you're crazy. Maybe you should deny everything you've told him - now that I have Enoch."

"What ever you say, Mr. Cassidy. Just be good to Enoch, and he'll be good to you."

Mr. Cassidy shook my hand. Then he and Enoch went away. I felt tired again. I went back to sleep for a long time.

It was night when I woke up. Charley Potter was banging on my cell door, bringing me supper.

"They got nine bodies out of the swamp!" he yelled. "You crazy murderer! I'm getting out of her right now. I'll leave you locked up for the night. The Sheriff will see that nobody breaks in to lynch you. If you ask me, he's wasting his time."

Then Charley went away. I heard him go out the front door and put the padlock on. I was all alone.

All alone! It was strange to be all alone, without Enoch, for the first time in years. I ran my fingers across the top of my head. It felt bare and strange.

Then I heard a fumbling at the door. The lock clicked down. Mr. Cassidy came running in. He was clawing at his head.

"Take him off me!" he yelled

"What's the matter?" I asked.

"Enoch! I thought you were crazy. Maybe *I'm* the crazy one. Take him off!"

"I told you what he's like," I said.

"He's crawling around up there now. I can feel him. I can *hear* him!"

"But I explained all that. Enoch wants something, doesn't he? You'll have to give it to him. You promised."

"I won't kill for him. He can't make me."

"He can. And he will."

Mr. Cassidy grabbed the bars of my cell. "Seth, you must help me. Call Enoch. Take him back. Hurry!"

I called Enoch. He didn't answer. I called again. There was silence.

"He won't come back," I said. "I guess he likes you."

Mr. Cassidy began to cry. I felt kind of sorry for him. I know what Enoch can do to you when he whispers that way. First he asks you. Then he threatens you.

"You'd better obey him," I said. "Has he told you to kill someone?"

Mr. Cassidy didn't say anything. He just cried. Then he took out the jail keys. He opened the cell next to mine. He went in and locked the door.

"I won't," he sobbed. "I won't."

"You won't do what?" I asked.

"I won't kill Dr. Silversmith and give Enoch his head. I'll stay in this cell, where I'm safe."

He slumped down to the floor. I could see him through the bars dividing our cells. His hands were tearing at his hair.

"You'd better," I said. "Or else Enoch will do something. Please, Mr. Cassidy!"

Mr. Cassidy gave a little moan. I guess he fainted, because he was quiet.

Then suddenly, he started to scream. Not loud, but deep down in his throat. He didn't move, just screamed. I knew it was Enoch, taking what he wanted.

What was the use of looking? You can't stop him, and I had warned Mr. Cassidy. So I turned away and held my hands over my ears until it was over.

When I turned around again, Mr. Cassidy was still slumped against the bars. There wasn't a sound to be heard.

Oh yes, there was! A purring. The purring of Enoch after he has eaten. Then I heard the scratching of Enoch's claws. The purring and scratching came from inside Mr. Cassidy's head.

Enoch was happy now.

I reached through the bars and pulled the jail keys from Mr. Cassidy's pocket. I opened my cell door. I was free again.

"Here, Enoch!" I called.

That was as close as I've ever come to seeing Enoch - a white streak that came flashing out of the big red hole in the back of Mr. Cassidy's skull.

Then I felt the soft, cold weight landing on my own head. Enoch had come home.

I walked to the door of the jail and opened it. Enoch's tiny feet began to patter on the roof of my brain.

Together we walked out into the night. The moon was shining - ever so softly - Enoch's happy laughter in my ear.

HOW TO GET AHEAD IN NEW YORK

Poppy Z. Brite

Consider this scene:

Four a.m. in the Port Authority bus terminal, New York City. The Port Authority is a bad place at the best of times, a place where Lovecraft's wrong geometry might well hold sway. The master of purple prose maintained that the human mind could be driven mad by contemplation of angles subtly skewed, of other planes where the three corners of a triangle might add up to less than a hundred and eighty degrees, or to more.

Such is the Port Authority: even in the bustle of midday, corners do not appear to meet up quite right; corridors seem to slope from one end to the other. Even in full daylight, the Port Authority terminal is a bad place. At five a.m. it is wholly soulless.

Consider two young men just off a Greyhound from North Carolina. They were not brothers, but they might be thought brothers, although they looked nothing alike: it was suggested in the way the taller one, crow-black hair shoved messily behind his ears, kept close to his fairhaired companion as if protecting him. It was implied in the way they looked around the empty terminal and then glanced at each other, exchanging bad impressions without saying a word. They were not brothers, but they had known each other since childhood, and neither had ever been to New York before.

The corridor was flooded with dead fluorescent light. They had seen an EXIT sign pointing this way, but the corridor ended in a steel door marked NO ADMITTANCE. Should anyone find this message ambiguous, a heavy chain had been looped through the door handle and snapped shut with a padlock as large as a good-sized fist.

The fair boy turned around in a complete circle, lifted his head and flared his nostrils. His pale blue eyes slipped halfway shut, the lids fluttering. His friend watched him warily. After a minute he came out of it, shook himself a little, still nervous. "I don't like it here, Steve. I can't find my way anywhere."

Steve didn't like it either, wished they could have avoided the terminal altogether. They'd planned to drive up, but Steve's old T-bird had developed an alarming engine knock which threatened to become a death rattle if not dealt with kindly. The trip was all planned; they were booked to play at a club in the East Village—but they also meant to embark on a cross-country road trip next month. Steve left the car with his mechanic, telling him to fix it or scrap the motherfucker, Steve didn't care which. Ghost stood by half-smiling, listening to this exchange. Then, while Steve was still bitching, he had walked up the street to the Farmers Hardware store that doubled as Missing Mile's bus station and charged two round trip tickets to his credit card. He hated using that card, hated the feel of the thing in his pocket, but this surely counted as an emergency. That same night they were New York bound.

"It's just the damn *bus station*," Steve said. "You ever know a town that could be judged by its bus station?" But as usual, there was no use arguing with Ghost's intuition. The place set Steve's teeth on edge too.

Ghost hitched his backpack up on his shoulder. They turned away from the padlocked door and tried to retrace their steps, but every corridor seemed to lead further into the bowels of the place. The soft sound of Ghost's sneakers and the sharp clatter of Steve's bootheels echoed back at them: *shush-clop, shush-clop*. Through Ghost's thin T-shirt Steve saw the sharp wing-like jut of his shoulderblades, the shadowed knobs of his spine. The strap of the backpack pulled Ghost's shirt askew; his pale hair straggled silkily over his bare, sweaty neck. Steve carried only a guitar case, the instrument inside padded with a spare shirt and a few extra pairs of socks.

They came to another dead end, then to the motionless hulk of an escalator with a chain strung across its railings. A KEEP OUT sign hung from the chain, swinging lazily as if someone had given it a push and then ducked out of sight just before Steve and Ghost came around the corner. Steve began to feel like a stupid hick, to feel like the place was playing tricks on them. *Came to the Big City and couldn't even find our way out of the bus station. We ought to sit down right here and wait for the next bus headed south, and when it comes, we ought to hop on it and go right back home. Fuck New York, fuck the big club date. I don't like it here either.*

But that was stupid. The city was out there somewhere, and it had to get better than this.

Port Authority, Ghost decided, was about the worst place he had ever been in. Everything about it looked wrong, smelled wrong, leaned wrong.

There were patterns on the floor made by the grime of a thousand soles; there was a bloody handprint on the tile wall. Looking at it, Ghost tried to close off his mind: he didn't want to know how it had gotten there. He managed to block out all but a faint impression of dirty knuckles plowing into a soft toothless mouth.

All at once the corridors shook and shuddered. The floor vibrated beneath his feet, throwing Ghost off balance. He had no way of knowing that this loss of equilibrium was caused by the subways constantly passing through; it made him feel as if the place were trying to digest him. *How did you ever get here?* he thought. *How did you get from the green mountains, from the kudzu traintracks and the lazy hot summers, all the way to this city that could chew you up and spit you out like a wad of gum that's lost its flavor? How did you get to this place where you can never belong?*

Immersed in his thoughts, he had let Steve get a little ahead of him. He looked up an instant before the apparition of death reeled around the corner; he heard Steve's curse, the sharp *"Fuck!"* that was nearly a gag, as the apparition lurched into Steve.

Steve's arms shot out reflexively, found the man's shoulders and shoved him away. The bum fell back against the wall, leaving a long wet smear on the tiles. His ragged suit jacket and the wattles of his throat were webbed with pale stringy vomit that dripped off his chin and made small foul splatters on the floor. His skin was gray, flaccid. It made Ghost think of a pumpkin that had sat too long in his grandmother's cellar once, waiting for Halloween; when he'd poked it, his finger had punched through the rind and sunk into the soft rotten meat. This man's skin looked as if it would rupture just as

easily. One of his eyes was filmed over with a creamy yellowish cataract. The other eye listed toward the ceiling, watered and seemed about to spill over, then managed to track. When the eye met his, Ghost felt ice tingle along his spine. There was no one home behind that eye.

A wasted claw of a hand came up clutching a Styrofoam cup in which a few coins rattled. Veins stood out on the back of the hand. In the dead light they were as stark and clear as a map of the man's ruined soul. "Spare change for my li'l girl," he muttered. His voice caught in his throat, then dragged itself out slow as a bad recording. "My li'l girl's sick. Gotta catch the mornin' bus to Jersey."

Ghost looked at Steve. The understanding passed clearly between them: *bullshit.* There was no little girl in Jersey, there was nothing waiting for this man except the love at the bottom of a bottle. But the reality of him staggering through the desolate corridors in his vomit-caked coat, with his lone empty eye - that was worse than any sob story. Steve pulled out his wallet; Ghost dug through the pockets of his army jacket. They came up with a dollar each and stuffed the bills into the broken Styrofoam cup.

The bum threw his head back and a weird hooting sound came from his cracked lips. It was not quite a word, not quite a whistle. It reverberated off the tiles and ceilings.

And then the walls and the corridors of the Port Authority seemed to split wide open, and the legions of the hopeless spilled forth.

The bums were everywhere at once, coming from every direction, their eyes fixed on Steve's wallet and Ghost's open hands and the crisp bills poking out of the cup. Most of them had their own jingling cups; they shoved them at Steve, at Ghost, and their eyes implored. Their voices

> The bums were everywhere at once, coming from every direction, their eyes fixed on Steve's wallet . . .

rose in a hundred meaningless pleas: *cuppa coffee...sick baby...hungry, mister, I'm hungry.* In the end the voices only meant one thing. *Give me. You who have, when I have none - give me.*

They kept coming. There seemed to be no end to them. Their hands reached for the money and grasped it. A persistent young brother grabbed a handful of Steve's hair and wouldn't let go until Steve reared back and punched him full in the face. He got a fistful of snot and ropy saliva for his trouble. As the boy fell away, Steve saw angry red holes in the pale flesh of his outstretched palms: needle marks. *He was my age,* Steve thought wildly; something in the eyes made him think the kid might have been even younger than twenty-four. *But he was already worn out enough to shoot up in the palms of his hands.*

Steve found himself flashing on *Dawn of the Dead,* a movie that had terrified him when he was a kid. He'd seen it again a couple of years ago and been surprised by how funny it really was: Romero's allegory of zombies roaming a modern mega-mall had escaped him at twelve. But now the original kid-terror flooded back. This was how it would be when the zombies ate you. They weren't very smart or quick, but there were a *lot* of them, and they would just keep coming and coming until you couldn't fight them any more.

Filth-caked nails scraped his flesh. The wallet was torn out of his grasp and dumped on the floor. Steve saw dirty hands shuffling through the trivia of his life. His driver's license. Ticket stubs from concerts he'd seen. A tattered review of Lost Souls?, his and Ghost's band, that had been written up in a Raleigh newspaper. Rage exploded like a crimson rocket in his brain. He had *worked* to get that money; he had *worked* to have a life, not see it trickle away from him like vomit on a dirty bus-station floor.

He hefted the guitar case - none of them seemed interested in that - and swung it in a wild arc. It connected with flesh, filthy hair, bone. Steve winced as he heard the jangling protest of the strings. He'd hit the first bum in his vomit-caked jacket, the only one they had willingly given money. *Try that for a handout, motherfucker.* The bum fell to his knees, clutching the back of his skull. Even the blood welling up between his fingers had an unhealthy look, like the watery blood at the bottom of a meat tray. It spattered the dirty floor in large uneven drops.

Ghost was grappling for his backpack. An old woman with skin like spoiled hamburger pulled at one shoulderstrap. The buttons of her flannel shirt had popped open and her shrivelled breasts tumbled out. The nipples were long and leathery as the stems of mushrooms. Her hair was a uniform grayish-yellow mat overlaid with a layer of white gauze which seemed to thicken, to form dense little balls, in several spots. Networks of delicate threads led away from these; dark shapes moved sluggishly within them. *Cocoons,* he realized sickly. *She has cocoons in her hair.* He grabbed the woman by the shoulders and shoved her away. Ghost's notebooks were in that backpack— the lyrics to every song they had written. Ghost's eyes met Steve's, pale blue gone darker with panic.

Then, for no discernible reason, the creeps began to lift their heads and scent the air. A silent alarm seemed to pass among them. One by one they shrank away, sidled along the walls and disappeared like wraiths into the maze of corridors. The money in their Styrofoam cups rustled and jingled. Steve thought of cockroaches scuttling for cover when the kitchen light snaps on. In less than a minute they were all gone.

Steve and Ghost stared at each other, sweating, catching their breaths. Ghost held up a shaky hand. The cocoon lady's nails had left a long, shallow scratch along the back of it, from his knuckles to the bony knob of his wrist. A moment later they heard heavy, measured footsteps approaching. They edged closer together but did not otherwise react; this was surely the soul of the city itself coming to claim them.

The cop came around the corner all hard-edged and polished and gleaming, stopped at the sight of them, saw Steve's wallet and its contents scattered on the floor, frowned. His face was broad, Italian-looking, freshly shaved but the beard beneath the skin already showing faintly blue-black. "Help you with something?" he asked, his voice sharp with suspicion.

Steve drew in a long trembling breath and Ghost spoke quickly, before Steve could. Cussing cops was never a good idea, no matter where you were. "I think we got a little lost," he said. "Could you tell us how to get out of here?"

He was relieved when the cop pointed them in the right direction and Steve bent and scooped up his wallet, then stalked off without a word. Ghost's brain still ached from the long bus ride and the attack of the homeless people - or the people who lived, perhaps, in Port Authority. Worse than their grasping hands had been the touch of their minds upon his, as many-legged and hungry as mosquitoes. Their raw pain, the stink of their dead dreams. On top of that he hadn't needed Steve to get himself arrested. But Ghost was used to being the occasional peacemaker between Steve and almost everyone they knew. Steve bristled and Ghost calmed; that was just the way things were.

The sky was already brightening when they came out of the bus terminal. The city soared around them, bathed in a clear lavender light. The first building Ghost saw was an old stone church; the second was a four-story sex emporium, its neon shimmering pale pink in the dawn. Steve leaned back against the glass doors and began to laugh.

"Good morning, Hell's Kitchen," he said.

Washington Square Park was in full regalia, though it was still early afternoon.

There were street musicians of every stripe, rappers clicking fast fingers and rattling heavy gold chains, old hippies with battered guitars and homemade pan pipes and permanent stoned smirks, young hippies singing solemn folk lyrics *a capella*, even a Dixieland brass band near the great stone arch. There was the savory mustard-chili tang of hot dogs, the harsh smoulder of city exhaust, the woodsy smell of ganja burning. There were homeboys and Rasta men and hairy-chested drag queens, slumming yuppies and street freaks. There were the folks for whom every day was Halloween, faces painted pale, lips slashed crimson or black, ears and wrists decorated with silver crucifixes, skulls, charms of death and hoodoo. They huddled into their dark clothes, plucked at their dyed, teased, tortured hair, cut their black-rimmed eyes at passersby. There were punks in leather; there were drug dealers chanting the charms of their wares (*clean crystal . . . sweetest smoke in the city...goooood ice, gooooood blow*). There were cops on the beat, cops looking the other way.

And, of course, there were two white boys from North Carolina whose feet had just this morning touched New York City asphalt for the first time.

They had drunk vile coffee from a stand in Times Square, then walked around for a while. They kept losing track of the Empire State Building, which was the only landmark they recognized. The tranquil light of early morning soon gave way to the hustle and shove of the day. The air came alive with shouts, blaring horns, the constant low thrum of the city-machine. Eventually—as soon as they could stand to go below street level again - they descended into the subway at Penn Station and didn't get out again until the Washington Square stop. At that point Ghost swore he would never enter a transit station or board any subway in New York City or anywhere else, ever again. It wasn't the crowds; since Port Authority the only panhandlers they'd seen had been shaking discreet cups or quietly noodling on saxophones. No one else had bothered them. It was the merciless white light in the stations and the bleak garbage-strewn deadliness of the tracks and the great clattering ratcheting roar of the trains. It was hurtling through sections of tunnel where the tracks split in two at the last heartstopping second before you smashed into solid stone. It was the abandoned tunnels that split off like dead universes. The very idea of the trains worming along beneath the city, in their honey-combed burrows, seemed horribly organic.

But topside, he was fine. Ghost found himself liking the stew of sounds and smells that comprised the city, and the colorful variety of the minds that brushed his, and the carnival of Washington Square. Steve stopped to watch the Dixieland band, and Ghost listened to the dipping, soaring brass for several minutes too.

But in his peripheral vision a man was rooting in a garbage can. He tried not to look, but couldn't help himself as the man pulled out a whole dripping chilidog, brushed flies away, and bit into it.

The man was old and white, with long gray dreadlocks and mummified hands and the universal costume of the drifter, army jacket, baggy pants, Salvation Army shirt that just missed being a rag: an ensemble ready to fade into the background at a moment's notice. The chilidog was a carnage of ketchup and pickle relish and flaccid meat, the bun limp, sponge-soggy. The man's face registered more pleasure than distaste. The 'dog might taste awful, but there was still warm sun on his shoulders and a half-full bottle in his pocket and a goddamn huge party going on right here, right now. His eyes were curiously clear, almost childlike.

But it was garbage, *he was eating* garbage. The wire trashcan was crammed with ripening refuse. A redolent juice seeped out at the bottom, a distillation of every disgusting fluid in the can, moonshine for bluebottle flies. Ghost felt his mind stretching, trying to accommodate something he had never had to think closely about before. There were poor people in Missing Mile, sure. Most of the old men who played checkers outside the Farmers Hardware store were on some kind of government or military pension. Lots of people got food stamps. But were there people eating out of garbage cans? Were there people so desperate that they would band together and attack you for the change in your pocket?

You bet there are. They're everywhere. Your life has been just sheltered enough, just sanitized enough, that you didn't see them. But you can't get away from it here . . . this city chews up its young and spits them back in your face.

Ghost looked up, startled. He wasn't sure what had just happened; it felt as if the world, for an instant, had split and then reconverged. As if someone had had the exact same thought as him, at the exact same time.

He saw a young black man leaning on the low concrete wall nearby, also watching the old drifter. The young man was handsome, trendily barbered, dressed in casual but expensive-looking sport clothes. He wore gold-rimmed glasses with little round lenses, carried a radio Walkman in his breast pocket and a copy of Spy tucked under his arm. In his face as he watched the old man chewing was an ineffable sadness, not quite sympathy, not quite pity.

The hearts that would swell with rage back home - if you could call them hearts - to see a black man looking upon

> . . . the man pulled out a whole dripping chilidog, brushed flies away, and bit into it.

a white man with anything resembling pity . . .

(Get outta that garbage, boy)

The man shifted on the wall and looked straight at Ghost, warm mocha eyes meeting startled pale blue. And suddenly Ghost knew many things about this man. He was from a tiny town in south Georgia - Ghost didn't get the name - and his family had been crushingly poor. Not trash-eating poor . . . but there had been a man in the town who *was*. Ancient and alone, black as midnight, brains pickled by half a century of rotgut wine. He was no town hobo of the sort people laughed at but looked out for; he had no colorful nickname, no family, no history. He was a smelly old wino who pissed his pants, and most of the whites in town, if they were aware of him at all, called him Hey Boy. As in *Hey, Boy, get outta that garbage.* As in *Hey, Boy, I'm talkin' to you.* As in *Hey, Boy, get off my property before I blow your nigger guts to Hell.*

And this young man, as a hungry scrawny child in this stagnant backwater of a town, had seen that happen.

Ghost saw the blood exploding through the air, smelled flame and cordite, redneck sweat and the raw sewage odor of Hey Boy's ruptured, blasted guts. He felt the giddy terror of a child hiding - where? - he couldn't get it - viewing death up close for the first time, afraid its twin black barrels would swing his way next. He could not move, could not look away from the young man's calm brown eyes, until Steve touched his shoulder. "Somebody just gave me directions to the club. It's real near here. You want to go check it out?"

Ghost glanced back over his shoulder as they left the park. The young man was no longer looking at him, and Ghost felt no urge to speak. They had already had the most intimate contact possible; of what use were words?

They crossed a wide traffic-filled avenue and turned east. Ghost wasn't sure just where the Village began, but the streets seemed to be getting narrower, the window displays more fabulous, the crowds decidedly funkier. People wore silver studs in their noses, delicate hoops through their lips and eyebrows. A boy in a black fishnet shirt had both nipples pierced, with a filigree chain connecting the rings. There were shaved and painted scalps, long snaky braids, leather jackets jangling with zippers and buckles, flowing hippie dresses of gossamer and gauze. The streets of the East Village by day seemed a shrine to mutant fashion.

Steve pulled a joint from his sock, lit up, took a deep drag and passed it to Ghost. Ghost grabbed the burning cigarette and cupped it gingerly between his palms, trying to hide it, expecting a big cop hand to fall on his shoulder at any second. "Are you *crazy?*"

Steve shook his head, then blew out a giant plume of smoke. "It's cool. Terry said you could smoke right on the street up here, as long as you're discreet. He gave me this as a going-away present."

Terry owned the record store where Steve worked, and was the best-travelled and most worldly of their crowd; also the biggest stoner, so he ought to know. But Ghost could not stretch his definition of *discreet* to include walking down one of the busiest streets in New York City with a cloud of pot smoke trailing behind. Still . . . He looked thoughtfully at the joint in his hand, then brought it up to his lips and took a cautious toke. The spicy green flavor filled his throat, swirled through his lungs and his brain. New York probably imported every exotic strain of reefer from every country in the world, but Southern homegrown had to beat them all.

A few blocks later the crowds thinned out. The streets here felt older, grayer, somehow more soothing. More like a place where you could actually live. There were little groceries on every block with wooden stands of flowers and produce in front. Ghost smelled ginger and ripe tomatoes, the subtle cool scent of ice, the tang of fresh greens and herbs. Sage, basil, onions, thyme, sweet rosemary and soapy-smelling coriander. As long as he could smell herbs he was happy.

New York, Steve decided, was a city bent upon providing its citizens with plenty of food and information. In other parts of the city there had been hot dog carts everywhere, pizza parlors and cappuccino shops, restaurants serving food from Thailand, Mongolia, Latino-China, and everywhere else in the world; newsstands on every corner carried hundreds of papers, magazines, and often a wide selection of hardcore porn. There were radios and TVs blaring, headlines shrieking. In the first part of the Village Steve had seen more restaurants, comics shops, and several intriguing bookstores he planned to check out later. Here you had the little groceries, though not quite so many restaurants. For information, there were the street vendors.

Steve had started noticing them a while back, though he'd been too busy noticing everything else to pay much attention at first. But here they were more frequent and less obscured by the flow of the crowd. They set up tables or spread out army blankets, then arranged the stuff they wanted to sell and sat down to wait until somebody bought it. There were tables of ratty paperbacks, boxes of old magazines, tie-dyed T-shirts and ugly nylon buttpacks, cheap watches and household appliances laid out on the sidewalk like the leftovers from somebody's yard sale.

But as they walked farther, the wares started to get a little strange. At first it was just stuff that no one could possibly want, like a box of broken crayon-ends or a shampoo bottle filled with sand. Then they passed a man selling what looked like medical equipment: bedpans in a dusty row, unidentifiable tubes and pouches, some jar-shaped humps covered with a tattered army blanket. In the center of his display was a single artificial leg that had once been painted a fleshy pink. Now the paint was chipped, the limb's surface webbed with a thousand tiny, grimy cracks. The toeless foot was flat and squared-off, little more than a block of wood. At the top was a nightmarish jumble of straps and braces meant, Steve supposed, to hold the leg onto a body. He could not imagine walking around on such a thing every day.

"Where is this club?" Ghost asked nervously.

"Well . . . I know we're near it." Steve stopped at the corner, shoved sweaty hair out of his face, and looked around hoping the place would appear. "The guy who gave me directions said it would be hard to find in the daytime. We're supposed to look for an unlit neon sign that says *Beware.*"

"Great."

"WHAT PLACE YEZ LOOKIN' FOR?" boomed a voice behind them. It took Steve several seconds to realize that the vendor had spoken and was now motioning them over.

"Yez look like gentlemen in search of the unusual," the vendor told them before they could say anything about clubs or directions. He was a white man of indeterminate age, dishwater-brown hair thin on top but straggling halfway down his back in an untidy braid. His eyes were hidden behind black wraparound shades, his grin as sharp and sudden as a razor. Steve noticed a strange

> Inside each jar, suspended in the murky liquid, was a large, pale, bloated shape: an undeniably real human head.

ring on the second finger of the guy's right hand: a bird skull cast in silver, some species with huge hollow eyesockets and a long, tapering, lethal-looking beak that jutted out over the knuckle. It was lovely, but it also looked like a good tool for putting an eye out or ventilating a throat.

"Well, right now we're looking for this club—"

"Something UNUSUAL," the vendor overrode. "A collector's item maybe." His hand hovered over his wares, straightened tubes and straps, caressed the artificial leg. "Something yez don't see every day." His face went immobile, then split back into that sharp crazy grin. "Or rather - something yez DO see every day, but most of the time yez can't take the fuckers HOME WITH YA!"

His hand twitched back the army blanket covering the jar-shaped humps. A small cloud of dust rose into the air. Sunlight winked on polished glass. Steve cussed, took two steps back, then came forward again and bent to look.

Ghost, who had never in his life felt so far from home, burst into tears.

The man had six big glass jars arranged in two neat rows, sealed at the tops and filled with what could only be formaldehyde. Inside each jar, suspended in the murky liquid, was a large, pale, bloated shape: an undeniably real human head.

The necks appeared to have been surgically severed. Ghost could see layers of tissue within the stumps as precisely delineated as the circles of wood inside a tree trunk. One head was tilted far enough to the side to show a neat peg of bone poking from the meat of the neck. Several had shaved scalps; one had dark hair that floated and trailed like seaweed. Parts of faces were pressed flat against the glass: an ear, a swollen nostril, a rubbery lip pulled askew. Blood-suffused eyeballs protruded from their sockets like pickled hard-boiled eggs.

"How much do you want for them?" Steve asked. Ghost sobbed harder.

The grin seemed to throw off light, it was so wide and dazzling. "Two apiece. Ten for all six of 'em."

"Ten *dollars*?"

"Hey, I'm in a hurry, I gotta unload these puppies today, yez think this is *legal* or somethin'?"

As if on cue, sirens rose out of the general distant cacophony, approaching fast. A pair of police cars rounded the corner and came shrieking up the block. Revolving blue light flickered across the lenses of the black wraparound shades. The grin disappeared. Without even a *good day to yez* the vendor scooped up the artificial leg and took off down the street. One car roared after him. The other slammed to a halt at the curb where Steve and Ghost still stood staring stupidly at the heads.

"You weren't really going to buy one, were you?" Ghost whispered.

"Course not." Steve snorted. "I don't have any money anyway, remember? The bums got it all. I'm lucky to have an I.D. to show this cop." He dug out his wallet and flipped it open. "We're just a couple of hicks from North Carolina, Officer. We lay no claim to these jars or their contents."

❖   ❖   ❖

Minds like butterflies preserved in brine, trapped under thick glass . . .

It seemed that their friendly vendor, a gentleman whose given name was Robyn Moorhead but who was known variously as Robyn Hood, Moorhead Robbins, and (aptly enough) "More Head," had robbed a medical transport truck en route from Beth Israel Hospital to the Mutter Medical Museum in Philadelphia while it was stopped at a gas station. The truck's door had not latched properly, and More Head and an unidentified girlfriend had simply climbed in and cleaned it out. He had already sold several items before Steve and Ghost came along. The artificial leg, though, was his own. He used it for display purposes only, to call attention to whatever shady wares he sold; it was a valuable antique and not for sale; he carried it everywhere.

No, Ghost told himself. *You did not feel their minds beating against the jars like dying insects. You did not feel the raw burn of formaldehyde against your eyeballs, the dead taste of it in your mouth; you did not feel the subtle breakdown of the molecular dream that was your brain. They were not alive. You could not feel them.*

"I gotta know," said the cop as he finished writing up their statement. "How much did he want for 'em?" Steve told him, and the cop shrugged, then sighed. He was a decent sort and the affair seemed to have put him in a philosophical mood. "Man, even'f I was a crook, even'f I was tryna sell yuman heads, I'd't least be askin' more'n ten bucks.

Kinda devalues the sanctity a'yuman life, y'know?"

Jewelled wings, beating themselves to powder against thick glass . . .

They had overshot the club by five blocks. The cops pointed them in the right direction and ten minutes later they were descending below street level again, past the unlit neon sign that said not *Beware* but *Be Aware*, though Ghost guessed it amounted to the same thing, and into the club. The poster they had sent was plastered everywhere: TONIGHT - LOST SOULS? They were too tired to consider doing a soundcheck yet, but it was just the two of them, Steve's guitar and Ghost's voice, and they didn't really need one. At any rate they wouldn't be going on till midnight. Right now they needed sleep. One of the bartenders was out of town and had left them the keys to her apartment, which was just upstairs.

Too tired for the stairs, they rode the ancient, terrifying elevator up seven stories. Steve had bummed two beers at the bar. He guzzled most of one as they rode up. "New York is pretty interesting," he said.

"No shit."

Steve snorted into his beer. And then at once they were both laughing, losing it in a rickety box suspended from an antique cable in a building that was taller than any building in Missing Mile but small by the standards of this magical, morbid, million-storied city. They fell against each other and howled and slapped high-five. They were young and the one had a voice like gravelly gold and the other could play guitar with a diamond-hard edge born of sex and voodoo and despair, and it was all part of the Great Adventure.

They staggered out at the top

still giggling, fumbled with three unfamiliar locks, and let themselves into the apartment. The place was decorated all in black: black walls, black lace dripping from the ceiling, black paint over the windows, black silk sheets on a huge futon that covered the floor. The effect was soothing, like being cradled in the hand of night. Their laughter wound down.

Steve stood his guitar case in a corner, gulped the second beer after Ghost refused it, and stretched his tired bones out on the futon. Ghost toed his sneakers off and lay down beside him. It was absolutely dark and, for the first time since Port Authority, nearly quiet. How strange to think that the whole teeming city was still out there, just beyond the walls of the building. Suddenly Ghost felt disoriented in the little pocket of blackness, as if the compass he always carried in his head had deserted him.

He shifted on the mattress so that his shoulder touched Steve's arm, so that he could feel Steve's familiar warmth all along the left side of his body. Steve heaved a great deep sigh like a sleeping hound. Ghost thought of all the highways, all the back roads, all the train tracks and green paths that led back home, and he did not feel so far away.

And there was music, there was always music to carry him wherever he wanted to go. Soon the distant thrum of the city and the tales it wanted to tell him faded completely, and the gouge -of Steve's bony elbow in his side lulled him to sleep.

Poppy Z. Brite's recently published first novel **Lost Souls**, *is the first hardcover in the acclaimed Abyss horror line. The characters in this story, Steve and Ghost appear in her novel.*

THE CAUSE

S.K. Epperson

"The witness claims he said what?"

"LSD. You know, as in the chemical? Acid?

"Anything else?" Murphy asked, and he looked at his watch in reflex. "Anything at all, Roy?"

"No," said his new partner.

Murphy looked at his watch again. "It's almost one o'clock. Coroner's had him four hours now. God, I hate hospital cafeterias. The lighting is for shit."

"Probably so you can't see what you're getting." Roy sipped at his glass of water and looked at his partner. No one liked Murphy very much. He was too smart. Too cocky. Too right all the time. Just watching him, Roy could see the wheels turning in his brain.

"Another play by play?" he asked.

Murphy looked at him. "What?"

"Are you going over it again? If you are, why don't you verbalize. Maybe I can pick up something you leave out."

Murphy's look said that was unlikely, but he nodded.

"All right. Mr. Gynecologist walks in the hospital, comes down here for tea and croissants with a lady patient, and a second after he sits down he starts freaking out. He up-

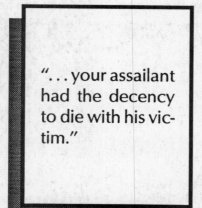

"... your assailant had the decency to die with his victim."

ends the table, grabs a knife and stabs the lady he's talking to, and thirty seconds later he's on the permanent inpatient list. A doctor at a nearby table rushes over and hears the guy say 'LSD' before he—"

"Not a trace of it," interrupted a bored voice, and Murphy looked up to see the blood-spattered whites of the coroner hovering over them.

"Well whatever you do, don't keep us in suspense."

The report hit the table with a slap. "Cardiac arrest. Your lucky Day, Murphy. I was free and your assailant had the decency to die with his victim. Have fun with the paperwork."

"All right." Roy was smiling as he stood.

"Wait a minute," said Murphy. "The guy's having a heart attack and in his final moments he's thinking of acid?"

The coroner shrugged for an answer and left them to stand in line for a cup of coffee. The woman in front of him glanced casually over her shoulder, then quickly fell out of line with a sudden loss of appetite. The coroner turned and winked at the two detectives.

"Let's get out of here," Roy suggested. "I need to stop by the dry cleaners and pick up some of Trudy's stuff." He emptied his cup, crumpled it in his hand, then sighed as his part-

> . . . a man having a heart attack didn't knife the lady next to him because he was pissed about dying.

ner made no motion to move. "What?"

"I'll see you later," Murphy said and waved a hand. "Go do your marital duty. I'm going to have another cup of coffee and talk to the witness again."

"Why?" Roy demanded. "This is ready to file."

"Hey, I like to be thorough in my reports, all right? You know how I hate secondhand information."

"I told you everything he said word for word."

Murphy nodded. "I know, and I'm sorry I was late, but I want to hear it for myself, Okay?"

Roy had to smile. "You better be wearing condoms with all these late night lovers. Why don't you find yourself a decent woman?"

"You got the last one," said Murphy.

Roy's smile wilted a bit as he left the cafeteria. He was wasting his time as far as his partner was concerned. Murphy claimed he had no time and none of the patience required to develop a decent relationship with a woman. He liked his life the way it was.

Roy glanced back through the glass before he headed for the eleva-tor and saw his partner pick up the report. Murphy was a damn good cop, no argument there. He was downright picky when it came to detail, and things he called *nuances*. Roy would never understand how his mind worked, how he made the connections he did and the weird associations that made sense to no one but Murphy.

But Murphy's mind did work. It was working now, Roy could tell. On what, he didn't know.

Just before the elevator doors closed, Murphy turned and looked at Roy. Murphy felt his partner watching him, wondering. He shrugged it off and went to the phone on the wall to call the witness back down. In his thinking, a man having a heart attack didn't knife the lady next to him because he was pissed about dying. There had to be more to it than that. There always was.

The witness, a fiftyish with a bad toupee, was perturbed at Murphy's request to repeat his statement.

"I told the other detective everything."

"I know you did, and I also know you're a very busy man, Dr. Curtis. What kind of doctor are you anyway?"

"Gynecologist. I knew Dr. Warren well. We sometimes referred patients to each other."

Murphy stared at the man's bulbous nose to keep from looking at the limp hairpiece. "Why did you do that?"

Curtis shrugged. "An occasional heavy case load."

"Can I get you anything, Dr. Curtis?" asked a sweet voice, and Murphy looked up to find a waitress at the table.

"No thanks," Curtis answered. "I won't be here long enough."

"You work here?" Murphy asked the girl.

"Behind the counter, usually," she said with a nod.

"Were you here this morning?"

"I cleaned up the mess, if that's what you mean."

"I might want to talk to you later."

She nodded and smiled at the doctor before moving away.

"Eleanor's a nice girl," said Curtis. "I helped her get on here."

Murphy watched her retreat behind the counter. Nice hips, perky breasts, bouncy hair. "She a relative?"

"No. Can we please get on with this?"

"Okay," Murphy said affably. "Start at the beginning and I'll stop you when I want elaboration."

Curtis sighed heavily, then repeated his story. Murphy stopped him twice. "Did you ever hear Dr. Warren talk about drugs? Maybe he dropped acid when he was younger."

"He never mentioned it if he did."

"What were he and the woman at the table discussing?"

"They didn't have a chance to discuss anything. They sat down and then Warren turned red and went crazy."

Murphy leaned back. "Did you know the woman?"

"Not personally, no. I knew she was Warren's patient, and that she was scheduled for a dilation and a curettage."

"How did you know that?"

"Warren asked me to do it for him."

Murphy rolled his coffee cup between his hands. "Okay, one more thing. Did you know Warren had heart problems?"

"It was common knowledge. He had a heart attack in the ICU unit two years ago. He never gave up cigarettes and the booze, though, and the stress of late was probably the topper."

"The stress of late?" Murphy repeated.

"The anti-abortionists making everyone crazy. Last week someone stole a container of aborted fetuses waiting for disposal. A day after the news was in the paper, the anti-abortionists claimed they were responsible. They said they wanted to provide decent burials."

"It's a hot issue," Murphy commented.

"No shit," the gynecologist said flatly, and he stood. "If there's nothing else, I need to get back upstairs." He stopped then. "If they want to bury aborted fetuses, then what about the millions of spontaneous abortions that occur in the form of miscarriage every year. If they consider these fetuses to be viable persons, are they going to search toilet bowls and pay for expensive funerals for fetuses?"

Murphy only lifted his brows. The doctor started off then turned and sat back down suddenly. He lifted his leg and looked at the bottom of his shoes. "What the hell? A damn lima bean. And they wonder why we hate to eat in this pig sty."

The doctor plucked the squashed bean from his sole and dropped in into the ashtray. Murphy looked at it and waited until the doctor was gone before calling the girl behind the counter over. She took the seat the doctor had vacated and made a face when Murphy shoved the ashtray at her.

"You didn't clean up very good. That was on the floor."

"I must've missed it in all the blood."

"Your name is Eleanor? Eleanor what?"

"Randall. I didn't catch your name."

He ignored her. "Tell me what happened this morning."

"I thought Dr. Curtis told you."

"He told me he got you this job. Are you friends?"

She frowned. "My mom knows him."

"Did you wait on Dr. Warren and his patient?"

"Behind the counter, yes. Did he have a heart attack?"

"Yeah. How did you know?"

"My dad had one. I know what they look like."

"Did you see him attack the woman?"

"Yes. None of us could believe it."

Murphy rubbed his face. "How old are you?"

"Twenty-two."

"Do you have a phone number at home?"

She frowned at him again, then wrote it down on a napkin and handed it over.

By the time Murphy made the office, Roy was already filling out the paperwork. He glanced up and smiled. "All over but the crying. Motive unknown."

"I'm not so sure." Murphy moved to his own desk.

Roy frowned. "Did you come up with something?"

Murphy didn't answer for a long moment. Suddenly he looked at Roy and said, "I went over to see Mrs. Warren after I left the hospital. The lady's not exactly overcome with grief. Got a pool and a big house to herself now. I asked her about the stress Warren was supposed to be under. She said he received some phone calls in the last week that made him borderline neurotic, but he wouldn't talk about it."

"What are you thinking? Blackmail?"

"I don't know, Roy."

Roy looked at his watch. "Come and eat with us tonight. We got blueberry pie for dessert. You need to relax that mental machine for an hour or so."

I can't. I need to call a little blonde."

Roy shook his head.

Murphy reached over and picked up his phone. He dialed the number on the napkin, then waved as Roy left.

When an older female answered, Murphy said, "This is Murphy calling for Eleanor Randall."

"Oh, are you the detective?"

"Yeah, are you the mother?"

She laughed. "I am. Hold on and I'll get her for you."

Eleanor came to the phone and said a cautious hello.

"This is Murphy. I need to talk to you again, and I thought we could do it while I eat. I'll even buy you dinner."

"Oh . . . what time?"

"Now. Give me your address and I'm on my way."

Two hours later Murphy tossed his napkin over the remainder of his lasagna and sat back to study Eleanor Randall. Her eyes were big and luminous, dark blue, and her blonde hair was loose and curly.

"How come you don't have a boyfriend, Eleanor?"

"Who says I don't?"

"Where is he?"

"In the military."

Murphy nodded. "Does he go out with other girls?"

"I don't think so."

"You came out with me."

"You're a detective. This isn't a date."

"Okay. Has Dr. Curtis known your mom a long time?"

"He's her gynecologist. Why?"

"She sounds nice. I bet she's pretty, too. Like you."

Eleanor smiled. "She has a phobia about aging. She nearly had a fit when—" Eleanor dropped her napkin and bent down to pick it up. "When she turned forty."

Murphy sent a hand under the table to set the beeper on his belt. The beeper went off and Murphy looked apologetically at the girl. He rose from the table on the pretense of finding a phone. When he returned, he said, "I have to go now. Come on, I'll take you home."

"What about your questions?"

"They'll keep."

Murphy rushed the girl home and drove back into town. If he hurried, he could make it over to Roy's house in time for pie.

Trudy looked through the peephole and smiled when she saw Murphy. She opened the door and stepped aside. "Tired of your dumpy little apartment and Chef Boyardee dinners?"

"Any pie left?" Murphy asked as he walked past her into the diningroom. Roy wiped his mouth with a napkin.

"What happened to the little blonde."

Murphy said down and Trudy moved to cut a huge piece of pie for him. "You want Cool Whip?"

"No thanks, Trudy. Hey, Roy, you talked to the girl behind the counter at the cafeteria this morning, right?"

Roy nodded. "Yeah. Blonde. Cute. Is that who you went out with?"

"Name's Eleanor Randall. Curtis got her the job at the hospital because her mother is his patient. In Dr. Warren's den today I saw a photo taken at some kind of pool party. You know, a bunch of people standing around holding drinks and trying to look California. Curtis and Warren looked pretty chummy with each other. And guess who just happened to be holding on to Warren's arm and showing her pearly whites to a guy in a marine uniform?"

"That's why you went out with

her?" Roy asked. "To find out why she was in a party photograph on a dead man's wall."

Murphy chewed his pie. After he swallowed, he reached into his pocket to find the napkin with Eleanor's number.

"Do one thing for me tomorrow," he asked. "Get me a list of the numbers called from this phone last week."

Roy looked at it. "You think she was the one calling Warren?"

"Tonight she told me she has a boyfriend in the military, and today Mrs. Warren told me the marine in the party picture is Dr. Curtis's son."

"So. What does that have to do with Warren?"

Murphy finished his pie and stood. "I don't know yet. Thanks for the pie, Trudy. It was great."

"What a minute," said Roy as Murphy headed for the door. "What will you be doing tomorrow?"

"Going to see a doctor," Murphy answered. "I can't seem to stop thinking about lima beans."

Roy stared as his partner closed the door behind himself. "You see what I have to put up with all day, Trudy? The guy's a basketcase."

"I thought you liked him?"

"I do," said Roy. "I just don't understand him."

Dr. Curtis seemed surprised to see Murphy the next morning. He offered a cup of coffee, then sat stirring his own without expression.

"Nice office you have here," Murphy commented.

Curtis cleared his throat. "I have patients waiting."

"Yeah, I saw them. Tell me, how long has your son been seeing Eleanor Randall?"

The toupee stayed in place while the brows rose. "What did she tell you?"

"That he's her boyfriend."

> "... it made your mom happy not to be a grandma, but it made you mad as hell."

Curtis frowned. "More like a one night stand."

"The night of the pool party at Warren's," Murphy said, and let the words hang.

"I did Eleanor a favor and got her invited because I know her mother. What does this have to do with anything? Just who are you investigating here?"

"Did Warren tell you he was receiving phone calls?"

The doctor blinked. "Yes. He said he was being harassed by someone calling and saying terrible things to him about performing abortions. Said it was driving him crazy. This was about the same time as the theft of those aborted fetuses occurred, so I assumed he meant the anti-abortionists had obtained his home phone number."

Murphy's beeper went off and he asked to use Curtis's phone. It was Roy.

"Warren's number was on the list, all right. About ten times, all of them late at night. Have we got anything?"

"I'll let you know," Murphy told him and he hung up. He turned back to the doctor. "Eleanor Randall made those calls, Dr. Curtis. I'm sure I'll be

able to sniff it out, but you could save both of us time and—"

"There's no reason for me to hide anything," Curtis said abruptly. "My son made her pregnant the night of the pool party. She came to me and I referred her to Warren, who also knew her mother. Warren took care of her."

Murphy nodded thoughtfully, then stood. "Thanks for your time, Dr. Curtis."

"Wanna tell me what's going on?" asked Roy, as Murphy led him to a table in the hospital cafeteria.

"They don't serve lima beans in here," said Murphy.

Roy groaned. "I give up on you, man."

"Had a little black spot on it," Murphy mused.

"Hello, Detective Murphy." Eleanor came to stand beside the table.

"Hello, El. Can you sit down a minute?"

She glanced at the counter, and then back again. "Only for a minute. How'd you know I'm called El?"

"Eleanor has three syllables. People always shorten names with three syllables. You've met Roy, my partner."

"Hell, Roy." Eleanor sat down.

Roy nodded to her and Murphy leaned forward suddenly and made his voice low and urgent. "What kind of things did you say to Dr. Warren on the phone, El?"

Her pupils dilated in shock and she jerked back.

"You probably talked about him murdering babies and things like that, didn't you? I'm thinking you didn't want an abortion. He may have tricked you into it or something, I don't know, and it made your mom happy not to be a grandma, but it made you mad as hell. You wanted to be the daughter-in-law of a rich doctor."

Eleanor's face was turning pink. She said, "How did you find out about that?"

Murphy ignored her. "I figure you decided to get a little revenge, and when those aborted fetuses were stolen from the hospital you saw a big opportunity to drive a guy with heart trouble right over the edge."

Roy looked first at Murphy, and then at Eleanor's ever reddening face. A tiny dot of blood appeared where she was biting her lip.

"He . . . he told me it was just a simple examination, but then he did something that made the baby abort. I couldn't prove he did it, but I knew why. Dr. Curtis didn't want me to screw up the affair he's been having with my mother for the past two years."

Murphy was oblivious to her. "You know, the thing that bothered me from the start was what Warren said. Why I asked myself, would he say something like 'LSD' before he croaked? But he didn't say 'LSD'. He said 'El's tea.' He was talking about something in the tea you gave him."

Hysterical laughter began to bubble in Eleanor. She covered her face with her hands and moaned. "You should've seen his face when he saw that lima bean floating in his tea. I even put a little eye on the thing to make it look like a real—"

Roy made a noise of disgust. "Did you think his killing a woman was funny?"

Eleanor immediately sobered. "How could I know he would do that? He probably thought she put the thing in his tea. He was so paranoid by then he didn't know up from down. He thought everyone was a member of the movement against him."

"You made sure of that, didn't you," said Roy.

Eleanor took a breath. She put a calming hand to her temple and said, "Good luck in proving any of this. You don't have anything but some phone calls and a story about a lima bean."

Murphy looked at her. "That's all we'll need, Eleanor. Trust me."

"What's on the menu tonight," Murphy asked Roy later.

"Chicken, I think. You wanna come over?"

"No, just asking."

Roy shook his head. "I don't know about you."

"What don't you know?"

"How you think, for one thing. Was there some *nuance* in that girl's makeup? How did you know what the hell you were looking for?"

Murphy sighed. "Ever hear of a guy named John Fletcher?"

"No. Should I?"

"Yeah. He's the guy who said, *Tell me the cause: I know there is a women in't.*"

Roy stared at him. "You love it, don't you. You love being so far away from the rest of us."

Murphy lifted his head to look at his partner. He smiled and said, "God, yes."

---

*S.K. Epperson's latest novel, **Nightmare**, was recently released to high praise. It is available through Donald I. Fine, Inc.*

BEHIND THE MASK

Matthew J. Costello

Fatal Subtraction, Pierce O'Donnell and Dennis McDougal (Doubleday, 1992)

The Privacy Poachers, Tony Lesce (Loompanics Unlimited,1992)

Bag of Toys, David France (Warner Books, 1992)

Head to Head, Lester Thurow (William Morrow & Co, 1992)

Subway Lives, Jim Dwyer, (Crown, 1991)

Double Cross, Sam and Chuck Giancana (Warner Books, 1992)

Recently I was talking to some Hollywood-slash-TV people about my possible involvement in a Hollywood-slash-TV project. And, since this was the early stages of discussions, the media folk wanted to see some ideas from me as part of my application for the gig. But, being no babe in the woods, the one thing that I knew was that you never, *ever* gave these people an idea. No, not without a contract, not without some cash on the barrel-head.

And so, while providing all sorts of High Expectations for the wonderful work to follow, I provided some pages devoid of a single concrete idea. . . . almost. There was, I'm afraid, one idea in my outline.

There was one idea. Just one. And when I finally spoke to the movie/tube people about the project, when they gave me an update on where they were going with the ball, they told me about this new concept they had. It was a great concept, really hot, they said. I nodded my head. And guess what the idea was?

The single idea I had shared had now miraculously become part of the bible of said project.

And maybe I didn't feel raped. It was, after all, only one idea . . . and I did allow it to squeak through. But I sure as hell felt as if someone goosed me.

Art Buchwald probably felt much stronger emotion when she saw his two and half page outline for a story of an African Prince coming to America dropped by Paramount, only to transmogrify into *Coming to America*. . . . based on an original story by Eddie Murphy.

Buchwald and his partner, Alain Bernheim sued Paramount, with Los Angeles Trial Lawyer Pierce O'Donnel spearheading their brave adventure into the web of Hollywood Profit & Loss.

Fatal Subtraction, by O'Donnell and Dennis McDougal, is an incredibly detailed account of this case. It should be mandatory reading for any writer hoping to be tapped by the barons of tinsel town, filled with insight into the financial machinations of film. Even after *Coming to America* grossed a suspected 350 million, Paramount claimed that the picture remained in the hole to the tune of

17+ million.

The book opens with lines form David Mamet's play, Speed-the-Plow . . . where one character asks about net profits and the other tell him that there are two things about the entertainment industry . . . "the first one is: there is no net . . . And I forget the second one."

But Buchawld's brave fight (which he won, but see above for his share of the 'net profits') is a victory for writers who have suffered insults, pilferage and downright thievery from the bubbleheads for way too long.

And we'd all have to be bubbleheads not to be concerned about the information in Tony Lesce's disturbing book *The Privacy Poachers*. Written is a flat, matter-of-fact style, Lesce first details all the lists that "they" are keeping about us.

From credit bureaus to the IRS, from telephone surveys to employment records, Lesce thoroughly documents that it is very doubtful that we have any privacy at all. What we eat, drink, rent at the video store, our finances, travel, political views - are all on record. And if that isn't alarming enough (and — let's face it — most people are hard to scare these days), Lesce shows some of the wonderful things that can happen to you. How your credit rating can be destroyed for no good reason, how you could find yourself on a list of 'bad tenants' unable to rent a new apartment, simply because you wanted some heat form your old landlord.

There's a chilling section here he talks about how psychological evaluations, routinely given at the time of employment, could find you labeled, somewhere, on someone's list, as a psychotic.

And boy, do these lists get shopped around.

Fortunately, not all is lost.

Lesce's last chapter is on protecting yourself. Though I suspect, Chicken Little said, that it is already too late, Lesce includes some neat tricks that can help protect you from everyone who wants to document your life. Protective measures include creating a perfectly legal 'Phantom', complete with a phony name and simply watching what organizations you join.

There's scary stuff here — this one's going on my fiction writers' reference shelf - and some good sensible advice on keeping as much from Big Brother as possible.

Andrew Crispo had no problem keeping his less-than-salutary interests from the customers of his fashionable Upper East Side Art Gallery.

In what might have been a heartwarming story, David France's book, *Bag of Toys*, describes how little Andy Crispo went from Philadelphia orphan to multi-million dollar art magnate. Using his good looks, his charm, his sexual appetite, and a willingness to lie and steal, Crispo became a major player in the competitive New York art world, building up a stock of Edward Hopper and Georgia O'Keefe paintings.

Crispo would borrow a painting for another gallery, jack up the price, and move in for the killer sale. Often Crispo charging a painting to a customer, then keep it for his own supply. He kept a complete set of double records, with the real financial dealings of his gallery, hidden away form the prying eyes of the IRS.

But Crispo's hidden life also included a robust interest in Sadomasochism. Weird homosexual scenes of young men being beaten with items from Crispo's 'Bag of Toys' while kneeling naked in Crispo apartment were common.

Meeting young, swarthy Bernard LeGeros was the catalyst that propelled Crispo into a more serious activity. Together they lured Eigil Vesti to LeGeros's family property in Rockland, where Vesti was shot, his body burned to a blackish mass. But Vesti's head, encased in a leather mask with a zipper remained relatively untouched by the flames. . . .

LeGeros ended up confessing to that actual shooting, and then testifying against his partner in debauchery, Andrew Crispo. But Crisp, ever lucky, was found not guilty. He didn't after all, pull any triggers. And after serving a few years for some tax difficulties (keeping ones' accounts straight can be so difficult), he returned to his apartment and his life in New York's art world.

Who says the 80s are over?

Lester Thurow, that's who. The dean of MIT's Sloan School of Management, has some good, and so bad news, for America.

But first, you should know that his book, *Head To Head*, is an excellent companion volume to Michael Crichton's novel, *Rising Sun* (Knopf). Crichton includes his own bibliography, so you can confirm that yes, we are getting our butts kicked by the Japanese. But Head-to-Head came out after Rising Sun, and it includes, as I said some good news. First, Japan's power will wane, if it hasn't already. Internal economic pressures will force retrenchment, and, in some cases, perhaps open closed markets to U.S. goods.

But — for the bad news — Thurow sees Europe, a unified EC, emerging as the real power, one that Japan will be unable to compete with or will, most likely, a beleaguered and isolated U.S. If the 20th Century was the American Century, then the start of the next millennium will inaugurate the Unified European Century.

Thurow's prescription for recovery isn't terribly dramatic. Consumption must fall here and investments rise. (But, damn, we want so many things.) The education system must improve (but I wish he'd talk more about our abandonment of cities where, hey, learning is as likely as moon men selling falafel.) He calls for teamwork, a concept that is antithetical to America individualism. Teamwork, he says, real teams of suppliers, distributors, and manufacturers is more important that less government or restrictive trade barriers.

Failure to follow his advice, Thurow says, will lead to our children not having a world-class standard of living . . . and deferring dealing with today's problems will lead to major problems in the next coming decades.

And what could be a bigger problem that the New York Subway? Oh, it runs regularly. And the new, graffiti-resistant cars, look good. But it is a dangerous place where token booth attendants can find themselves torched and murder and assault are common events.

Jim Dwyers' *Subway Lives* in a wonderful book for anyone who loves New York and once loved the Subway. The New York Subway used to be my toy, my personals train whisking me from Coney island to the American Museum of Natural History. And while I rode it on a regular basis, alone, as early as eleven years old, now adults face genuine risk once they descend below the streets.

Dwyer gives the history of the various subway lines - the famed IRT, BMT, and IND — including the political controversy of the never-started Second Avenue Subway, a line that has been promised, even budgeted for, and yet never begun.

But his book is really about the people, over one 24 hour period, from MTA Chief David Gunn to

Anna Lans inside her armored token booth. The New York Subway still has massive ridership, slightly over 1 Billion (down from 2 billion in 1946.)

But in the same period, when ridership halved, reported crimes went from 6,147 a year to over 40,000. Nevertheless, Dwyer's book is filled with love for the troubled system, from the transit cops and the once-beautiful stations with frescoes with broken tiles, to the mammoth control room that keeps the nearly 3 million riders a day moving.

And finally, as Wayne might say, here are some real secrets . . . not! The cottage industry of Kennedy Assassination theorists shows no sign of abating and *Double Cross* promised the much-publicized revelations of Chuck Giancana, brother to the Chicago Mafia Don, Sam Giancana.

Double Cross narrates the rise of "Mooney" Giancana, as he was called, from two-bit hood to someone who could push the button on J.F.K. and Marilyn Monroe.

But despite the heavy-duty players, this book is mostly about Mooney's rise, told second-hand. The latter part of the story seems to rush by, perhaps indicative of the lack of support for the Giancana's claims. The story's grand denouement of mob involvement in the JFK assassination and poor Marilyn's death is unconvincing—but the book remains entertaining throughout.

Real secrets, though, lie elsewhere. . . .

Matthew J. Costello is **Gauntlet's** *non-fiction reviewer. His latest novel,* **Homecoming***, is slated for November. He will have a short story in our next issue.*

THE HOUSE OF FICTION

Reviews

T. Liam McDonald

Gerald's Game
by Stephen King
Viking, $23.50

Gerald Burlingham likes to handcuff his wife to the bed during sex.

A minor kink, yes, but one which has grown exceedingly tiresome for Gerald's wife, Jessie.

She found it amusing the first time; faintly tolerable thereafter. But recently, it has become more of a nuisance. It is tripping little switches in her brain, telling her things about her husband's darker side, calling up unpleasant memories.

When Gerald snaps the cuffs into place—up at their isolated lakeside summer home—Jessie suddenly knows she must be set free. In no uncertain terms, she tells Gerald that the game is over, and it was never very pleasant to begin with. For a moment, she sees the glimmer of recognition in Gerald's eyes: he knows she is serious.

Except . . . Gerald chooses to pretend it's part of the game, and Jessie's anger and struggle only provide a little extra turn-on. The stage is set for an act of marital rape, but Jessie places two well-aimed kicks to his stomach and genitals, knocking the air out of Gerald and stopping his advances.

And then —

Gerald is unable to breath. He clutches at his chest, mutters "heart," and drops dead.

It would almost be poetic justice.

That is: if both of Jessie's wrists weren't still handcuffed to the bed. She is naked, unable to move, unable to reach the phone or the keys to the handcuffs; and a long long way from anyone.

Jessie Burlingham is trapped in the premise to a Stephen King novel.

With its faint echoes of *Cujo* (trapped woman most overcome danger to escape), *Gerald's Game* is in territory familiar to most King fans. But there's something different about this book. Something hard to trace. Where *Cujo* resembles part domestic novel and part Wild Kingdom episode — *Gerald's Game* is definitely focused on a woman's inner life and the trauma she has suffered.

Though many of King's most avid readers are women, one criticism his books have encountered over the years is that he doesn't do female characters very well. This could present a particularly prickly problem in *Gerald's Game* — which is a woman's book from start to finish — if King misstepped. In fact, he not only didn't misstep, but he delivered one of the best female-perspective novels turned out by a male writer in recent years.

If this sounds a bit like "dancing dog" criticism (ie, you're just amazed that the dog CAN dance, even if he ain't Fred Astaire), it's far from it. *Gerald's Game* is a brilliant stretch of internal storytelling, calling to mind another title of this literary season: Joyce Carol Oates' Black Water. Both books take isolated women driven to revelations about themselves by extreme circumstances and the immanence of death. It's the stuff grand drama is made of, and, like Oates, King has scored a winner.

Aside from Gerald — who does his swan dive of death early on — and some men near the end, there is no one but Jessie in *Gerald's Game*. If

there was just the faintest trace of falseness in King's portrayal of her, the book would fall apart before it ever started. Instead, it takes off like a missile directed at the darkest recesses of a tormented woman's psyche. As the terror of Jessie Burlingham's situation becomes increasingly more apparent to her, lost parts of her life — horrible memories long suppressed — begin to bubble to the surface, aided by a Greek chorus of inner voices that either goad her to new epiphanies or warn her of the dangerous landscape ahead.

It becomes quite clear that until Jessie goes all the way through her personal hell, there will be no escape — literal or metaphorical — for her. Drawing on a well of strength she didn't even know she had, Jessie confronts the demons of the dark and of the mind, knowing all the time that she will either be freed of the burden of the past or die.

There is more to this book — MUCH MORE — than has been hinted at here. To say more would deprive the reader of the joy of discovery. Rest assured: there is fear here aplenty. The trademark Stephen King edge-of-the-seat suspense and violence are here too.

But there's something more. Something that has moved the author into a new territory. The beauty of the writing, of places and people that live and breath, of that special magic that makes King more than just someone who writes scary books, are all here. The prose sings with heartbreak and tragedy and joy. The stark portraits of a woman's psyche, etched on the page with all the vividness of memory, take this book over the top. Stephen King never "just" writes about fear. He writes about experience, about people we've known and loved and been. That's the secret to his success, and it's all in *Gerald's Game*.

**The Secret History
by Donna Tartt
Knopf, $23.00**

Every once in a while an author explodes on the literary scene with so much fanfare and hoopla that the writing itself often gets lost in the shuffle. Publicity people work overtime, magazines like *People* run profiles, reviewers reach into their bag of adjectives and flash words like "brilliant" and "genius" as though they were going out of style. When the smoke clears, the book just as often as not turns out to be merely so-so.

This is NOT the case with Donna Tartt, whose first novel — *The Secret History* — has already garnered heaps of praise and generated a flurry of excitement. For a first book by a previously unheard-of twenty-eight-year-old to snatch a half- million dollars and be optioned while still in manuscript for film either points to phenomenal talent or effective management.

Rest assured, Donna Tartt is a phenomenal talent. The Secret History is worthy of every bubbling adjective, and probably more. Tartt's effortless blending of the popular novel (mystery/suspense/pick-your-genre) and the literary and the high-minded has created a work that keeps the reader turning the pages, while exploring psychological and intellectual realms with acute skill.

The story centers around a tight clique of young Classical scholars at a college in Vermont. These five students have only one teacher, the eccentric Julian Morrow, and access to this inner circle is strictly limited. The narrator, an unexceptional transfer from California named Richard Papen, is accepted into Morrow's group after proving his skill at Greek to the other nstudents. The group is an odd collection of quirky intellectuals, very tight and very secretive. Gradually, Papen becomes part of their group, and he learns that they have a secret. Their absorption, bordering on obsession, with the Classics has led them to attempt a bacchanal: a primal frenzy of the senses used by the ancients as vent for the emotions they felt their intellect could control. In the process of the bacchanal, a man is killed, and the group covers it up. When it appears that one of their own — Bunny — is getting recklessly close to disclosing their secret, they kill him, too.

This may all seem very simple and almost conventional. It is anything but. The murder and murderers are known from the first page, so it certainly isn't a mystery in the traditional sense of "who did it," but more a look at the circumstances and motives and relationships of the murderers. The penetrating analysis of an idealistic experiment with Classical thought — living in the Appolonian intellect while attempting to indulge, but control, the Dionysian emotion — is in itself a grand mystery: the mystery of human nature and how people act and react in the face of violence and death. There is the primal, emotional murder on the one hand, and the intellectual murder of necessity other. The clique lives in an bubble of thought in a world 1 with feelings. They are guilty of over- intellectualizing, and their hubris is in thinking they can confront the primal without being affected by it, that they can release their Dionysian emotions and return safely to their Appolonian ideal. As Tartt grippingly relates in *The Secret History*, both roads end in ruin.

Lost Souls
by Poppy Z. Brite
Dell Abyss, $18.00

With only a handful of stories, Poppy Brite has proven herself to be one of the most unique and talented horror writers to emerge in recent years. Now, she has written her first novel, *Lost Souls*, and those strengths of style and tone that set her apart are all in evidence. But there is something odd about this book, something that doesn't quite work despite the high quality of writing.

Lost Souls could be flippantly described as a gay vampire novel, but it is, of course, much more than that. (There is only one major woman character, and even she doesn't have much of a role.) The alternating storylines concern Ghost and Steve of the alternative band Lost Souls?; Christian, a 383 year old vampire; Nothing, a teenage runaway; and Zillah, Twig and Molochai, three vampires roaming the countryside in a black van. We follow these people as their paths converge, cross, and converge again, with Nothing becoming the nexus point around which everyone eventually revolves.

Brite's strength lies in her exquisite, highly evocative, decadent prose, which creates a mood and atmosphere wholly unlike that found in the work of any other writer. She has meticulously crafted a subculture of vampires and alternative rock, not unlike that created by Wendy Snow-Lang in her *Night's Children* series of graphic novels. Everyone in *Lost Souls* looks and acts like refugees from a Bauhaus concert, with punked out hair, black eye-liner, and enough clove cigarettes to choke Peter Murphy. This subculture lives and breathes, and hardly a hint of the "real world" intrudes. Brite plunges the reader into a perverse, ugly world of her own invention, and she never falters in the creation and depiction of that world.

Unfortunately, there isn't a whole lot beyond this. *Lost Souls* is a book desperately in search of a plot and some sense of narrative drive. The characters are so brutal and ugly that we simply cannot like or care for them, and so we merely wallow in their angst-ridden nihilism. The only character that borders on being sympathetic — Ghost — is a cipher who is passive throughout most of the story, a mere observer. This tends to be the problem with what is described as "the new horror": we simply do not care about these people, so how can we care about what happens to them or involve ourselves intimately in their world?

If this sounds like a negative review, it is a reluctant one. Poppy Brite is a brilliant writer, there is no doubt about that, and she will certainly continue to be a force in the field of horror. *Lost Souls*, for all its strengths of style, mood, and atmosphere, is just not a completely likable book. It is undoubtedly unique, and there is much to read and enjoy in it. But in the end, it simply fails to involve the reader in its story, and so must exist simply as a wonderful evocation of evil and a herald of great things to come.

T. Liam McDonald is Gauntlet's regular fiction reviewer.